American Economic History

ECONOMICS INFORMATION GUIDE SERIES

Series Editor: Robert W. Haseltine, Associate Professor of Economics, State University College of Arts and Science at Geneseo, New York

The above series is part of the
GALE INFORMATION GUIDE LIBRARY

The Library consists of a number of separate series of guides covering major areas in the social sciences, humanities, and current affairs.

General Editor: Paul Wasserman, Professor and former Dean, School of Library and Information Services, University of Maryland

Managing Editor: Denise Allard Adzigian, Gale Research Company

American Economic History

A GUIDE TO INFORMATION SOURCES

Volume 16 in the Economics Information Guide Series

William K. Hutchinson

*Assistant Professor of Economics
Miami University
Oxford, Ohio*

Gale Research Company
Book Tower, Detroit, Michigan 48226

Library of Congress Cataloging in Publication Data

Hutchinson, William Kenneth, 1945-
    American economic history.

    (Economics information guide series ; v. 16) (Gale
information guide library)
    Includes indexes.
    1. United States—Economic conditions—Bibliography.
I. Title.
Z7165.U5H89   [HC103]   016.330973   73-17577
ISBN 0-8103-1287-5

To Bryan and Jennifer
Both of Them, A Father's Delight

VITA

William K. Hutchinson is an assistant professor at Miami University in Oxford, Ohio. He received his B.A. from State University of New York at Geneseo and his M.A. and Ph.D. from the University of Iowa.

His current research projects include analysis of U.S. regional exports to foreign countries, social security and private saving, and time and technology. Hutchinson has contributed to the JOURNAL OF ECONOMIC HISTORY and is the editor of HISTORY OF ECONOMIC ANALYSIS (Gale Research Co., 1976). He is a member of the American Economic Association and the Economic History Association.

CONTENTS

Contents

ACKNOWLEDGMENTS

I wish to express my appreciation to my graduate students, Gary VanCamp and Sang-gon Lee, and to Susan Kozak, an undergraduate who contributed greatly in the original screening of many articles and books. They all saved me numerous hours of research and writing time. I also want to thank Mimi Farr for her expert typing of the original manuscript, and for her considerable patience with a difficult author.

I would like to thank Professor Stanley Engerman for taking the time to read the first five chapters of this work. The suggestions that he made served to improve this book and any errors and/or omissions remain mine. The editorial assistance provided by Denise Allard Adzigian and others at Gale Research Co. has been of inestimable value to me.

Finally, I would like to thank Dianne, Bryan, and Jennifer for their patience and understanding during the period in which I was working on this book.

INTRODUCTION

The purpose for writing a book such as this one is to provide, for the beginning student of American economic history, a source of information regarding the important topics in the field. Since economic history is, generally speaking, the explanation of historical events through the use of economic theory, varying degrees of competence in both history and economics will be necessary to utilize the sources provided in this book. Most of the works cited may, however, be used by nearly anyone, whether or not the person is a specialist.

There has been, in recent years, a significant shift in the type of economic history produced by both economists and historians. The earlier works were similar to traditional historical writing, where large amounts of data were gathered and conclusions were drawn from this information. The so-called new economic history emphasizes the use of statistics, data processing with the aid of computers, and the application of rigorous economic models to the available data. The result in many cases has been the rewriting of economic history, in the sense that the historians' conclusions did not withstand the more rigorous testing. One significant example of this reversal has been in the study of American Negro slavery and the development of the South during the antebellum period. Studies of urban settlement and migration have also advanced our knowledge with respect to this aspect of the process of development.

Every aspect of economic life is a potential area of study for the economic historian. Since most human behavior has an economic side, economic history may be viewed as the study of the past behavior of the people and the results of this behavior on the remainder of the economy.

METHOD OF COVERAGE

The works included in this study treat topics from the colonial period to the present. That is to say, economic history may pertain to last year's occurrences. The usual cutoff date will, however, be around 1960 which is a common dividing line. Articles or books that treat topics or issues in the period since 1960 will appear in bibliographies of current macroeconomic or microeconomic literature available in the reference section of most libraries.

There are ten chapters; the first is addressed to the topic of methodology and the remaining nine are devoted to special topics. The sources for each chapter are divided into two parts: (1) those sources that are annotated; and (2) those sources that are listed as possible further references for the interested reader.

If the title of the source does not indicate the time period studied, then the annotation will describe the period of study. The user may find that the time span of studies in various fields is far more limited than others. The reason is usually the lack of sufficient information about the topic during the other periods, and not that it was an uninteresting topic or period.

An attempt has been made to incorporate all types of studies in this work so that the user may have the benefit of observing all viewpoints regarding a particular topic. The reader may find that the circumstances are not that unlike those observed at other times, and, consequently, the methodology may be applied to the other circumstances as well.

OUTLINE OF THE BOOK

In addition to the above description of this book, there are two appendixes, as well as author, subject, and title indexes. The first appendix contains the names and addresses of the major organizations that are particularly concerned with American economic history. The second appendix contains the names and addresses of the major journals that contain articles pertaining to American economic history.

Chapter 1
METHODOLOGY AND GENERAL WORKS

The first chapter of any book serves to introduce the reader to what follows in the remaining chapters. In that vein, this chapter provides the user of this information guide with a set of sources that will introduce him to the general methodological approaches which have been employed by various scholars. The listings in this chapter include works purporting various types of methodological approaches because it was felt that there were benefits to be derived from such a broad survey of the various approaches.

In addition to the methodological listings, there are a few general works that are annotated. There are two sections of unannotated listings, one of which is devoted to general works that encompass many areas of research. These works serve as beginning reading for the student before he moves on to the more specialized works listed in the specific chapters. The other group of unannotated listings contains further sources on methodology and types of research.

Many of these methodological works also pertain to a specific area of economic history, and for that reason they may appear in later chapters. The user is urged to consult also the many philosophy of science works that are available, if he wishes to study methodology in depth. One may also wish to avail himself of the vast number of methodological works that pertain to pure economic analysis.

1.1 ANNOTATED LISTINGS

1   Aydelotte, William O. QUANTIFICATION IN HISTORY. Reading, Mass.: Addison-Wesley Publishing Co., 1971. 181 p.

> From the point of view of a historian, answers are proffered for the following three questions: (1) of what value are quantitative methods; (2) what is the significance of the theoretical purposes for which quantitative methods can be used; and (3) what is the extent to which it is feasible to use such methods at all. A well-written piece, it uses particular examples as support for the arguments.

2   Bassmann, R.L.   "The Role of the Economic Historian in Predictive Test-
     ing of Proffered 'Economic Laws'."   EXPLORATIONS IN ECONOMIC
     HISTORY   2 (Summer 1965):   159–86.

     This is an assessment of the role of the econometrician as a
     tester of economic theories vis-a-vis the role of the economic
     historian in explaining history through economic models. Their
     roles are viewed as complementary and are discussed on the
     basis of the logical form that must be used by both types of
     investigators.

3   Clark, J.M.   "Relations of History and Theory."   JOURNAL OF ECO-
     NOMIC HISTORY   2 (December 1942):   132–41.

     This is one of four papers from the Economic History Associa-
     tion's annual meeting which considers aspects of entrepreneurial
     research. Clark analyzes in great detail the methods for exam-
     ining the role of the entrepreneur, and emphasizes the great
     difficulty involved in determining what should be measured as
     well as how it should be measured.

4   Cochran, Thomas C.   "The Economics in a Business History."   JOURNAL
     OF ECONOMIC HISTORY   5 (December 1945):   54–65.

     A detailed explanation of how to write a business history is
     provided. Aspects that are relevant to the economist or eco-
     nomic historian are singled out for extended discussion. The
     history of the brewing industry is used as an example.

5   Cole, Arthur H.   "Business History and Economic History."   JOURNAL OF
     ECONOMIC HISTORY   5 (December 1945):   45–53.

     An outline or format for the cooperation of the two fields is
     provided, with the emphasis placed on the task of the business
     historian to provide a cross-section of the economy or of eco-
     nomic activity. The economic historian is to contribute by ad-
     dressing himself to some of the broader issues, that is, those
     issues that are generally important to all businesses.

6   _____.   "The Committee on Research in Economic History: An Historical
     Sketch."   JOURNAL OF ECONOMIC HISTORY   30 (December 1970):   723–
     41.

     A survey of the work prompted by the committee during its
     life and the intentions of the founders as well as those who
     transformed it into the council in the 1950s. An extensive
     bibliography of the works published by the committee (council)
     is provided at the end of the article.

7   _____.   "Economic History in the United States: Formative Years of a

Discipline." JOURNAL OF ECONOMIC HISTORY 28 (December 1968): 556-89.

The author provides an excellent chronology of the progress of this field of study in the United States, describing each of the phases and the motive forces that he believes lay behind each.

8   Conrad, Alfred H. "Econometrics and Southern History." EXPLORATIONS IN ECONOMIC HISTORY 6 (Fall 1968): 34-53.

Conrad sets for himself the task of explaining who exactly an econometrician is and what differentiates him from others, such as statisticians, who also analyze data. The main distinguishing characteristic is the econometricians' concern with models of economic behavior. Through a discussion of the econometric work produced on southern history, Conrad considers the various problems that one might encounter in doing econometric history.

9   Conrad, Alfred H., and Meyers, John. "Economic Theory, Statistical Inference, and Economic History." JOURNAL OF ECONOMIC HISTORY 17 (December 1957): 524-44.

Assuming that the historian wants to find causes and to explain, rather than merely to record facts, this article contains an extensive examination of the ways in which one may approach history in this way. The problems encountered in scientific explanation are examined with respect to economic history.

10   Davis, Lance E. "'And It Will Never Be Literature' the New Economic History: A Critique." EXPLORATIONS IN ECONOMIC HISTORY 6 (Winter 1968): 75-92.

An attempt is made to demonstrate the relationship between the new economic history and traditional economic history. The contribution of the use of economic models is also assessed with respect to their ability to clarify the view of the past. The use of the counterfactual method is also discussed.

11   Davis, Lance E.; Easterlin, Richard A.; and Parker, William N., eds. AMERICAN ECONOMIC GROWTH: AN ECONOMIST'S HISTORY OF THE UNITED STATES. New York: Harper & Row, 1972. 683 p.

One of the more recent texts, this work also serves as an excellent source book for anyone just beginning to examine a particular area of economic history. Each of the chapters is written by one of the best researchers in that particular subject area, and an adequate bibliography is provided after each chapter. The only deficiency is the lack of a treatment of the economics of slavery and southern development.

12   Davis, Lance E.; Hughes, Jonathan R.T.; and Reiter, Stanley. "Aspects of Quantitative Research in Economic History." JOURNAL OF ECONOMIC HISTORY 20 (December 1960): 539-47.

> This article treats the various aspects of writing quantitative history as opposed to literary history, dealing with model formulation and data collection as well as data processing. The latter is an area where the computer has made major contributions. Examples of studies are used to illustrate the salient points.

13   Fishlow, Albert, and Fogel, Robert W. "Quantitative Economic History: An Interim Evaluation; Past Trends and Present Tendencies." JOURNAL OF ECONOMIC HISTORY 31 (March 1971): 15-42.

> This is a very extensive review of the methodological issues that have preoccupied economic historians during past years, and some of the expected directions of future research. It is a good review of the more salient literature in the major areas.

14   Floud, Roderick. AN INTRODUCTION TO QUANTITATIVE METHODS FOR HISTORIANS. Princeton, N.J.: Princeton University Press, 1973. 220 p.

> A very well written work, this book introduces the student of history to the uses and techniques for handling quantitative data. Requiring only an initial knowledge of arithmetic and algebra, the author does an excellent job of illustrating the quantitative techniques that are useful to the historian, and closes the book with a chapter dealing with the physical equipment used in such quantitative analysis.

15   Fogel, Robert W. "The Specification Problem in Economic History." JOURNAL OF ECONOMIC HISTORY 27 (September 1967): 283-308.

> Starting with an extensive discussion of uses of counterfactual models, the author moves to a discussion of efficient models, that is, models that make the most use of existing information. Finally, in a section which comprises about one-half of the article, Fogel discusses the problems of misspecification, using as an example an article by Peter Temin, "Labor Scarcity and the Problem of American Industrial Efficiency in the 1850's." JOURNAL OF ECONOMIC HISTORY 26 (September 1966): 277-98.

16   Fogel, Robert W., and Engerman, Stanley, eds. THE REINTERPRETATION OF AMERICAN ECONOMIC HISTORY. New York: Harper & Row, 1971. 494 p.

> This is a collection of works by various experts in particular

fields of economic history. It is a fairly rigorous theoretical treatment which might prove rather difficult for those who have only a minimum background in economic theory. A separate table of contents is provided for those who might wish to use the book for teaching traditional economic theory.

17   Gallman, Robert E. "Some Notes on the New Social History." JOURNAL OF ECONOMIC HISTORY 37 (March 1977): 3-12.

This presidential address delivered at the 1976 meeting of the Economic History Association calls for at least a mutual awareness if not an actual interchange between the new social historians and the economic historians. This plea results from Gallman's observation of the similarities in the two fields and the contention that both could benefit greatly from such an encounter.

18   Gerschenkron, Alexander. "The Discipline and I." JOURNAL OF ECONOMIC HISTORY 27 (December 1967): 443-59.

Gerschenkron's presidential address, this work is an assessment of the methodology which he used in his studies of Europe. He has, however, selected those issues that have significance to economic history in general. References are made to the "new economic history," and to the general effect of economic history upon economists.

19   Goodrich, Carter. "Economic History: One Field or Two?" JOURNAL OF ECONOMIC HISTORY 20 (December 1960): 531-38.

Although this is only an introduction to two papers that follow, this article serves to delineate the importance of distinctions in the study of economic growth and business cycles by (1) quantitative methods and (2) the traditional "literary" method of the economic historians. The articles introduced are cited as number 12 above and number 47 below.

20   Heaton, Herbert. "Criteria of Periodization in Economic History." JOURNAL OF ECONOMIC HISTORY 15 (September 1955): 267-72.

The author discusses the efficiency of assigning period limits in the study of economic history and the various views on such a policy. Periodization becomes much more necessary when one deals with quantitative or measurable data, since the analysis is dependent upon the data series. The necessity for remembering the institutional constraints is never for a moment forgotten.

21   Hempel, Carl G. "The Function of General Laws in History." JOURNAL OF PHILOSOPHY 39 (January 1942): 35-51.

Stating that "history can 'grasp the unique individuality' of its objects of study no more and no less than can physics or chemistry," the author develops in a very thorough manner the concept of explanation as it is used in both natural and social sciences. The concept of an "explanation sketch" is developed as being the most commonly used in history, and this study provides one of the clearest explanations of how one should use theory for purpose of explanation in history.

22   Hexter, J.H.   "A New Framework for Social History."   JOURNAL OF ECONOMIC HISTORY 15 (December 1955): 415-26.

This article presents a critique of uses of the Marxist model for analyzing social history, and proffers an alternative method for analyzing social groupings and/or socioeconomic classes along a time axis.

23   Hicks, Sir John R. A THEORY OF ECONOMIC HISTORY. Oxford: Clarendon Press, 1969. 181 p.

A highly successful attempt by one of the world's greatest economists to provide a general theory for dealing with economic history. Sir John develops this theory by using it in conjunction with various issues in the general developmental process, for example, rise of the market, money, law, credit, the labor market, and the industrial revolution.

24   Hughes, J.R.T.   "Fact and Theory in Economic History."   EXPLORATIONS IN ECONOMIC HISTORY 3 (Winter 1966): 75-100.

The argument contained in this article is that neither historical facts nor logical theories by themselves are useful avenues of discovery. One must combine the two in order to explain in any meaningful way why a particular event may have occurred. It is in this paper that the concept of "explanation sketches" is discussed.

25   Knooss, Herman E.   "Economic History and the New Business History." JOURNAL OF ECONOMIC HISTORY 18 (December 1958): 467-85.

Knooss discusses the benefits that an economic historian can derive from the works of the new business historians. He argues that business history, as an independent field of study, has raised various economic issues and provided insights for those who wish to study the more aggregated economy.

26   Kuznets, Simon.   "The State as a Unit in Study of Economic Growth." JOURNAL OF ECONOMIC HISTORY 11 (Winter 1951): 25-41.

After first outlining the conditions for setting upon analysis of

economic growth, the author demonstrates how these conditions
are best satisfied by using the sovereign state as the unit of
study. The remainder of the article considers the possible difficulties involved in using the state as a unit of analysis.

27 _____. "Statistics and Economic History." JOURNAL OF ECONOMIC
HISTORY 1 (May 1941): 26-41.

An excellent treatment of this issue, the author shows how the
statistical analysis of economic inquiry might benefit the economic historian, and how economic history might "raise critical
standards in economic inquiry."

28 Lampard, Eric E. "The Price System and Economic Change, A Commentary
on Theory and History." JOURNAL OF ECONOMIC HISTORY 20 (December 1960): 617-37.

Beginning with a quotation about the role of the price system,
the author provides a discussion of the "nature and uses of historical sociology" and how economic historians might benefit
from and/or contribute to this field of inquiry. In closing,
the author warns that although much can be learned from economic sociology, other fields must also be developed in order
for analysis to be complete.

29 Letwin, William, ed. A DOCUMENTARY HISTORY OF AMERICAN ECO-
NOMIC POLICY SINCE 1789. Garden City, N.Y.: Doubleday & Co.,
1961. 406 p.

This collection of documents by various persons and committees
covers a very wide variety of economic aspects prior to World
War II. Some of the topics covered are monetary policy, railroad regulation, taxation, agriculture, immigration, and foreign
trade. Each section has a brief introduction which provides the
setting for the subsequent works.

30 McClelland, Peter D. CAUSAL EXPLANATION AND MODEL BUILDING
IN HISTORY, ECONOMICS, AND THE NEW ECONOMIC HISTORY.
Ithaca, N.Y.: Cornell University Press, 1975. 296 p.

31 McCloskey, Donald N. "Does the Past Have Useful Economics?" JOUR-
NAL OF ECONOMIC LITERATURE 14 (June 1976): 434-61.

A very cleverly written piece, this article delineates the role
of economic history qua economics in a manner which is, I
am sad to say, seldom observed. Economic history's contributions to policy and the general development of theory are the
primary emphasis. It is a very useful piece for both the economic historian and the general economists.

32   Mann, J. de L., ed. "The Teaching of Economic History in Universities: Parts I and II." ECONOMIC HISTORY REVIEW 3 (October 1931): 197-218; (April 1932): 325-45.

> This is a survey of not only the actual course listings in economic history but also the economic history content of courses taught at universities in the various countries of the world. The United States was reported (pp. 330-34) to be the country with the greatest emphasis on economic history. The discussion for each country is written by a scholar from that country.

33   Morgenstern, Oskar. ON THE ACCURACY OF ECONOMIC OBSERVATIONS. 2d ed. Princeton, N.J.: Princeton University Press, 1963. 322 p.

> The author spends the first 130 pages discussing errors in data and their effect on various forms of economic analytic processes. The remaining 180-plus pages are devoted to a discussion of errors that appear in particular data series which economists use in their analyses.

34   Murphy, George G.S. "The 'New' History." EXPLORATIONS IN ECONOMIC HISTORY 2 (Winter 1965): 132-46.

> The author discusses the grounds on which one might justify this title, maintaining that is a result of the increasing empirical rigor with which economic historians are approaching history. He also develops a strong argument for why the "movement towards a 'new' history will continue."

35   Nef, John U. "What Is Economic History." JOURNAL OF ECONOMIC HISTORY 4 (December 1944): 1-19.

> This is a discussion of the role of the economic historian as perceived by others and as perceived by himself vis-a-vis the other disciplines. Many references are made to issues that were to surface in the 1950s and 1960s regarding the use of economic theory and other such issues. Two comments follow this article, one by Richard H. Shryock and the other by Harold F. Williamson.

36   Parker, William N. "From Old to New to Old in Economic History." JOURNAL OF ECONOMIC HISTORY 31 (March 1971): 3-14.

> In this presidential address before the Economic History Association, Parker attempts to set out for us what it is that the "economic historian" is all about and why American writers have altered what this name has connoted at other times and places. It is a very thought-provoking piece.

37   Popper, Karl R. THE POVERTY OF HISTORICISM. New York: Harper &
      Row, 1964. 166 p.

      The thesis is that "there can be no prediction of the course of
      human history by scientific or any other rational methods." This
      does not preclude the testing of economic theories by comparison
      with the real world. One cannot, however, predict historical
      developments which will result from the accumulation of knowl-
      edge. Historicism as a method of research therefore collapses,
      according to Popper.

38   Redlich, Fritz. "American Banking and Growth in the Nineteenth Century:
      Epistemological Reflections." EXPLORATIONS IN ECONOMIC HISTORY
      10 (Spring 1973): 305-14.

      Although this is not a purely methodological work, most of the
      discussion centers around issues which arise as a result of the
      author's basic methodological differences with Professor Sylla,
      whose paper he is criticizing (see no. 50). It is a presen-
      tation of the standard traditional view on methodology.

39   _____. "New and Traditional Approaches to Economic History and Their
      Interdependence." JOURNAL OF ECONOMIC HISTORY 25 (December
      1965): 480-95.

      In this piece Redlich analyzes both the broad and narrow con-
      cepts of "new economic history" and compares their usefulness
      in conducting the study of economic history. He specifically
      attacks the use of "figments" which have appeared in America
      under the name of "counterfactual or subjunctive conditional."

40   _____. "Potentialities and Pitfalls in Economic History." EXPLORATIONS
      IN ECONOMIC HISTORY 6 (Winter 1968): 93-108.

      This statement is very critical of the excessive use of quantita-
      tive methods in economic history. The author develops the
      methodology of history from both sides, illustrating the inherent
      problems, but emphasizes the fruitlessness of mathematical manip-
      ulation of poor quantitative data for purposes of explanation.

41   Redman, Barbara J. "On Economic Theory and Explanation." JOURNAL
      OF BEHAVIORAL ECONOMICS 5 (April 1977): 161-76.

      Although this article is more strictly concerned with traditional
      economics, the discussion of model building and testing and
      the use of theory for explanation are most appropriate for eco-
      nomic historians. It is easily read and provides many references
      for further methodological study.

42   Rostow, W.W.   "The Interrelation of Theory and Economic History."
      JOURNAL OF ECONOMIC HISTORY 17 (December 1957): 509-23.

      It is proposed that "the most natural meeting place of theory
      and history is the study of comparative patterns of dynamic
      change in different societies, focused around the problems of
      economic growth." This conclusion is reached on the assump-
      tion that the economic historian is primarily engaged in Mar-
      shallian long-run analysis, and of necessity must be something
      of a "general dynamic theorist."

43   Schumpeter, Joseph A.   "The Creative Response in Economic History."
      JOURNAL OF ECONOMIC HISTORY 7 (November 1947): 149-59.

      Distinguishing between "adaptive" and "creative" responses to
      changes in economic variables, the author asks for much great-
      er study of the creative responses, so that we can one day in-
      clude those situations under the heading of adaptive responses,
      that is, responses that can be consistently predicted.

44   Schweitzer, Arthur.   "Economic Systems and Economic History." JOUR-
      NAL OF ECONOMIC HISTORY 25 (December 1965): 660-79.

      In this article the author attempts to show the degree of com-
      plementarity of these two areas and the benefits that each may
      gain from the other as well as the general benefits to the re-
      searcher from embracing both areas.

45   Segal, Harvey H.   "Business Cycles: Methodology, Research, and Public
      Policy." JOURNAL OF ECONOMIC HISTORY 14 (June 1954): 164-74.

      This review of six new works on business cycles discusses and
      compares the various types of methodologies that were being
      used during the 1950s. A good introduction to some of the
      issues for a student of cyclical fluctuations.

46   Shen, T.Y.   "Job Analysis and Historical Productivities in the American
      Cotton Textile Industry: A Study in Methodology." REVIEW OF ECO-
      NOMICS AND STATISTICS 40 (May 1958): 149-58.

      In an attempt to analyze the degree of substitution between
      labor and machines, the author initiates the use of a new
      source of data--job analysis studies. These are mostly time
      and motion studies for which a method is developed to use
      these data in an analysis of cotton industry behavior.

47   Spiethoff, Arthur.   "The 'Historical' Character of Economic Theories."
      JOURNAL OF ECONOMIC HISTORY 12 (Spring 1952): 131-39.

      In this article we are shown how history is important for the
      formulation of economic theory, especially in establishing the

background conditions from which the axioms are derived. The economic historian can learn from this discussion, for he must always be sure his theories are appropriate for the particular problem.

48 Supple, Barry E. "Economic History and Economic Growth." JOURNAL OF ECONOMIC HISTORY 20 (December 1960): 548-56.

The author acknowledges the usefulness of the economic historian's concern with growth but also cautions against becoming too narrowly specialized, that is, to the point where he is no longer a true economic historian.

49 Swanson, Joseph A., and Williamson, Jeffrey G. "Explanations and Issues: A Prospectus for Quantitative Economic History." JOURNAL OF ECONOMIC HISTORY 31 (March 1971): 43-57.

The article contains a discussion of the various possible future uses of quantitative analysis. The microeconomic foundations of macroeconomics are developed and the use of such models is discussed extensively. The last section uses a specific model of financial intermediaries in factor markets for purposes of exposition.

50 Sylla, Richard. "Economic History 'von unten nach oben' and 'von oben nach unten': A Reply to Fritz Redlich." EXPLORATIONS IN ECONOMIC HISTORY 10 (Spring 1973): 315-18.

This is a very short reply to Professor Redlich's comment (see no. 38) on an article by the author, and represents a further installment in the methodological debate between the traditional economic historians and the new economic historians.

51 Tawney, R.H. "The Study of Economic History." ECONOMICA 13 (February 1933): 1-22.

This was the author's inaugural lecture upon becoming a professor, and the subject chosen was the methods by which economic history has been conducted and the methods by which such analysis should be conducted. It is a very early version of the move toward the use of quantitative information and the advocacy of moving slightly away from the total literary approach.

52 Temin, Peter. "General Equilibrium Models in Economic History." JOURNAL OF ECONOMIC HISTORY 31 (March 1971): 58-75.

Temin argues that the reason for a continued lack of consensus on such issues as labor scarcity, the 1930s, and the late nineteenth-century deflation has been the reluctance of analysts to

use general equilibrium approaches. He illustrates how each
of the nongeneral equilibrium approaches has failed. The use
of the counterfactual in this approach is also discussed.

53 _____, ed. NEW ECONOMIC HISTORY. Baltimore: Penguin Books,
1973. 445 p.

This is a collection of essays on various topics in the field of
economic history: measurement of growth; agriculture; land
policy; railroads; banking and cycles; and slavery.

54 Thrupp, Sylvia L. "The Role of Comparison in the Development of Economic Theory." JOURNAL OF ECONOMIC HISTORY 17 (December
1957): 554-70.

Outlining three basic types of comparisons, the author argues
that analysts must use comparative analysis to avoid labeling
an atypical event typical. Caution is also urged lest one
become overzealous in attempting to find similarities and differences and not studying various systems intensively enough.

55 Tunzelmann, G.N. von. "The New Economic History: An Econometric
Appraisal." EXPLORATIONS IN ECONOMIC HISTORY 5 (Winter 1968):
175-200.

The article is an attempt to evaluate critically the economic
historians' use of applied econometrics. By reference to various econometric difficulties, von Tunzelmann illustrates the
shortcomings of most writers in economic history. It is a fairly
thorough treatment of the econometric problems that the analysts
might encounter.

56 Usher, Abbott Payson. "Institutional Methodology in Economic History."
JOURNAL OF ECONOMIC HISTORY 1 (May 1941): 88-96.

As a review of Louis B. Hacker's THE TRIUMPH OF AMERICAN
CAPITALISM, this article points out many of what the author
considers to be dangerous methodological errors on Hacker's
part.

57 _____. "The Significance of Modern Empiricism for History and Economics." JOURNAL OF ECONOMIC HISTORY 9 (November 1949):
137-55.

This is a very thorough and careful treatment of the issues involved in applying empirical analysis and economic theory to
the study of economic history.

58 Williamson, Harold F. "Business History and Economic History." JOUR-
NAL OF ECONOMIC HISTORY 26 (December 1966): 407-17.

This is not an argument for the amalgamation of the two fields but rather an argument for cooperation and exchange of information. The argument is put forth via an analysis of the development of business history as a field of study, with illustrations of how it has interacted with economic history. It is an excellent discussion.

59   Williamson, Jeffrey G. "Embodiment, Disembodiment, Learning by Doing, and Returns to Scale in Nineteenth-Century Cotton Textiles." JOURNAL OF ECONOMIC HISTORY 32 (September 1972): 691-705.

This comment on a paper by Paul A. David, "Learning by Doing and Tariff Protection." JOURNAL OF ECONOMIC HISTORY 30 (September 1970): 521-601, serves as a good discussion of particular issues in methodology dealing with technology and productivity change. A rejoinder to this article follows: Paul A. David, "The Use and Abuse of Prior Information in Econometric History." JOURNAL OF ECONOMIC HISTORY 32 (September 1972): 706-27.

1.2 METHODOLOGY LISTINGS

60   Andrews, Charles M. BRITISH COMMITTEES, COMMISSIONS AND COUNCILS OF TRADE AND PLANTATIONS, 1622-1675. Baltimore: Johns Hopkins Press, 1908. 151 p.

61   _____. GUIDE TO THE MATERIALS FOR AMERICAN HISTORY, TO 1783, IN THE PUBLIC RECORD OFFICE OF GREAT BRITAIN. Washington, D.C.: Carnegie Institution, 1912-14. 773 p.

62   Andrews, Charles M., and Davenport, Frances G. GUIDE TO THE MANUSCRIPT MATERIALS FOR THE HISTORY OF THE UNITED STATES, TO 1783, IN THE BRITISH MUSEUM, IN MINOR LONDON ARCHIVES, AND IN LIBRARIES OF OXFORD AND CAMBRIDGE. Washington, D.C.: Carnegie Institution, 1908. 499 p.

63   Buckingham, J.S. AMERICA: HISTORICAL, STATISTICAL, AND DESCRIPTIVE. 3 vols. London: Fisher, Son, and Co., 1841.

64   Chapin, William. A COMPLETE REFERENCE GAZETTEER OF THE UNITED STATES. New York: Phelps and Ensign, 1840. 347 p.

65   Cole, Arthur H. "Business Manuscripts: A Pressing Problem." JOURNAL OF ECONOMIC HISTORY 5 (May 1945): 43-59.

66   Dunbar, Robert G. "The Role of Agricultural History in Economic Development." AGRICULTURAL HISTORY 41 (October 1967): 329-44.

67 Hasse, Adelaide R. INDEX OF ECONOMIC MATERIAL IN DOCUMENTS OF THE STATES OF THE UNITED STATES. Washington, D.C.: Carnegie Institution, 1908. 393 p.

68 Miskimin, Harry. "Agenda for Early Modern Economic History." JOURNAL OF ECONOMIC HISTORY 31 (March 1971): 172-83.

69 Paullin, Charles O., and Paxson, Frederic L. GUIDE TO MATERIALS IN LONDON ARCHIVES FOR THE HISTORY OF THE UNITED STATES SINCE 1783. Washington, D.C.: Carnegie Institution, 1914. 642 p.

70 Scheiber, Harry N. "On the New Economic History--and Its Limitations: A Review Essay." AGRICULTURAL HISTORY 41 (October 1967): 383-96.

71 Wright, Gavin. "Note on the Manuscript Census Samples." AGRICULTURE HISTORY 44 (January 1970): 95-100.

1.3 GENERAL LISTINGS

72 Anderson, A. AN HISTORICAL AND CHRONOLOGICAL DEDUCTION OF THE ORIGIN OF COMMERCE. Vol. 4. New York: A.M. Kelley, 1967. 696 p.

73 Avery, E.M. A HISTORY OF THE UNITED STATES AND ITS PEOPLE. 7 vols. Cleveland: Burrows Brothers Co., 1904-10.

74 Bancroft, George. HISTORY OF THE UNITED STATES. 10 vols. Boston: Little, Brown and Co., 1834-75.

75 Blowe, Daniel. A GEOGRAPHICAL, COMMERCIAL, HISTORICAL, AND AGRICULTURAL VIEW OF THE UNITED STATES OF AMERICA. London: Edwards and Knibb, 1820. 746 p.

76 Bogart, Ernest L. ECONOMIC HISTORY OF THE UNITED STATES. New York: Longmans, Green, and Co., 1912. 597 p.

77 Callender, Guy S. SELECTED READINGS IN THE ECONOMIC HISTORY OF THE UNITED STATES, 1765-1860. New York: Ginn and Co., 1909. 819 p.

78 CAMBRIDGE MODERN HISTORY. 2 vols. New York: Macmillan Co., 1903.

79   Channing, Edward. STUDENT'S HISTORY OF THE UNITED STATES. New York: Macmillan Co., 1902. 606 p.

80   Chevalier, Michel. SOCIETY, MANNERS, AND POLITICS IN THE UNITED STATES, 1834-35. Boston: Weeks, Jordan, and Co., 1839. 467 p.

81   Clay, Henry. WORKS. 10 vols. New York: G.P. Putnam's Sons, 1904.

82   Cochran, Thomas C. "The New York Committee on Business Records." JOURNAL OF ECONOMIC HISTORY 5 (May 1945): 60-64.

83   _____. "Recent Contributions to Economic History: The United States, The Twentieth Century." JOURNAL OF ECONOMIC HISTORY 19 (March 1959): 64-75.

84   Cooper, Thomas. SOME INFORMATION RESPECTING AMERICA, 1793. London: J. Johnson, 1795. 240 p.

85   Coxe, Tench. A VIEW OF THE UNITED STATES OF AMERICA. Philadelphia: William Hall, 1794. 513 p.

86   Davis, Lance E.; Hughes, J.R.T.; and McDougall, Duncan M. AMERICAN ECONOMIC HISTORY. Homewood, Ill.: Irwin, 1965. 482 p.

87   Dodd, William E. "Economic Interpretation of American History." JOURNAL OF POLITICAL ECONOMY 24 (May 1916): 489-95.

88   Goodrich, Carter. "Recent Contributions to Economic History: The United States, 1789-1860." JOURNAL OF ECONOMIC HISTORY 19 (March 1959): 25-43.

89   Hacker, Louis B. THE TRIUMPH OF AMERICAN CAPITALISM: THE DEVELOPMENT OF FORCES IN AMERICAN HISTORY TO THE END OF THE NINETEENTH CENTURY. New York: Simon and Shuster, 1940. 460 p.

90   Hardy, Charles O. "Recent Economic Changes in the United States." JOURNAL OF POLITICAL ECONOMY 38 (April 1930): 213-27.

91   Harper, Lawrence A. "Recent Contributions to American Economic History: American History to 1789." JOURNAL OF ECONOMIC HISTORY 19 (March 1959): 1-24.

92   Harris, Seymor E. AMERICAN ECONOMIC HISTORY. New York: McGraw-Hill, 1961. 560 p.

93   Hart, A.B. GUIDE TO AMERICAN HISTORY. Boston: Ginn and Co., 1903. 471 p.

94   Hutchins, John G.B. "Recent Contributions to Business History: The United States." JOURNAL OF ECONOMIC HISTORY 19 (March 1959): 103-21.

95   Krooss, Herman E. AMERICAN ECONOMIC DEVELOPMENT. Englewood Cliffs, N.J.: Prentice-Hall, 1955. 536 p.

96   LeDuc, Thomas. "Recent Contribution to Economic History: The United States, 1861-1900." JOURNAL OF ECONOMIC HISTORY 19 (March 1959): 44-63.

97   MacDonald, William. DOCUMENTARY SOURCE BOOK OF AMERICAN HISTORY. New York: Macmillan Co., 1926. 713 p.

98   MacKay, Alexander. THE WESTERN WORLD. 3 vols. London: R. Bentley, 1849.

99   National Bureau of Economic Research. TRENDS IN THE AMERICAN ECONOMY IN THE NINETEENTH CENTURY. Studies in Income and Wealth, no. 24. Princeton, N.J.: Princeton University Press, 1960. 682 p.

100   Rhodes, J.F. A HISTORY OF THE UNITED STATES, FROM THE COMPROMISE OF 1850. 8 vols. New York: Macmillan Co., 1916.

101   Ries, Heinrich. ECONOMIC GEOLOGY OF THE UNITED STATES. New York: J. Wiley and Sons, 1916. 856 p.

102   Robertson, Ross. HISTORY OF THE AMERICAN ECONOMY. New York: Harcourt Brace, 1955. 593 p.

103   Schieber, Harry N. UNITED STATES ECONOMIC HISTORY. New York: Knopf, 1964. 583 p.

104   Schouler, J. HISTORY OF THE UNITED STATES OF AMERICA. 7 vols. New York: Dodd, Mead, and Co., 1894-1913.

105   Semple, Ellen C. AMERICAN HISTORY AND ITS GEOGRAPHIC CONDITIONS. New York: Houghton Mifflin and Co., 1903. 466 p.

106 Seybert, Adam. STATISTICAL ANNALS. Philadelphia: Thomas Dobson and Son, 1818. 803 p.

107 Smart, William. ECONOMIC ANNALS OF THE NINETEENTH CENTURY, 1801-1830. London: Macmillan and Co., 1910. 280 p.

108 Thwaites, R.G. THE COLONIES, 1492-1750. New York: Longmans, Green, and Co., 1902. 301 p.

109 Tyler, L.G. ENGLAND IN AMERICA. New York: Harper and Brothers, 1904. 355 p.

110 Urquhart, M.C. "Historical Statistics of the United States, Colonial Times to 1957." JOURNAL OF ECONOMIC HISTORY 21 (September 1961): 361-63.

111 Warden, David B. A STATISTICAL, POLITICAL, AND HISTORICAL ACCOUNT OF THE UNITED STATES. 3 vols. Edinburgh: A. Constable and Co., 1819.

112 Webster, W.C. A GENERAL HISTORY OF COMMERCE. New York: Ginn and Co., 1918. 453 p.

113 Williamson, Harold F. THE GROWTH OF THE AMERICAN ECONOMY. New York: Prentice-Hall, 1951. 946 p.

114 Wilson, Woodrow. THE HISTORY OF THE AMERICAN PEOPLE. 5 vols. New York: Harper and Brothers, 1902.

Chapter 2

POPULATION AND THE LABOR FORCE

The citations included in this chapter relate to the various issues in migration, immigration, and labor force developments from the colonial period to the present. These are only a selection of the multitude of sources available on population and labor, especially from the more historical view. Many of the major sources of data and the works dealing with controversial issues are included. These analytic works concentrate on the economic aspects. The user is encouraged to explore the citations in chapter 8 on regional development for additional works on slavery in the antebellum South.

The CENSUS OF THE UNITED STATES provides exceptionally good information on population, and the U.S. Treasury's ANNUAL REPORT ON COMMERCE AND NAVIGATION also provides information on immigration since approximately 1867. If assistance with sources of data is needed, consult the available government documents librarian.

2.1 ANNOTATED LISTINGS

115 Abbott, Edith. "History of the Employment of Women in The American Cotton Mill." JOURNAL OF POLITICAL ECONOMY 16 (November 1908): 602-21; (December 1908): 680-92; 17 (January 1909): 19-35.

> The composition of workers, the patterns and conditions of employment, and the lifestyle of American cotton mill workers are examined in this study. The last of the three parts examines the sanitary conditions in cotton mills and the impact of the crisis of 1848-49 as well as the impact of immigration and internal migration.

116 _____. "The History of the Industrial Employment of Women in the United States: An Introductory Study." JOURNAL OF POLITICAL ECONOMY 14 (October 1906): 461-501.

> In an attempt to test the hypothesis that cheap female labor drives out less cheap male labor, the author has examined employment statistics for women in manufacturing between 1800

and 1900 as well as early attitudes toward women working in industry. This paper is critiqued in Rubinow, I.M. "Women in Manufactures: A Critique." JOURNAL OF POLITICAL ECONOMY 15 (January 1907): 41–47.

117 _____. "The Wages of Unskilled Labor in the United States, 1850–1900." JOURNAL OF POLITICAL ECONOMY 13 (June 1905): 321–67.

The intent is to statistically analyze whether unskilled labor received its share of the increase in productivity, given the increase in real wages.

118 Adams, Donald R., Jr. "Some Evidence on English and American Wage Rates, 1790–1830." JOURNAL OF ECONOMIC HISTORY 30 (September 1970): 499–520.

By analyzing the magnitude of wage differentials between skilled and unskilled and rural and urban labor in the United States and England, the author attempts to account for the relatively capital-intensive industry in the United States by comparing relative factor costs in the two countries.

119 _____. "Wage Rates in the Early National Period: Philadelphia, 1785–1830." JOURNAL OF ECONOMIC HISTORY 28 (September 1968): 404–426.

The analysis sheds light on the problems of skilled-unskilled wage differentials, rural-urban wage differentials, and the impact of industrialization and international events on the wage earner. Both money and real wages are examined.

120 Aldrich, [Terry] Mark. "Earnings of American Civil Engineers, 1820–1859." JOURNAL OF ECONOMIC HISTORY 31 (June 1971): 407–19.

Changing conditions of competition altered the economic structure of the engineering profession as it became continually more technical. These engineers were of crucial importance to the development of transportation systems, especially in the South. More emphasis is placed upon the changing economic structure than on the role of engineers in development.

121 _____. "Rates of Return Earned on Investments in Formal Technical Education in the Antebellum American Economy." JOURNAL OF ECONOMIC HISTORY 30 (March 1970): 251–55.

Attention is focused on the educational process that produced the stock of technically trained people who developed the transportation revolution. After analyzing both the direct and the opportunity costs of acquiring an education, the author concludes that there were other investments which had higher rates of return than education. This was particularly true for the

U.S. Military Academy, where many of the early technically trained people received their education.

122 Aufhauser, R. Keith. "Slavery and Scientific Management." JOURNAL OF ECONOMIC HISTORY 33 (December 1973): 811-24.

In an attempt to decide whether the southern slaveholder followed the most efficient practice, this author compares the methods used with those laid out by F.W. Taylor for scientific management. The practices used by the managers of free workers were the same as those used by most slave managers, especially the managers of workers in the large corporations of the late nineteeth century.

123 Bell, Philip W. "Cyclical Variations and Trend in Occupational Wage Differentials in American Industry Since 1914." REVIEW OF ECONOMICS AND STATISTICS 33 (November 1951): 329-37.

A critique of previous work on shifts in occupational wage differentials is presented along with further empirical analysis of changes in the wage structure. The depression years of 1929-33 are also included in his analysis, whereas others excluded them.

124 Bernstein, Irving. "The Growth of American Unions." AMERICAN ECONOMIC REVIEW 44 (June 1954): 301-18.

Relying heavily upon quantitative data, Bernstein analyzes the growth of unionism with respect to the following variables: (1) growth of the labor force; (2) growing social acceptability of unions; (3) increasing homogeneity of labor; (4) the extension of collective bargaining; (5) wars; and (6) severe depressions. A comment by Charles W. Fristoe and a reply by Bernstein appear in AMERICAN ECONOMIC REVIEW 45 (June 1955): 386-93.

125 Bowley, A.L. "Comparison of the Changes in Wages in France, the United States, and the United Kingdom, from 1840-1891." ECONOMIC JOURNAL 8 (December 1898): 474-89.

This deals strictly with the rates of increase of wages rather than the comparison of average wages.

126 _____. "Comparison of the Rates of Increase of Wages in the United States and in Great Britain 1860-1891." ECONOMIC JOURNAL 5 (September 1895): 369-83.

This is an examination of the changes in the purchasing power of money, which resulted from changes in the ratio of the rates of increase in average wages in the two countries.

127 Brito, D.L., and Williamson, Jeffrey G. "Skilled Labor and Nineteenth Century Anglo-American Managerial Behavior." EXPLORATIONS IN ECONOMIC HISTORY 10 (Spring 1973): 235-52.

Avoiding the debates of other writers with respect to labor scarcity, this treatment zeroes in on the differences between U.S. and British managerial behavior during the antebellum and pre-World War I periods. It is argued that the cost of capital services was less dear in the United States, when one compares interest rate differentials.

128 Brogan, D.W. "The American Negro Problem." ECONOMIC HISTORY REVIEW 15 (April 1945): 73-78.

Reviewing Gunnar Myrdal's AN AMERICAN DILEMMA: THE NEGRO PROBLEM AND MODERN DEMOCRACY (New York: Harper and Brothers, 1944), this article provides perspective on the problems rooted in economics, history, and sociological separation.

129 Campbell, Robert, and Siegel, Barry N. "The Demand for Higher Education in the United States, 1919-1964." AMERICAN ECONOMIC REVIEW 57 (June 1967): 482-94.

This is an analysis of post-World War I demand for higher education, using income and price (tuition) as explanatory variables.

130 Closson, Carlos C. "The History of 'Unemployment'." JOURNAL OF POLITICAL ECONOMY 3 (September 1895): 461-69.

The development of charitable agencies and methods during previous periods of unemployment are the topic of this article.

131 Cobb, Charles W. "Some Statistical Relations between Wages and Prices." JOURNAL OF POLITICAL ECONOMY 37 (December 1929): 728-36.

Presents data supporting the theory that an attempt to straighten any one of the ratio curves of prices, employment, real wages, or labor's share will straighten the other series. The author argues that as long as the trend ratio curves of employment and prices move in like directions, stability will be enhanced by such straightening attempts.

132 Cobb, Charles W., and Douglas, Paul H. "A Theory of Production." AMERICAN ECONOMIC REVIEW 18 (March 1928): 139-65.

In this article the authors lay out the model for a production function that was to be used repeatedly by economic historians.

133 Coelho, Philip R.P., and Ghali, Molteb A. "The End of the North-

South Wage Differential." AMERICAN ECONOMIC REVIEW 16 (December 1971): 932-37.

Admitting that investments in human capital will alter one's level of productivity, the authors argue that in terms of real wages there is no difference between wages in the North and those in the South. Therefore, the market mechanism has not failed to equalize real return to factor inputs. A comment by Mark L. Ladenson and a reply by Coelho and Ghali appear in AMERICAN ECONOMIC REVIEW 63 (September 1973): 754-62.

134 Coen, Robert M. "Labor Force and Unemployment in the 1920's and 1930's: A Re-Examination Based on Postwar Experience." REVIEW OF ECONOMICS AND STATISTICS 55 (February 1973): 46-55.

Taking into account some commonly ignored factors, a model is developed which produces more accurate estimates of post-war and prewar labor force and employment statistics. The estimates for the prewar years imply there were unemployment rates of 5 percent or greater during five of the eight years 1922-29.

135 Conrad, Alfred H.; Dowd, Douglas; Engerman, Stanley; Ginzberg, Eli; Kelso, Charles; Meyer, John R.; Scheiber, Harry N.; and Sutch, Richard. "Slavery as an Obstacle to Economic Growth in the United States: A Panel Discussion." JOURNAL OF ECONOMIC HISTORY 27 (December 1967): 518-60.

The purpose of the panel discussion is to examine thoroughly the model and underlying rationale of Conrad and Meyer in their seminal article (see no. 1114) on the profitability of slavery. After examining all possible aspects, the panel concludes that the model had contributed to the development of precision and measurement in economic history.

136 Cox, Lawanda F. "The American Agricultural Wage Earner: 1865-1900: The Emergence of a Modern Labor Problem." AGRICULTURAL HISTORY 22 (April 1948): 95-113.

An attempt is made in this paper to examine the roots of farm labor unrest.

137 Cullen, Donald E. "The Industry Wage Structure, 1899-1950." AMERICAN ECONOMIC REVIEW 46 (June 1956): 353-69.

In contrast to previous studies, this one finds that in the long run the interindustry wage structure has been constant during these fifty years. Narrowing was found to occur only temporarily at the extremes of business cycles.

138   Diamond, D.E.   "The Service Worker in U.S. Manufacturing and Employ-
       ment Stability."   OXFORD ECONOMIC PAPERS   14 (February 1962): 81-
       93.

       The article addresses whether the lower lay-off rate in the
       service sector served as a stabilizing force counterbalancing
       effects from production workers being laid off.

139   Douglas, Paul. REAL WAGES IN THE UNITED STATES, 1890-1926. New
       York: Houghton Mifflin Co., 1930. 682 p.

       Attempting to measure the material progress of American work-
       ers, the author computes a new cost-of-living index, a refined
       series of wage rates, averages of the annual earnings of em-
       ployed workers, the probable amount of unemployment, and the
       earnings of the wage-earning class as a whole. These data are
       examined to assess the material progress obtained.

140   Easterlin, Richard A.   "Influences in European Overseas Emigration before
       World War 1."   ECONOMIC DEVELOPMENT AND CULTURAL CHANGE
       9 (April 1961): 331-51.

       This article is an attempt to discern various differences in the
       patterns of emigration, with special emphasis on the country
       differences in the secular level of emigration, differences in
       the long-term trend, and the long swing cycles. An analysis
       of relative peaks and troughs is conducted for immigration and
       income levels.

141   _____. POPULATION, LABOR FORCE, AND LONG SWINGS IN ECO-
       NOMIC GROWTH. New York: National Bureau of Economic Research,
       1968. 298 p.

       This is an examination of the interrelation of demographic and
       economic swings, fertility rates, the labor force, and the vari-
       ous sources of data on these topics.

142   _____. "Population Change and Farm Settlement in the Northern United
       States." JOURNAL OF ECONOMIC HISTORY 36 (March 1976): 45-83.

       Contrary to the usual Malthusian framework, this work empha-
       sizes that a decline in fertility and not a rise in mortality gen-
       erated the declining size of farm families. The pattern of
       farm settlement is addressed and then the decline in the fertil-
       ity of the farm population is discussed. A hypothesis is ad-
       vanced that such fertility declines were conscious attempts to
       forestall the wider distribution of one's wealth among the children.

143   Eisemann, Doris M. "Inter-Industry Wage Changes, 1939-1947." REVIEW
       OF ECONOMICS AND STATISTICS 38 (November 1956): 445-48.

Utilizing Census Bureau and Bureau of Labor Statistics data, the author analyzes the significance of interindustry wage differentials for fifty-seven industries. The relationships examined include those between earnings changes and the original earnings level as well as changes in production, employment, productivity, the importance of wages in total costs, and the extent of unionization.

144 Engerman, Stanley. "The Effect of Slavery upon the Southern Economy: Review of the Recent Debate." EXPLORATIONS IN ECONOMIC HISTORY 4 (Winter 1967): 71-97.

Examines the positions of U.B. Phillips and C.W. Ransdell, concentrating on three points: (1) profitability of slavery; (2) the viability of slavery as a system; and (3) the effect of slavery on the development of the South.

145 Ermich, John, and Weiss, Thomas. "The Impact of the Rural Market on the Growth of the Urban Workforce, U.S. 1870-1900." EXPLORATIONS IN ECONOMIC HISTORY 11 (Winter 1973-74): 137-54.

By concentrating on the market for manufactured goods, an attempt is made to examine the hypothesis that urban growth resulted partially from an expansion of its role as a supplier to the rural sector. The service sector is also examined, with the conclusion that it was of lesser importance than manufacturing in this urban-rural relationship.

146 Fine, Sidney. "The Origins of the United Automobile Workers, 1933-1935." JOURNAL OF ECONOMIC HISTORY 18 (September 1958): 249-82.

Examining the power struggles and the nature of the auto industry, the author traces the rise of the U.A.W. The reasons why it was so difficult to unionize the industry's workers are also laid out.

147 Fishlow, Albert. "Levels of Nineteenth-Century American Investment in Education." JOURNAL OF ECONOMIC HISTORY 26 (December 1966): 418-36.

The mandate for public education was manifest by 1850. Both legally and financially the scene was set. The magnitude of resources spent on education is evaluated, and a comparison of public and private outlays is made. An attempt is also made to compare the expenditure with the opportunity cost of not working and to compare this period with European and present expenditures.

148 Fleisig, Heywood. "Slavery, the Supply of Agricultural Labor, and the Industrialization of the South." JOURNAL OF ECONOMIC HISTORY 36 (September 1976): 572-96.

This is an argument that slavery's relief of the labor constraint on production increased absolute profits and retarded the mechanization of southern agricultural production and industrialization in general. A very thorough analysis of an extremely evasive question.

149 Foust, James D., and Swan, Dale E. "Productivity and Profitability of Antebellum Slave Labor: A Micro Approach." AGRICULTURAL HISTORY 44 (January 1970): 39-62.

Examining the productivity of slaves across time, the authors provide another estimate of cotton output per slave for 1850 and 1860, taking into account geographic regions, soil types, and slaveholding classes. Internal rates of return and varying rates of profitability are also examined with respect to these same variations.

150 Gallaway, Lowell E. "The North-South Wage Differential." REVIEW OF ECONOMICS AND STATISTICS 45 (August 1963): 264-72.

First an attempt is made to explain wage differentials by the existence of barriers to the free flow of labor. Various empirical tests are performed on other explanations of the wage differential, such as the monopolistic exploitation argument, the excess labor supply argument, and the regional production function argument. See also Kaun, David E., "The North-South Wage Differential: A Comment." REVIEW OF ECONOMICS AND STATISTICS 47 (August 1965): 337-38.

151 Gallaway, Lowell E., and Vedder, Richard K. "Emigration from the United Kingdom to the United States: 1860-1913." JOURNAL OF ECONOMIC HISTORY 31 (December 1971): 885-97.

Attempting to discover whether the pull of the new economy or the push of the old was the motive force behind immigration during this period, the authors apply regression analysis to the data. Since there was little in the sociopolitical environment to generate the flow of immigrants, the question was what had caused the seemingly unorganized flows of people. Pull is found to have been slightly more important than push, although both were important.

152 _____. "The Increasing Urbanization Thesis--Did 'New Immigrants' to the United States Have a Particular Fondness for Urban Life?" EXPLORATIONS IN ECONOMIC HISTORY 8 (Spring 1971): 305-20.

After examining the existing theoretical and empirical work regarding the settlement of new immigrants, the authors conclude that the increasing urbanization hypothesis--that the immigrants followed the pattern of the U.S. population--is not substantiated.

153 _____. "Mobility of Native Americans." JOURNAL OF ECONOMIC HISTORY 31 (September 1971): 613-49.

> The factors underlying the patterns of migration are analyzed through the use of economic theory, historical data, and techniques of statistical estimation. People appear to have become increasingly more responsive to factors such as distance. The period of time covered was 1850 to 1960.

154 Gallaway, Lowell E.; Vedder, Richard K.; and Chukla, Vishwa. "The Distribution of the Immigrant Population in the United States: An Economic Analysis." EXPLORATIONS IN ECONOMIC HISTORY 11 (Spring 1974): 213-26.

> Concentrating on early twentieth-century data, a very strong argument is made that immigrants were very accurate in tracing out the areas with abundant economic opportunities. Mobility is treated as an investment in human capital decisions, and a gravity-flow model is used.

155 Genovere, Eugene D. THE POLITICAL ECONOMY OF SLAVERY. New York: Pantheon Books, 1965. 304 p.

> Argues that slavery produced a social system and civilization in the South that was distinctly different from the remainder of the country. Many of the relevant economic factors are discussed and compared with those data for the North. Much of the force of this book has been reduced by more recent study of the antebellum South.

156 Goodrich, Carter, et al. MIGRATION AND ECONOMIC OPPORTUNITY. Philadelphia: University of Pennsylvania Press, 1936. 763 p.

> This is an extensive analysis of the regional impact of migration and how the changing demand for labor altered the flow of migration. The second part of the book deals with various aspects of migration control used by other countries, namely; Russia, Germany, and Great Britain, as well as the United States.

157 Grant, Arthur. "Issues in Distribution Theory: The Measurement of Labor's Relative Share, 1899-1929." REVIEW OF ECONOMICS AND STATISTICS 45 (August 1963): 273-79.

> Arguing that the work of others has erroneously used national income as a basis upon which to examine the relative share of labor of output, an alternative method of measurement is offered. The new method measures the ratio of employee compensation to the production of the particular sector of the economy.

158   Gray, L.C.   "Economic Efficiency and Competitive Advantages of Slavery under the Plantation System." AGRICULTURAL HISTORY 4 (April 1930): 31–47.

The advantages that produced competitive superiority as well as the history of the process of substituting slave labor for free labor are extensively discussed. This is one of the earlier works on this topic.

159   Grob, Gerald N.   "The Knights of Labor and the Trade Unions, 1878–1886." JOURNAL OF ECONOMIC HISTORY 18 (June 1958): 176–92.

The long-standing rift between trade unions and unions that admit general laborers is examined for the particular case of the Knights of Labor. Such differences in structure and ideology still exist but to a lesser extent.

160   Grubel, H.G., and Scott, A.D. "The Immigration of Scientists and Engineers to the United States, 1949–61." JOURNAL OF POLITICAL ECONOMY 74 (August 1966): 368–78.

Evaluating the magnitude of the "brain drain," the authors estimate the human capital content of these immigrants on the basis of a similarly qualified person in the United States. Time series data are used for both the United States and for countries experiencing the loss.

161   Haddy, Pamela, and Tolles, N. Arnold.   "British and American Changes in Interindustry Wage Structure under Full Employment." REVIEW OF ECONOMICS STATISTICS 39 (November 1957): 408–14.

Prior to World War II both the United States and Great Britain were moving toward full employment. This situation allows the authors to examine the effect on the structure and level of wages as well as the stability of relative wages. The forces that maintained such an environment are also examined.

162   Hall, John Phillip.   "The Knights of St. Crispin in Massachusetts, 1869–1878." JOURNAL OF ECONOMIC HISTORY 18 (June 1958): 161–75.

Analyzing a single local's activities and philosophy, the author attempts to discover the experimental aspect of the knights and to investigate the opposition. The method used is to study the local personalities and environment instead of relying solely upon the media releases of the tradition-bound national leaders.

163   Hall, Prescott F.   "The Recent History of Immigration and Immigration Restriction." JOURNAL OF POLITICAL ECONOMY 21 (October 1913): 735–51.

Describing the pattern of immigration between 1907 and 1913, the article also contains an examination of federal immigration restrictions and the supporting political arguments.

164 Hanna, Frank A. "Age, Labor Force, and State Per Capita Incomes, 1930, 1940, and 1950." REVIEW OF ECONOMICS AND STATISTICS 37 (February 1955): 63-69.

Examines the effects of variations of family size and composition, birth and death rates, participation in the labor force, and other demographic variables on per capita income by state. The effect of using various denominators on the distribution of "per capita" income among states is also discussed.

165 Heald, Morrell. "Business Attitudes toward European Immigration, 1880-1900." JOURNAL OF ECONOMIC HISTORY 13 (Summer 1953): 291-304.

After years of exploiting the availability of cheap abundant labor, businessmen and laborers alike began to oppose free immigration, which was to be gradually closed during the 1880s. The declining quality of immigrants and the rise of unionism generated a concern for the stability of the United States. This article analyzes these changes and events.

166 Higgs, Robert. "Mortality in Rural America, 1870-1920: Estimates and Conjectures." EXPLORATIONS IN ECONOMIC HISTORY 10 (Winter 1973): 177-96.

This is an examination of the effects of advances which improved both urban and rural health conditions after 1870, thus lowering the mortality rates of both areas.

167 _____. "Race, Skills, and Earnings: American Immigrants in 1909." JOURNAL OF ECONOMIC HISTORY 31 (June 1971): 420-28.

Two explanations have been offered to explain the fact that "old" immigrants were paid higher wages than "new" immigrants: (1) skill differentials, and (2) ethnic discrimination. The evidence assembled supports the first argument and not the second. The evidence does not support the accusations that immigrants were exploited, unskilled laborers.

168 Hill, Peter J. "Relative Skill and Income Levels of Native and Foreign Born Workers in the United States." EXPLORATIONS IN ECONOMIC HISTORY 12 (January 1975): 47-60.

This article is an attempt to discern whether, on an economic basis, foreign-born fared any worse than native-born workers. Using a large amount of quantitative data, the author concludes that there was little economic difference. Peter R. Shergold argues that although these foreign-born were economically as well off as native-born, the presence and costs of discrimination may not be ruled out. He argues that in fact a large amount of discrimination existed, which leads one to believe that the foreign-born must have compensated in some way. See Shergold, "Relative Skill and Income Levels of Native and Foreign Born Workers: A Reexamination." EXPLORATIONS IN ECONOMIC HISTORY 13 (October 1976): 451-62.

169 Hoover, Edgar M., Jr. "Interstate Redistribution of Population, 1850-1940." JOURNAL OF ECONOMIC HISTORY 1 (November 1941): 199-205.

Population density movements and the rate of population redistribution for particular ethnic groups are examined for various decades. A redistribution coefficient is derived for the purpose of estimating the net result of birth-death ratios and migration patterns. Census data for the United States are used and comparisons are made on a state-by-state basis.

170 Jones, Ethel B. "New Estimates of Hours of Work Per Week and Hourly Earnings, 1900-1957." REVIEW OF ECONOMICS AND STATISTICS 45 (November 1963): 374-85.

Due to the increased presence of paid vacations for workers, the Bureau of Labor Statistics data on earnings per week understate the actual situation for hourly earnings per week. The "hours per week worked" are adjusted for these discrepancies, and data for the years since 1900 are provided where not covered by the B.L.S. data.

171 Keat, Paul G. "Long-Run Changes in Occupational Wage Structure, 1900-1956." JOURNAL OF POLITICAL ECONOMY 68 (December 1960): 584-600.

Examining a composite sample of many occupations in a variety of industries, this study corroborates the evidence from less extensive studies regarding the narrowing of wage differentials associated with skill differentials. The possible causes of such a narrowing in wage differentials are also discussed.

172 Kelley, Allen C. "Demographic Cycles and Economic Growth: The Long Swing Reconsidered." JOURNAL OF ECONOMIC HISTORY 29 (December 1969): 633-56.

Through the use of a life-cycle savings model the author analyzes the effect of a demographic shock on the economy, especially with respect to the generation of Kuznets cycles. The demographic shocks from immigration supposedly generated many of the long swings in economic activity, because of their effect on aggregate saving.

173 _____. "Scale Economics, Inventive Activity, and the Economics of American Population Growth." EXPLORATION IN ECONOMIC HISTORY 10 (Fall 1972): 35-52.

A timely piece on the impact of population growth, the historical record is first examined and compared with the present situation. It is concluded that it was the rate of technological change which made rapid population growth important, but such rapid growth of technological development no longer prevails. Therefore, the benefits of population growth are diminishing.

174 Kravis, Irving B. "Wages and Foreign Trade." REVIEW OF ECONOMICS AND STATISTICS 38 (February 1956): 14-30.

Although manufacturing is the primary sector, agriculture and mining are also discussed in this study of wage levels in export and import-competing industries. Export industries were found to have relatively higher wages. The rationale for this was the higher proportion of durable goods industries in the export sector than in the import-competing sector.

175 Kuznets, Simon. POPULATION, CAPITAL, AND GROWTH. New York: W.W. Norton & Co., 1973. 342 p.

This collection of essays by Kuznets emcompasses more than strictly population issues, but three of the ten articles deal with various aspects of population and growth. The first essay is an especially good piece.

176 Kuznets, Simon, et al. POPULATION REDISTRIBUTION AND ECONOMIC GROWTH, UNITED STATES, 1870-1950. 3 vols. Philadelphia: American Philosophical Society, 1957. 759, 289, 368 p.

Given that a continuous chain of independent variables links economic growth and population redistribution, the authors attempt to provide information on these various independent variables. It is probably the best single source available on population, per capita income trends, employment trends, and redistribution of these variables over the period 1870 to 1950.

177 Landes, William M., and Solmon, Lewis C. "Compulsory Schooling Legislation: An Economic Analysis of Law and Social Change in the Nineteenth Century." JOURNAL OF ECONOMIC HISTORY 32 (March 1972): 54-91.

This is a systematic empirical analysis of the determinants of different schooling levels, both across states and over time. The hypothesis that legislation was responsible for increases in the levels of schooling is rejected and alternative hypotheses are proffered.

178 Lebergott, Stanley. MANPOWER IN ECONOMIC GROWTH. New York: McGraw-Hill, 1964. 561 p.

Two general questions are addressed: (1) how has manpower in the United States been rewarded and utilized since 1800; and (2) what are the more significant consequences for growth that have resulted from this pattern of use and reward. Various new series are constructed. It is considered to be one of the best sources for labor force information.

179 _____. "Migration within the U.S., 1800-1960: Some New Estimates." JOURNAL OF ECONOMIC HISTORY 30 (December 1970): 839-47.

A new method of population estimation is derived using the census data, and it is applied to the period 1870-1960. The results are quite consistent with those derived by the Wharton School project on population flows for 1800-1870. Migration is viewed as both a cause and consequence of the redistribution of resources and changing productivity patterns and levels.

180 Lerner, Eugene M. "Money, Prices, and Wages in the Confederacy, 1860-65." JOURNAL OF POLITICAL ECONOMY 63 (February 1955): 20-40.

Because of the reduced area in which confederate notes were acceptable, the money stock effectively increased along with the rise in velocity and the decline of real output. Money and price indexes are constructed for various areas of the South to examine the effects of inflation. The impact of the northern blockade, the effect on the real value of money, wage movements, and the popular response to inflation are also examined.

181 Lester, Richard A. "Effectiveness of Factory Labor: South-North Comparisons." JOURNAL OF POLITICAL ECONOMY 54 (February 1946): 60-75.

Allegations that southern wages were lower because southern labor was less efficient than northern labor have prevailed for years. This study examines the record for firms that had plants in the North and the South as a test case to learn the causes of wage differentials and the experience of unions.

182 _____. "Effects of the War on Wages and Hours." AMERICAN ECONOMIC REVIEW 33 (March 1943): 218-37.

Tracing the trend of wages through the war period, attention is finally focused on the potential problem of postwar wage distortions resulting from an excess of liquid assets including money. The author recommends that wartime controls be extended and that government provide guidance for production and investment.

183 _____. "Negotiated Wage Increases, 1951-1967." REVIEW OF ECO-
NOMICS AND STATISTICS 50 (May 1968): 173-81.

This is a comparison of negotiated wage settlements series in
manufacturing and more specifically building construction, with
straight-time average earnings in manufacturing. By comparing
these series for the unemployment rate in manufacturing industries, light is shed on such topics as "wage drift" and wage
price guidelines of the 1960s. The influence of guidelines on
negotiated wage increases is also investigated.

184 Levasseur, Emile. "Wages in the United States." JOURNAL OF POLITI-
CAL ECONOMY 4 (March 1896): 166-86.

Determinants of wages such as custom, supply and demand,
productivity of labor, cost of living, competition, and the
production and consumption of capital are considered after
the author considers whether the wage system is a permanent
mode of organization.

185 Lockridge, Kenneth A. "The Population of Dedham, Massachusetts, 1636-
1736." ECONOMIC HISTORY REVIEW 19 (August 1966): 318-44.

Highlighting the difficulties of historical demography, the
study contains a comparison of the American village with
European villages that had similar population trends.

186 Logan, Frenise A. "Factors Influencing the Efficiency of Negro Farm
Laborers in Post-Reconstruction North Carolina." AGRICULTURAL HIS-
TORY 33 (October 1959): 185-89.

The efficiency of black farm workers is examined with respect
to the effects of barriers to entry in skilled jobs, wages, tenancy laws, and the mortgage and lien bond system.

187 Long, Clarence D. THE LABOR FORCE UNDER CHANGING INCOME
AND EMPLOYMENT. Princeton, N.J.: Princeton University Press, 1958.
439 p.

This is an attempt to answer the questions left by less complete
studies, for example, has income and employment influenced
participation rates? Are the effects of income and employment
dominant? and do any one of the other influences furnish a
rather complete explanation of labor force behavior? It is
especially concerned with the role of women in the labor force.

188 _____. WAGES AND EARNINGS IN THE UNITED STATES, 1860-1890.
Princeton, N.J.: Princeton University Press, 1960. 169 p.

The author studies various time periods and real versus nominal
wage changes. He provides comparisons of wage differences
by industry, region, occupation, and sex.

189 McMurry, Donald L. "Labor Policies of the General Managers' Association of Chicago, 1886-1894." JOURNAL OF ECONOMIC HISTORY 13 (Spring 1953): 160-78.

> An account of collective action on the part of management is presented in the case of the General Managers Association in Chicago. This article describes the commonly obscured facts regarding the activity of the association both prior to and as a counter-measure to the American Railway Union strike of 1894.

190 Maddox, James G. "Private and Social Costs of the Movement of People Out of Agriculture." AMERICAN ECONOMIC REVIEW 50 (May 1960): 392-402.

> The cost of off-farm migration and their implications for policy formulation are the topic of this article. Types of costs considered include cost of the migrants, costs to the community from which they came, and cost to the community to which they migrate.

191 Maher, John E. "The Pattern of Wage Movements in the United States Since 1945--Its Meaning and Significance." REVIEW OF ECONOMICS AND STATISTICS 43 (August 1961): 277-82.

> An attempt to assess the impact of collective bargaining on wage structure by accounting for both wage and earnings differentials, this article examines differences among thirteen industries.

192 Mansfield, Edwin. "Wage Differentials in the Cotton Textile Industry, 1933-1952." REVIEW OF ECONOMICS AND STATISTICS 37 (February 1955): 77-82.

> Unlike most studies, this one focuses upon a single industry and examines wage differentials within that industry. The purpose of such an approach is to provide a format for later, more intensive studies of the relationship between cyclical movements and wage differentials, and with the industry's total wage dispersion.

193 Markham, Jessie W. "Regional Labor Productivity in the Textile Industry." AMERICAN ECONOMIC REVIEW 33 (March 1943): 110-15.

> Examining data from two large corporations that operated plants in the North and the South that were identical in every possible way, an investigation is made of the possible causes of productivity differences. Areas considered include occupational heritage, racial and ethnic attributes, temperament, cultural background, intelligence, and education.

194 Mears, Eliot G. "Financial Aspects of American Immigration." ECO-
NOMIC JOURNAL 33 (September 1923): 332-42.

> This is an examination of the economic motives and strictly
> financial aspects of migration, for example, the resulting
> money transfers.

195 Mecker, Edward. "The Improving Health of the United States, 1850-1915."
EXPLORATIONS IN ECONOMIC HISTORY 9 (Summer 1972): 353-74.

> It is argued that very little was accomplished prior to the 1880s
> with respect to mortality rates, but that after that time the
> sanitation movement yielded significant reductions in the mor-
> tality rate.

196 Mills, H., and Montgomery, R. ORGANIZED LABOR. New York:
McGraw-Hill, 1945. 930 p.

> Dealing with the evolution of the labor movement, the authors
> carefully elucidate the history, structure, government, policies,
> interrelationships, institutionalism, and relationship with the
> courts, as well as various problems arising from unionism. Since
> it is a capsulized account, some acquaintance with the nature
> of organized labor is assumed.

197 Mood, Fulmer. "A British Statistician of 1854 Analyzes the Western Movement in the United States." AGRICULTURAL HISTORY 19 (July 1945):
142-51.

> The essential issue of this paper is the effect the westward
> movement had on the information gathered in the 1850 U.S.
> Census.

198 Mooney, Peter J., and Orsagh, Thomas J. "A Model for the Dispersion
of the Migrant Labor Force and Some Results for the United States, 1880-
1920." REVIEW OF ECONOMICS AND STATISTICS 52 (August 1970):
306-12.

> As an attempt to explain geographical distribution and labor
> force mobility, the author develops and tests a theoretical
> model. The model is developed to distinguish demand and
> supply forces in labor movements.

199 Murphy, George G.S., and Zellner, Arnold. "Sequential Growth, the
Labor-Safety-Value Doctrine and the Development of American Unionism."
JOURNAL OF ECONOMIC HISTORY 19 (September 1959): 402-21.

> Frederick Jackson Turner's safety-value doctrine is applied to
> labor. Sequential growth and the legislative climate are said
> to have provided alternative activities for the unions. Sequen-
> tial growth is credited for unions as well as other institutions.

A comment is provided by August C. Bolins in this same journal, volume 20 (June 1960): 314-17, and a reply by Murphy appears in volume 21 (March 1961): 81-84.

200 National Bureau of Economic Research, ed. ASPECTS OF LABOR ECO-
NOMICS. Princeton, N.J.: Princeton University Press, 1962. 349 p.

Comprising eight papers: the first three, by S. Rottenberg, A. Alchian and R. Kessel, and R. Evans, deal with market organization and structure; the next two papers by H.G. Lewis and M.W. Reder deal with relative wage differentials among sections of the labor force; the sixth paper by T.W. Shultz analyzes the functioning of the labor market especially for female clerical workers; the seventh by J. Mincer examines the usefulness of the backward bending supply curve argument for explaining the empirical evidence; and the eighth paper by A. Siegel explores the form and structure of labor protest and its relation to industrialization.

201 Neal, Larry, and Uselding, Paul. "Immigration, A Neglected Source of American Economic Growth, 1790 to 1912." OXFORD ECONOMIC PAPERS 24 (March 1972): 68-88.

Ignoring the more general question of whether immigrants merely displaced domestic-born laborers, the authors calculate the contribution made by immigrants to the growth of output. The uses to which resources that were freed by the immigrants were applied are explored along with the effects of these uses on the contribution to total output.

202 North, Douglas C. "Agenda for a History of Management Policies towards Labor in the United States." JOURNAL OF ECONOMIC HISTORY 16 (June 1956): 206-10.

Attempting to fill a void in the literature on industrial labor relations, the author analyzes the expansion of scientific management, which he views as a change in the role of management vis-a-vis the labor unions and government. How well has management been able to control labor, is the question he asks.

203 Novack, David E., and Perlman, Richard. "The Structure of Wages in The American Iron and Steel Industry, 1860-1890." JOURNAL OF ECO-
NOMIC HISTORY 22 (September 1962): 334-47.

This period is free from significant government and union interference and therefore provides a testing ground for the theory of wages. Very strong movements influenced the wage structure during this period, reducing the effects of random movements. Good use is made of the rather scanty wage data.

204 Page, Thomas Walker. "The Distribution of Immigrants in the United States before 1870." JOURNAL OF POLITICAL ECONOMY 20 (July 1912): 676-694.

The reasons why immigrants settled where they did and why native-born people migrated are the subject of this essay.

205 _____. "Some Economic Aspects of Immigration before 1870." JOURNAL OF POLITICAL ECONOMY 20 (December 1912): 1011-28; 21 (January 1913): 34-55.

Examining efforts to diminish the burdens of immigration, the author also examines the ethnic composition of paupers and criminals as well as aspects of the lives of immigrants, such as their lack of capital and their different agricultural methods. The process of assimilation of the employed and the effect of laboring immigrants on various sectors is also examined.

206 Papenfuse, Edward C., Jr. "Planter Behavior and Economic Opportunity in a Staple Economy." AGRICULTURAL HISTORY 46 (April 1972): 297-312.

This is a study of planter reactions to soil exhaustion in a tobacco growing region during the eighteenth century.

207 Peppers, Larry. "Full-Employment Surplus Analysis and Structural Change: The 1930's." EXPLORATIONS IN ECONOMIC HISTORY 19 (Winter 1973): 197-210.

By recalculating the full-employment budget surplus under the assumption of unit elasticity of taxes with respect to GNP, the conclusions of earlier works are refined. The author's recalculations are based on the clarification of the changing restrictiveness of fiscal policy.

208 Peterson, John M. "Employment Effects of Minimum Wages, 1938-50." JOURNAL OF POLITICAL ECONOMY 65 (October 1957): 412-30.

In an attempt to reconcile an apparent contradiction between the empirical evidence and predictions of the competitive model, the evidence for employment is reexamined on a cross-sectional basis instead of time series. The cross-sectional evidence for particular industries is consistent with the competitive model with respect to minimum wages.

209 Phillips, Ulrich B. LIFE AND LABOR IN THE OLD SOUTH. Boston: Little, Brown and Co., 1929. 375 p.

This study of the people, the region, and the institutions of the South provides a very detailed view of labor, both slave and free.

210   Poulson, Barry W., and Holyfield, James, Jr. "A Note on European
      Migration to the United States: A Cross Spectral Analysis." EXPLORA-
      TIONS IN ECONOMIC HISTORY 11 (Spring 1974): 299-310.

      Spectral analysis is applied in an attempt to discern whether
      it was push or pull factors that induced immigration during
      the years 1835-1950. Differences in relative income between
      the United States and the European countries appears to be
      the most relevant force for immigration.

211   Raimon, Robert L. "Interstate Migration and Wage Theory." REVIEW
      OF ECONOMICS AND STATISTICS 44 (November 1962): 428-38.

      Focusing on long distance labor mobility, an attempt is made
      to test the hypothesis that labor responds to employment oppor-
      tunities rather than wage differentials.

212   Rasen, Sherwin. "Short-Run Employment Variation on Class-I Railroads
      in the U.S., 1947-1963." ECONOMETRICA 36 (July-October 1968):
      511-29.

      After reviewing both the "specific investment" and the "sub-
      stitution" hypotheses regarding the short-run variations in em-
      ployment, the author considers the implications of occupational
      differences among railroad workers.

213   Rees, A. REAL WAGES IN MANUFACTURING, 1890-1914. Princeton,
      N.J.: Princeton University Press, 1961. 163 p.

      The question is, why did real wages cease to grow during this
      period? By reestimating the necessary data series, the author
      succeeds in shedding new light on this question. Some of the
      previous arguments are reviewed and compared and the move-
      ments in the new real wage series are compared with trends
      in productivity.

214   Reitell, Charles. "Mechanical Evolution and Changing Labor Types."
      JOURNAL OF POLITICAL ECONOMY 26 (March 1918): 274-90.

      Does mechanization require more or less highly skilled workers?
      This article examines forty seven open-hearth steel operations
      with respect to the following characteristics: (1) nature of
      process introduced; (2) effect on safety; (3) effect on number
      of workers required; and (4) the level of work required by
      mechanization as measured by physical needs, intelligence,
      and wages earned.

215   Rezneck, Samuel. "Unemployment, Unrest, and Relief in the United
      States during the Depression of 1893-97." JOURNAL OF POLITICAL
      ECONOMY 61 (August 1953): 324-45.

Using a large quantity of quantitative data on unemployment and relief, as well as information on unrest, the author examines the depression of 1893-97, with special emphasis on the Pullman strike. The role of unions in these three areas is also analyzed.

216 Richardson, W.H. "British Emigration and Overseas Investment, 1870-1914." ECONOMIC HISTORY REVIEW 25 (February 1972): 99-113.

This is an examination of the possible link between international factor flows and factor price differentials. The impact of British overseas investment and emigration is also analyzed.

217 Rosenberg, Nathan. "Anglo-American Wage Differences in the 1820's." JOURNAL OF ECONOMIC HISTORY 27 (June 1967): 221-29.

Using the data published in Zachariah Allen's book THE SCIENCE OF MECHANICS (1829), the author attempts to compare skilled and unskilled wage differentials between countries. He also updates other interpretations of Allen's data.

218 Russel, Robert R. "The Economic History of Negro Slavery in the United States." AGRICULTURAL HISTORY 11 (October 1937): 308-21.

The economic aspects of slavery and the impetus for introducing slavery are the topics of this paper.

219 _____. "The Effects of Slavery upon Nonslaveholders in the Ante Bellum South." AGRICULTURAL HISTORY 15 (April 1941): 112-26.

This is a critique of the commonly held belief that slaveholding planters crowded the nonslaveholding planters out of the more productive regions, thus reducing their standard of living.

220 Schoenberg, Erika H., and Douglas, Paul H. "Studies in the Supply Curve of Labor: The Relation in 1929 between Average Earnings in American Cities and the Proportions Seeking Employment." JOURNAL OF POLITICAL ECONOMY 45 (February 1937): 45-79.

Paralleling an earlier work by Douglas (see no. 139), the present study uses a forty-one-city sample in attempting to determine a short-run supply curve for labor. A comparison is made between the results in this study and those for an earlier period, 1890-1921, which were reported in Douglas's earlier article.

221 Schultz, T.W. "Capital Formation by Education." JOURNAL OF POLITICAL ECONOMY 68 (December 1960): 571-83.

The contribution of human capital from education to economic growth is the topic of this study. The size of the investment in human capital is estimated from the direct and opportunity cost of education since 1900. Calculation of the rate of return on investment in education is left for later work.

222 Schultz, T.W.; Becker, Gary S.; et al. "Investment in Human Beings." JOURNAL OF POLITICAL ECONOMY 70 (October 1962): supplement, 1-157.

This is a collection of papers appearing as a supplement to the October issue, and is generally concerned with the effect of people investing in themselves. Such investment in human capital was found to produce changes in economic growth, the structure of relative earnings, and the distribution of personal income. Types of investment in human capital dealt with were education, on-the-job training, migration, information, and health.

223 Scoville, Warren C. "Minority Migrations and the Diffusion of Technology." JOURNAL OF ECONOMIC HISTORY 11 (Fall 1951): 347-60.

After a brief discussion of the phases of technical change, the author examines the impact of minority migration on the diffusion of technology. Many instances are cited for the world as well as the United States. A rather unfavorable prospect is presented for such technical diffusion in the future.

224 Scroggs, William I. "Interstate Migration of Negro Population." JOURNAL OF POLITICAL ECONOMY 25 (December 1917): 1034-43.

Going back to 1865 in order to understand northern migration during 1916-17, the author explores the motives, organizational patterns, and composition of the migration.

225 Seastone, Don A. "The History of Guaranteed Wages and Employment." JOURNAL OF ECONOMIC HISTORY 15 (June 1955): 134-50.

There have been many movements to obtain guaranteed wage and employment plans. This is a chronological discussion of the various attempts to establish such plans.

226 Shanahan, E.W. "Economic Factors in the Changing Distribution of Population between Urban Centers and Rural Areas." ECONOMIC JOURNAL 37 (September 1927): 395-403.

This is a consideration of the factors facilitating the population shift between rural and urban centers. The author discusses the question, what allowed the smaller population to produce a sufficient amount to support the urban areas?

227 Shipton, Clifford K. "Immigration to New England, 1680-1740." JOUR-
NAL OF POLITICAL ECONOMY 44 (April 1936): 225-39.

On the basis of the limited data available, an attempt is made
to analyze the socioeconomic and political positions of these
people, the reasons why they immigrated, and the impact of
their coming. The general New England area is covered,
with emphasis on Boston.

228 Shofner, Jerrell H. "A Merchant Planter in the Reconstruction South."
AGRICULTURAL HISTORY 42 (April 1972): 291-96.

The plight of a post-Civil War Floridian planter is examined
with respect to his lifestyle, his handling of disasterous economic conditions, and his debt management.

229 Smith, Walter B. "Wage Rates on the Erie Canal, 1828-1881." JOUR-
NAL OF ECONOMIC HISTORY 23 (September 1963): 298-311.

Static institutional conditions and adequate data on wages and
jobs provide a laboratory-like situation for this study. Wage
levels, trends, and fluctuations are analyzed.

230 Spears, J.R. THE AMERICAN SLAVE TRADE. New York: C. Scribner's
Sons, 1900. 232 p.

Relying upon public documents, biographies, stories of travelers,
and other sources of original information, the book is devoted
to the history, conditions, and consequences of the slave trade
industry in the United States.

231 Spengler, Joseph J. "Population Movements and Economic Equilibrium in
the United States." JOURNAL OF POLITICAL ECONOMY 48 (April
1940): 153-82.

By partitioning the population according to occupation, race,
region, and age group, changes in group-to-group growth differentials are examined for their economic significance. The
investigation seeks to discover the ways in which these population movements affect the equilibrating and disequilibrating
socioeconomic process.

232 Spengler, Joseph J., and Duncan, Otis Dudley, eds. POPULATION
THEORY AND POLICY. Glencoe, Ill.: Free Press, 1956. 519 p.

This book contains papers by thirty different authors on nearly
every aspect of population and economic activity that might
be related to population growth. Both theoretical and policy
issues are discussed for domestic as well as international aspects.

233 Sultan, Paul E. "Unionism and Wage-Income Ratios: 1929-1951." RE-VIEW OF ECONOMICS AND STATISTICS 36 (February 1954): 67-73.

This study compares the inter- and intra-industry wage income structures in the context of union growth. The hypothesis that where wage earners are strongly organized in trade unions one might expect labor to succeed in obtaining a larger share of the product is tested, using the statistics on aggregate distributive shares.

234 Sutch, Richard. "The Profitability of Ante-Bellum Slavery-Revisited." SOUTHERN ECONOMIC JOURNAL 31 (April 1965): 365-77.

Reviewing the previous studies on this topic the author produces his own estimates of the profitability of slavery, concentrating especially on the production function for cotton and the yield of cotton per share.

235 Swerling, Boris C. "Capital Shortage and Labor Surplus in the United States?" REVIEW OF ECONOMICS AND STATISTICS 36 (August 1954): 286-89.

This is one of the many attempts to analyze the factor intensity of exports and imports vis-a-vis the domestic economy. An input-output technique is used with data for 1947.

236 Temin, Peter. "Labor Scarcity and the Problem of American Industrial Efficiency in the 1850's." JOURNAL OF ECONOMIC HISTORY 26 (September 1966): 277-98.

After approximately 1850, American technology began to amaze Europeans, especially the British. The observed high price of American labor was felt to have been one of the forces providing the impetus for innovation. This study reexamines this situation using a formal production function approach, and compares the resulting implications with the evidence. See also the article by Fogel (no. 15), for a lengthy critique of this study. A comment by Ian M. Drummond appeared in this journal, volume 27 (September 1967): 383-90, and a reply by Temin to both Fogel and Drummond also appears in this journal, volume 28 (March 1968): 124-25.

237 _____. "Labor Scarcity in America." JOURNAL OF INTERDISCIPLINARY HISTORY 1 (Winter 1971): 251-64.

The author attempts to clarify the issues that were the source of many misunderstandings regarding his previous article (no. 236).

238 Thomas, Brinley. MIGRATION AND ECONOMIC GROWTH. Cambridge, Engl.: Cambridge University Press, 1954. 498 p.

This work provides a very comprehensive examination of migration and the related issues for economic growth. Contemporary themes are discussed in addition to the usual historical issues, such as regional growth, nonwhite immigration in Britain, the faltering of the trans-Atlantic brain drain since 1950, the urban dilemma in the United States, and the U.S. international economy since 1945. A fifty-six page summary article by Thomas may also be helpful: "Migration and the Rhythm of Economic Growth, 1830-1913." MANCHESTER SCHOOL OF ECONOMIC AND SOCIAL STUDIES 19 (September 1951): 215-71.

239 Thomas, Robert Paul, and Anderson, Terry L. "White Population, Labor Force and Extensive Growth of the New England Economy in the Seventeenth Century." JOURNAL OF ECONOMIC HISTORY 33 (September 1973): 634-67.

Recognizing that labor payments constitute a predominant share of any economy's income, an attempt is made to estimate an upper and lower bound for population growth as well as a labor force series. A stable population model is used, and the results allow the authors to infer that a rather high rate of growth was attained.

240 Troy, Leo. "Trade Union Membership, 1897-1962." REVIEW OF ECONOMICS AND STATISTICS 47 (February 1965): 93-113.

Through a compilation of trade union membership statistics, the historical trends are revealed. The method of compilation is also discussed and compared to that of the Bureau of Labor Statistics. Suggestions for improving the collection process used by the bureau are also proffered.

241 Uselding, Paul [J.]. "Conjectural Estimates of Gross Human Capital Inflows to the American Economy: 1790-1860." EXPLORATIONS IN ECONOMIC HISTORY 9 (Fall 1971): 49-62.

This is one of the better attempts at accounting for the capital content (the skill level) of immigrants to the United States before 1860. It also attempts to assess the significance of this capital transfer for aggregate economic growth.

242 _____. "Factor Substitution and Labor Productivity Growth in American Manufacturing, 1839-1899." JOURNAL OF ECONOMIC HISTORY 32 (September 1972): 670-81.

This is an attempt to measure the importance of the apparent capital intensity of U.S. manufacturing with respect to its influence on the measurement of labor productivity. Although the results are not inconsistent with the labor scarcity hypothesis, the factor-saving bias in U.S. technology and the economic influence on invention are beyond the scope of the paper.

243 Usher, Abbott Payson. "The Resource Requirements of an Industrial Economy." JOURNAL OF ECONOMIC HISTORY 7 (1947): supplement, 35-46.

World War II aroused the industrial ambitions of many under-developed countries. This author suggests that after considering the institutional and cultural factors one must compare the present level and the possible potential of industry, given resource availability for each country. A rather dismal picture is presented for the future of the less developed countries, despite their large endowments of untapped resources.

244 Wachter, Michael L. "Relative Wage Equatron's for United States Manufacturing Industries, 1946-1967." REVIEW OF ECONOMICS AND STATISTICS 52 (November 1970): 405-10.

By attempting to develop a model that deals with relative wages for two-digit industries, one encounters the difficulty of creating district aggregate labor markets for each industry. The author concludes that relative wages depend on a supply factor (relative aggregate unemployment) and a demand factor (relative value added or productivity).

245 Waldorf, William H. "Labor Productivity in Food Wholesaling and Retailing, 1929-1958." REVIEW OF ECONOMICS AND STATISTICS 48 (February 1966): 88-93.

By utilizing various indexes, the author attempts to derive a new measure for the growth of productivity in wholesale and retail foods of farm origin headed for domestic consumption.

246 Weiss, Thomas. "The Industrial Distribution of the Urban and Rural Workforces: Estimates for the United States, 1870-1910." JOURNAL OF ECONOMIC HISTORY 32 (December 1972): 919-37.

With particular emphasis on the service sector, the author presents evidence on the industrial distribution of the U.S. work force in urban and rural areas, and relates this evidence to structural change in the economy.

247 Williamson, Jeffrey G. "The Sources of American Inequality, 1896-1948." REVIEW OF ECONOMICS AND STATISTICS 58 (November 1976): 387-452.

This is a very extensive paper in which an attempt is made to construct an intertemporal framework for approaching migration and to demonstrate its empirical relevance for explaining U.S. income distribution changes. The human investment approach to migration is reconfirmed.

248 Wolman, Leo. "Labor Policy and Economic History." JOURNAL OF ECONOMIC HISTORY 5 (December 1945): 86-92.

It is a short but concise paper, and one which provides the student with new directions for research and some guidelines on how to address these research topics. An eclectic view is purported for answering questions regarding structure of wage rates and labor policies.

249 Woodhouse, Chase G. "The Standard of Living at the Professional Level, 1816-17 and 1926-27." JOURNAL OF POLITICAL ECONOMY 37 (October 1929): 552-72.

This is a comparison of two very similar families at these two dates on the basis of standard of living differences, cost of living, commodities purchased, the lifestyle, and the level of money and real income.

250 Wright, Wilson. "Impact of the War on Technical Training and Occupational Mobility." AMERICAN ECONOMIC REVIEW 33 (March 1943): 238-48.

This is an analysis of the ways business and government solved the problems that arose from the increased intensity with which the United States used its resources during World War II. The development of new training techniques and cooperative efforts between government authorities, educators, and industrial management served as solutions to the problems.

251 Yasuba, Y. BIRTH RATES OF THE WHITE POPULATION IN THE UNITED STATES, 1800-1860: AN ECONOMIC STUDY. Baltimore: Johns Hopkins Press, 1962. 198 p.

Concentrating on the plight of a coal mining region, this analysis from the very early stages of development through the final stages, before the coming of the new order, demonstrates the effect when ideology subordinates economics in a society.

252 Zabler, Jeffrey. "Further Evidence on American Wage Differentials, 1800-1830." EXPLORATION IN ECONOMIC HISTORY 10 (Fall 1972): 109-17.

In an attempt to further corroborate Habakkak's thesis on U.S.-British skill differentials, the author extrapolates from evidence on eastern Pennsylvanian iron producers to industries of other regions. A comment appeared: Adams, Donald R., Jr. "Wage Rates in the Iron Industry: A Comment." EXPLORATIONS IN ECONOMIC HISTORY 11 (Fall 1973): 89-94, with a reply in the same issue of the journal, pages 95-99.

253 Zeichner, Oscar. "The Transition from Slave to Free Agricultural Labor

in the Southern States." AGRICULTURAL HISTORY 13 (January 1939):
22-31.

> The world of the wage laborer was a foreign place to most
> slaves, where they faced the problems of unemployment, re-
> distribution of plantations, and tenancy. These are the issues
> of this paper.

2.2 GENERAL LISTINGS

254 Barnett, George E. "American Trade Unionism and the Standardization of
Wages during the War." JOURNAL OF POLITICAL ECONOMY 27 (October 1919): 670-93.

255 Behman, Sara. "Wage Changes, Institutions, and Relative Factor Prices
in Manufacturing." REVIEW OF ECONOMICS AND STATISTICS 51
(August 1969): 277-38.

256 Brems, Hans. "Growth Rates of Output, Labor Force, Hours and Productivity." REVIEW OF ECONOMICS AND STATISTICS 39 (November 1957):
415-20.

257 Clark, Lindley D. "Workmen's Compensation and the Railroads: A Hesi-
tating Revolution." JOURNAL OF POLITICAL ECONOMY 41 (December
1933): 806-20.

258 Coen, Robert M. "Labor Force and Unemployment in the 1920's and 1930's:
A Reply." REVIEW OF ECONOMICS AND STATISTICS 55 (November
1973): 527-28.

259 Conrad, Alfred H.; Dowd, Douglas; Engerman, Stanley; et al. "Slavery
as an Obstacle to Economic Growth in the U.S.: A Panel Discussion."
JOURNAL OF ECONOMIC HISTORY 27 (December 1967): 518-60.

260 Davis, Joseph S. "The Population Upsurge and the American Economy."
JOURNAL OF POLITICAL ECONOMY 61 (October 1953): 369-88.

261 Dewey, Donald. "Negro Employment in Southern Industry." JOURNAL
OF POLITICAL ECONOMY 60 (August 1952): 279-93.

262 Domar, Evsey D. "The Causes of Slavery or Serfdom: A Hypothesis."
JOURNAL OF ECONOMIC HISTORY 30 (March 1970): 18-32.

263 Evans, Robert, Jr. "Some Notes on Coerced Labor." JOURNAL OF
ECONOMIC HISTORY 30 (December 1970): 861-66.

264 Ferenczi, I. INTERNATIONAL MIGRATIONS. New York: National Bureau of Economic Research, 1929. 381 p.

265 Foner, P. HISTORY OF THE LABOR MOVEMENT IN THE UNITED STATES. New York: International Publishers, 1947. 423 p.

266 Ginger, Ray. "Managerial Employees in Anthracite, 1902: A Study in Occupational Mobility." JOURNAL OF ECONOMIC HISTORY 14 (June 1954): 146-56.

267 Gitelman, H.M. "The Labor Force at Waltham Watch during the Civil War Era." JOURNAL OF ECONOMIC HISTORY 25 (June 1965): 214-43.

268 Goodrich, Carter. "The Australian and American Labor Movements." ECONOMIC RECORD 4 (November 1928): 193-208.

269 Greenwood, Michael J. "An Analysis of the Determinants of Geographic Labor Mobility in the United States." REVIEW OF ECONOMICS AND STATISTICS 51 (May 1969): 189-94.

270 Hourwich, Isaac A. "The Social-Economic Classes of the Population of the United States." JOURNAL OF POLITICAL ECONOMY 19 (March 1911): 188-215; (April 1911): 309-37.

271 Johnson, Hildegard Binder. "Factors Influencing the Distribution of the German Pioneer Population in Minnesota." AGRICULTURAL HISTORY 29 (January 1945): 39-57.

272 Kao, Charles H.C., and Lee, Jae Won. "An Empirical Analysis of China's Brain Drain into the United States." ECONOMIC DEVELOPMENT AND CULTURAL CHANGE 21 (April 1973): 500-513.

273 Lucas, Robert E., Jr., and Rapping, Leonard A. "Unemployment in the Great Depression: Is There a Full Explanation?" JOURNAL OF POLITICAL ECONOMY 80 (January-February 1972): 186-91.

274 McBrearty, James C. AMERICAN LABOR HISTORY AND COMPARATIVE LABOR MOVEMENTS: A SELECTED BIBLIOGRAPHY. Tucson: University of Arizona Press, 1973. 262 p.

275 McKinnon, Ronald I. "Wages, Capital Costs, and Employment in Manufacturing: A Model Applied to 1947-58 U.S. Data." ECONOMETRICA 30 (July 1962): 501-21.

278   Miller, Ann Ratner.   "Components of Labor Force Growth."   JOURNAL
       OF ECONOMIC HISTORY 22 (March 1962): 47-58.

279   Northrup, Herbert R.   "Organized Labor and Negro Workers."   JOURNAL
       OF POLITICAL ECONOMY 51 (June 1943): 206-21.

280   Okun, Bernard.   "Interstate Population Migration and State Income In-
       equality: A Simultaneous Equation Approach."   ECONOMIC DEVELOP-
       MENT AND CULTURAL CHANGE 16 (January 1968): 297-313.

281   _____.   TRENDS IN BIRTH RATES IN THE UNITED STATES SINCE 1870.
       Baltimore: Johns Hopkins Press, 1958. 203 p.

282   Olson, Helen, and Wolfe, A.B.   "War-Time Industrial Employment of
       Women in the United States."   JOURNAL OF POLITICAL ECONOMY 27
       (October 1919): 639-69.

283   Page, Thomas W.   "The Causes of Earlier European Immigration to the
       United States."   JOURNAL OF POLITICAL ECONOMY 19 (October 1911):
       676-93.

284   _____.   "The Transportation of Immigrants and Reception Arrangements in
       the Nineteenth Century."   JOURNAL OF POLITICAL ECONOMY 19
       (November 1911): 732-49.

285   Perlman, Richard.   "Forces Widening Occupational Wage Differentials."
       REVIEW OF ECONOMICS AND STATISTICS 40 (May 1958): 107-15.

286   Sanderson, Warren.   "The Fertility of American Women since 1920."
       JOURNAL OF ECONOMIC HISTORY 30 (March 1970): 271-72.

287   Saville, Lloyd.   "Earnings of Skilled and Unskilled Workers in New England
       and the South."   JOURNAL OF POLITICAL ECONOMY 62 (October 1954):
       390-405.

288   Schmidt, Emerson P.   "Union and Non-union Wages and Hours in the Street
       Railway Industry."   JOURNAL OF POLITICAL ECONOMY 42 (October
       1934): 654-59.

289   Segal, Martin.   "Regional Wage Differences in Manufacturing in the Post-
       war Period."   REVIEW OF ECONOMICS AND STATISTICS 43 (May 1961):
       148-55.

290   Shannon, Fred A.   "A Post Mortem on the Labor-Safety-Value Theory."
       AGRICULTURAL HISTORY 19 (January 1945): 31-38.

291   Simler, Norman J.   "Unionism and Labor's Share in Manufacturing In-
      dustries."   REVIEW OF ECONOMICS AND STATISTICS 43 (November
      1961): 369-78.

292   Smith, Daniel Scott.   "The Demographic History of Colonial New England."
      JOURNAL OF ECONOMIC HISTORY 32 (March 1972): 165-83.

293   Spengler, Joseph J.   "Right to Work: A Backward Glance."   JOURNAL
      OF ECONOMIC HISTORY 28 (March 1968): 171-96.

294   Stocking, G.W.   "Labour Problems in the American Bituminous Coal In-
      dustry."   ECONOMIC JOURNAL 37 (June 1927): 213-25.

295   Taylor, Paul S.   "Some Aspects of Mexican Immigration."   JOURNAL OF
      POLITICAL ECONOMY 38 (October 1930): 609-15.

296   Terbargh, G.W.   "The Application of the Sherman Law to Trade-Union
      Activities."   JOURNAL OF POLITICAL ECONOMY 37 (April 1929):
      203-24.

297   Waud, Roger N.   "Man-Hour Behavior in U.S. Manufacturing: A Neo-
      classical Interpretation."   JOURNAL OF POLITICAL ECONOMY 76
      (May-June 1968): 407-27.

298   Weaver, Robert C.   "Recent Events in Negro Union Relationships."   JOUR-
      NAL OF POLITICAL ECONOMY 52 (September 1944): 234-49.

299   Weintraub, Robert E.   "The Productive Capacity of Rural and Urban Labor:
      A Case Study."   JOURNAL OF POLITICAL ECONOMY 63 (October 1955):
      412-26.

300   Welch, Finis.   "Labor-Market Discrimination: An Interpretation of Income
      Differences in the Rural South."   JOURNAL OF POLITICAL ECONOMY
      75 (March-April 1967): 225-40.

301   Wilkinson, Maurice.   "European Migration to the United States: An Econo-
      metric Analysis of Aggregate Labor Supply and Demand."   REVIEW OF ECO-
      NOMICS AND STATISTICS 52 (August 1970): 272-79.

Chapter 3

LAND AND AGRICULTURAL DEVELOPMENT

This chapter comprises a collection of works that will allow the student to ac-
quaint himself with land policy, agricultural growth, and the interaction of the
two. There is a near even mixture between the more rigorous and less rigorous
types of studies.

Some of the studies in chapter 4 regarding technical innovation in agriculture
are not annotated in this chapter. There will of necessity be some overlap of
topics among both previous and subsequent chapters. This is particularly true
of the literature dealing with the economic self-sufficiency of the antebellum
South, which is primarily covered in chapter 8.

For more information on twentieth-century agriculture the reader is referred to
the publications that the U.S. Department of Agriculture has produced. The
U.S.D.A. library and the one at University of Illinois--Urbana are two of the
best libraries for agricultural research. There are other libraries that would be
more appropriate for specialized topics, for example, the University of North
Carolina at Chapel Hill for research on southern plantation agriculture.

The areas of research in agricultural economics are varied and rewarding, so
the areas of analysis in the economic history of agriculture are quite logically
even greater. Thus there is much that remains unsettled and in need of further
study. That, I think, will become evident as one surveys the annotated sources.

3.1 ANNOTATED LISTINGS

302 Abbott, Martin. "Free Land, Free Labor, and the Freedmen's Bureau."
     AGRICULTURAL HISTORY 30 (October 1956): 150-56.

     This article examines the success of the Freedman's Bureau in
     providing jobs and land for the freedmen.

303 Allen, S.G. "Inventory Fluctuations in Flaxseed and Linseed Oil, 1926-
     1939." ECONOMETRICA 22 (July 1954): 310-27.

Using a system of linear equations, an attempt is made to explain quarterly inventory fluctuations and no attempt is made to develop a forecasting model.

304   Anderson, Russell H.   "Agricultural Frontiers in the United States: Advancing across the Eastern Mississippi Valley."   AGRICULTURAL HISTORY 17 (April 1943):   97-104.

Historically tracing the movement of settlers across the eastern Mississippi Valley between 1790 and 1860, the author examines land and water transportation, timbering, canals, steamboats, population, and the plantation system.   An attempt is made to identify the agricultural "frontier" of the period.

305   Arnold, B.W.   HISTORY OF TOBACCO INDUSTRY IN VIRGINIA.   Baltimore: Johns Hopkins Press, 1897.   86 p.

Dealing with the post-Civil War era, the author focuses primarily on markets, prices, distribution of profits, and methods of sale.   Changes in methods of production are not considered extensively.

306   Barger, H., and Landsberg, H.   AMERICAN AGRICULTURE, 1899-1939.   New York: National Bureau of Economic Research, 1942.   440 p.

After defining agricultural output and enterprises, the authors discuss the factors that affect the size and composition of farm output over time.   An examination of output behavior for each product and the nutritional standards of farm output are presented along with estimates of the per capita consumption of calories, vitamins, and other food elements.   Employment, technological change, and changes in agricultural productivity are also investigated.

307   Bateman, Fred.   "Improvement in American Dairy Farming, 1850-1910."   JOURNAL OF ECONOMIC HISTORY 28 (June 1968):   255-73.

In examining dairy improvement, the author analyzes changes in breeding, feeding, and care of dairy animals, because any increase in yields during this period was not from mechanization of dairying.   The underlying argument is that agricultural improvements are an important aspect of economic development.

308   _____.   "Labor Inputs and Productivity in American Dairy Agriculture, 1850-1910."   JOURNAL OF ECONOMIC HISTORY 29 (June 1969):   206-29.

By comparing the changes in average annual dairy labor requirements per animal, and their relationship with changes in the average annual milk yields, an attempt is made to calculate the increase in labor productivity.   Gerald Gunderson has a comment in the same journal, volume 29 (September 1969): 501-5, followed by Bateman's reply.

309 Battalio, Raymond C., and Kagel, John. "The Structure of Antebellum Southern Agriculture: South Carolina, A Case Study." AGRICULTURAL HISTORY 44 (January 1970): 25-38.

This is an analysis of whether the distinction between large slaveholding plantations and small farms is warranted. The status of the southern foodstuff market is also examined, to determine if there was specialization in staple commodities.

310 Bicha, Karel Denis. "The Plains Farmer and the Prairie Province Frontier, 1897-1914." JOURNAL OF ECONOMIC HISTORY 25 (June 1965): 263-70.

This analysis of the role of the U.S. farmers in the settlement of Alberta and Saskatchewan examines the motivating factors such as the increased price of wheat that resulted from the end of the 1890 depression. The impact of immigrants on the frontier is also analyzed.

311 Billington, Ray Allen. "The Origin of the Land Speculator as a Frontier Type." AGRICULTURAL HISTORY 19 (October 1945): 204-11.

This is an investigation of the importance of the land jobber and the origins of the land speculator in the westward movement of the U.S. development.

312 Bogart, Ernest L. ECONOMIC HISTORY OF AMERICAN AGRICULTURE. New York: Longmans, Green and Co., 1923. 173 p.

This is a discussion of colonial, antebellum, and postbellum agricultural development, including such topics as slavery, western movement, and mechanization. The development of agriculture as a business is also considered.

313 Bogue, Allen G. "Farming in the Prairie Peninsula, 1830-1890." JOURNAL OF ECONOMIC HISTORY 23 (March 1963): 3-29.

This is an account of how readily farmers in this area adapted to new technology and the area itself during a relatively short period of time. Increase in the productivity of land is analyzed vis-a-vis such activities as speculation, inventiveness, extensions of credit, and mechanization.

314 _____. FROM PRAIRIE TO CORNBELT, FARMING ON THE ILLINOIS AND IOWA PRAIRIES IN THE NINETEENTH CENTURY. Chicago: University of Chicago Press, 1963. 310 p.

This is an attempt to consider the problems of tenancy, freight rates, marketing problems, profits, and community economic structures that confronted the operator of a farm business.

315 _____. "The Land Mortgage Company in the Early Plains States." AGRICULTURAL HISTORY 25 (January 1951): 20-33.

Using the Watkins Company as a prime example, the author examines the characteristic management, scope, and policies of land mortgage companies. He considers the agrarian protests against money lenders.

316 Bogue, Allen G., and Bogue, Margaret [Beattie]. "Profits and the Frontier Land Speculator." JOURNAL OF ECONOMIC HISTORY 17 (March 1957): 1-24.

Besides examining the concentration of capital and the rates of return realized, the authors also analyze the effects such speculators had on the rates of economic development.

317 Bogue, Margaret Beattie. "The Swamp Land Act and Wet Land Utilization In Illinois, 1850-1890." AGRICULTURAL HISTORY 25 (October 1951): 169-80.

This is a general consideration of the problems of the drainage of farm land, and a specific analysis of the Swamp Land Act.

318 Bonner, James C. "Advancing Trends in Southern Agriculture, 1840-1860." AGRICULTURAL HISTORY 22 (October 1948): 248-59.

This study is a comparison of the similarities between the development of southern agriculture between 1840 and 1860 and that after World War I. Topics considered include land improvement, land values in proportion to the value of labor, livestock husbandry, crop diversification, and the foreign influence.

319 Bowman, John D. "An Economic Analysis of Mid-Western Farm Land Values and Farm Land Income, 1860-1900." YALE ECONOMIC ESSAYS 5 (Fall 1965): 317-54.

Given the political turmoil that prevailed in the agricultural sector during this period, the author examines the economic conditions of farmers in an attempt to ascertain whether the farmer was justified in complaining about his supposed depressed condition.

320 Bowman, John D., and Keehn, Richard H. "Agricultural Terms of Trade in Four Midwestern States, 1870-1900." JOURNAL OF ECONOMIC HISTORY 34 (September 1974): 592-609.

Using data for Illinois, Indiana, Wisconsin, and Iowa the authors examine the hypothesis about the secular price movements, which supposedly hurt the agricultural terms of trade. Short-run fluctuations are found in some of the price series but no secular decline in the terms of trade.

321 Bowman, Mary Jean. "The Land-Grant Colleges and Universities in Human-Resource Development." JOURNAL OF ECONOMIC HISTORY 22 (December 1962): 523-46.

This is an examination of the kinds and quantities of human resources created by the land grand institutions. These contributions are compared with those of parallel forces and agencies with respect to economic growth.

322 Broyer, Herbert O. "The Influence of British Capital on the Western-Range Cattle Industry." JOURNAL OF ECONOMIC HISTORY 9 (1949): supplement, 85-98.

This is an analysis of the role played by British capital, knowledge, and livestock in the development of the western-range cattle industry during the last half of the nineteenth century.

323 Bristed, John. THE RESOURCES OF THE UNITED STATES OF AMERICA. New York: James Eastburn and Co., 1818. 505 p.

A brief account of the physical, intellectual, and moral character, capacity, and resources of the United States. Such capacities as population, the territorial aspect, agriculture, and navigable waters are examined. The development of the arts, religions, sciences, habits, manners, and character of the United States are included in the analysis.

324 Brogan, D.W. "The Rise and Decline of the American Agricultural Interests." ECONOMIC HISTORY REVIEW 5 (April 1935): 1-23.

During the 1920s there was a decline in the amount of cultivated land which produced both an emotional and an economic impact. This change is analyzed along with a brief historical account of the western movement and agricultural land creation.

325 Brown, Harry Gunnison. "Land Rent as a Function of Population Growth." JOURNAL OF POLITICAL ECONOMY 34 (June 1926): 274-88.

With special references to tax policy this article contains an analysis of land rents and values using classical rent theory to consider the effects of population.

326 Brunger, Eric. "Dairying and Urban Development in New York State, 1850-1900." AGRICULTURAL HISTORY 29 (October 1955): 169-73.

Urban growth and the presence of western competition are examined with respect to their effect on the New York dairy industry.

327 Bulkley, Robert J. "The Federal Farm Loan Act." JOURNAL OF POLITICAL ECONOMY 25 (February 1917): 129-47.

The structure and availability of credit to the farmers are examined in an attempt to determine what precipitated the creation of the Federal Farm Loan Act. The impact of this act on speculation and farm land values is also considered.

328 Burnett, Edmund C. "The Continental Congress and Agricultural Supplies." AGRICULTURAL HISTORY 2 (July 1928): 111-28.

Concentrating on the importance of supplying the army, the author reviews the congressional policy toward agricultural development.

329 Camp, William R. "The Organization of Agriculture in Relation to the Problem of Price Stabilization, Parts I & II." JOURNAL OF POLITICAL ECONOMY 32 (June 1924): 282-314; (August 1924): 414-67.

This is a two-part study of the marketing methods of producers' organizations and the effects these had on the stabilization of prices, wages, and industrial costs in general. The system, limitations, problems, and extent of organization of farm producers are also examined.

330 Cassels, John. "The Fluid-Milk Program of the Agricultural Adjustment Administration." JOURNAL OF POLITICAL ECONOMY 43 (August 1935): 482-505.

Concentrating upon the short-run effects of price supports for fluid milk, the author examines the techniques used. He does not, however, look at the longrun effects on marketing techniques in this industry.

331 Clements, Robert V. "The Farmers' Attitude toward British Investment in American Industry." JOURNAL OF ECONOMIC HISTORY 15 (June 1955): 151-59.

This is an account of the reaction to British investment during 1887-91, when the farmer was preoccupied with the economic power of monopolistic industries and trusts. The farmers generally viewed these investments as imperialistic moves by London bankers.

332 Colman, Gould P. "Innovation and Diffusion in Agriculture." AGRICULTURAL HISTORY 42 (July 1968): 173-88.

Using a methodology which minimizes the necessary resource materials, this is an investigation of the adoption of the reaper in New York in 1850. The adoption process and the characteristics of the adopters are discussed.

333　Coulter, E. Merton. "The Movement for Agricultural Reorganization in the Cotton South during the Civil War." AGRICULTURAL HISTORY 1 (January 1927): 3-17.

This is an exploration of the efforts of the South to remain self-sufficient during the Civil War, with special emphasis on the importance of corn and livestock.

334　Cox, Lawanda Fenlason. "Tenancy in the United States, 1865-1900: A Consideration of the Validity of the Agricultural Ladder Hypothesis." AGRICULTURAL HISTORY 18 (July 1944): 97-104.

Comparing and analyzing the corn and wheat belts of the North Central region with the cotton belt of the South, the theory of a progression from laborer to tenant to owner is challenged.

335　Danhof, Clarence H. "Farm-Making Costs and the 'Safety Value': 1850-60." JOURNAL OF POLITICAL ECONOMY 49 (June 1941): 317-59.

The safety valve thesis entails many assumptions regarding the ability of labor to make effective their desires for moving. Cheap land is not sufficient for the thesis to hold. This assumption is examined along with the others.

336　David, Paul A. "Mechanization of Reaping in the Ante-Bellum Midwest." In INDUSTRIALIZATION IN TWO SYSTEMS, edited by Henry Rosovsky, pp. 3-39. New York: John Wiley & Sons, 1966.

This is an excellent paper dealing with the early problems of agricultural growth and the mechanization process.

337　Decanio, Stephen. "Cotton 'Overproduction' in Late Nineteenth-Century Southern Agriculture." JOURNAL OF ECONOMIC HISTORY 33 (September 1973): 608-33.

After defining what is meant by "overproduction," the author further examines the reasons why southern agriculture remained engaged primarily in the production of cotton. A general equilibrium framework is utilized for this analysis.

338　Dick, Everett. "Agricultural Frontiers in the United States: Going beyond the Ninety-Fifth Meridian." AGRICULTURAL HISTORY 17 (April 1943): 105-12.

The examination of the Great Plains settlement after 1873 considers problems with fuel, irrigation, food, timber, and drought.

339   Donald, W.J. "Land Grants for Internal Improvements in the United States." JOURNAL OF POLITICAL ECONOMY 19 (May 1911): 404-10.

This is a study of the amount of land granted and actually patented for internal improvement in transportation.

340   Dovring, Folke. "European Reactions to the Homestead Act." JOURNAL OF ECONOMIC HISTORY 22 (December 1962): 461-72.

Looking at the lives of immigrants prior to their departure for the United States, the author attempts to measure the effect of the passage of the Homestead Act on immigration.

341   Dunham, Harold H. "Some Crucial Years of the General Land Office, 1875-1890." AGRICULTURAL HISTORY 11 (April 1937): 117-41.

In an effort to study the sources and effects of the trend toward concentration of agricultural land, the author focuses upon the land development policies of the General Land Office.

342   Edwards, Everett E. "Europe's Contribution to the American Dairy Industry." JOURNAL OF ECONOMIC HISTORY 9 (1949): supplement, 72-84.

The author traces the development of the dairy and cattle industry from ancient times, outlining the technological developments and the refinements in raising techniques.

343   Ellis, David M. "Land Tenure and Tenancy in the Hudson Valley, 1790-1860." AGRICULTURAL HISTORY 18 (April 1944): 75-82.

The distinctive characteristics and development of land tenure and tenancy in the Hudson Valley are examined with respect to conflicts between tenants and autocratic land owners. The effects of agrarian revolts and the eventual elimination of the leasehold are also considered.

344   Feller, Irwin. "Inventive Activity in Agriculture 1837-1890." JOURNAL OF ECONOMIC HISTORY 22 (December 1962): 560-77.

Using previously unavailable data, the author examines the level and composition of inventions in order to determine the role of the market mechanism and economic conditions in generating inventive activity.

345   Fleisig, Heywood. "Slavery, The Supply of Agricultural Labor, and the Industrialization of the South." JOURNAL OF ECONOMIC HISTORY 36 (September 1976): 572-97.

The author addresses the questions of whether it was due to the

existence of slavery that the entrepreneurs shifted their resources into agriculture, that is, was cotton farming really as
profitable as people believed? The evidence for 1860 on both
free and slave agriculture allows for a test of the intermediate
predictions of the model used.

346   Fogel, Robert W., and Engerman, Stanley L. "The Relative Efficiency of
Slavery: A Comparison of Northern and Southern Agriculture in 1860."
EXPLORATIONS IN ECONOMIC HISTORY 8 (Spring 1971): 353-67.

Explanations are offered for why, on the basis of geometric
indexes of factor productivity, the South was found to utilize
resources more efficiently in 1860.

347   Forbes, Gerald. "Oklahoma Oil and Indian Land Tenure." AGRICUL-
TURAL HISTORY 15 (October 1941): 189-94.

This article explores the interrelationships of oil industry development and Indians and their landholding. The author examines questions such as what ultimately produced tenancy
among the Indians. State government corruption is also explored.

348   Galambos, Louis. "The Agrarian Image of the Large Corporation, 1879-
1920: A Study in Social Accommodation." JOURNAL OF ECONOMIC
HISTORY 28 (September 1968): 341-62.

Using the material that appeared in the agricultural publications
during the period, an analysis is made of the accommodations
granted large corporations.

349   Gallman, Robert E. "Changes in Total U.S. Agricultural Factor Productivity in the Nineteenth Century." AGRICULTURAL HISTORY 46 (January 1972): 191-210.

This is an examination of the rate of change in output relative to the factor inputs for the period 1790 to 1840 in agriculture.

350   _____ . "A Note on the Patent Office Crop Estimates, 1841-1848."
JOURNAL OF ECONOMIC HISTORY 23 (June 1963): 185-95.

A report on how the Patent Office produced crop estimates
and how the results were checked to ascertain their usefulness
as historical data. Since the 1840s the methods used have
been quite accurate and the data series are broadly correct,
a fact which is quite significant for historical research.

351   Gates, Paul W. THE FARMER'S AGE: AGRICULTURE 1815-1860. New
York: Holt Rinehart and Winston, 1960. 460 p.

This study covers both regional issues and various topics of agricultural development in general; very extensive coverage.

352 _____. "The Homestead Act as an Incongruous Land System." AMERI-CAN HISTORICAL REVIEW 41 (July 1936): 652-81.

This is an examination of the various hypotheses regarding the Homestead Act as the chief distributor of land. The sources of such hypotheses are examined and the hypotheses are tested.

353 _____. "Land Policy and Tenancy in the Prairie States." JOURNAL OF ECONOMIC HISTORY 1 (May 1941): 60-82.

The Jeffersonian ideal for economic democracy through the existence of small land owners was not realized even with the increased liberalization of land policy in the nineteenth century. The author attributes the lack of success of the system to the revenue principle and the right to unrestricted entry.

354 _____. "The Promotion of Agriculture by the Illinois Central Railroad, 1855-1870." AGRICULTURAL HISTORY 5 (April 1931): 57-76.

This is an examination of the ways the railroad affected agricultural development, for example, crop diversification, grade of stock improvements, and improved tilling methods.

355 Gray, Lewis. HISTORY OF AGRICULTURE IN THE SOUTHERN U.S. TO 1860. Washington, D.C.: Carnegie Institution of Washington, 1933. 943 p.

Although a relatively old work, this is one of the best generally complete works on agriculture in the South. It has withstood the repeated tests of new economic historians and has served them as a valuable source on nearly all aspects of agriculture.

356 _____. "The Market Surplus Problems of Colonial Tobacco." AGRICUL-TURAL HISTORY 2 (January 1928): 1-34.

This is an analysis of the effect the Spanish conquest of America had on agriculture. The long-run effects on Latin American agriculture are also discussed.

357 Griliches, Zvi. "Research Costs and Social Returns: Hybrid Corn and Related Innovations." JOURNAL OF POLITICAL ECONOMY 66 (October 1958): 419-31.

Analyzing the period since 1955, the author estimates the return from investment on research. The returns on both private and public investment in hybrid corn research are compared with the returns on alternative investment possibilities.

358 _____. "The Sources of Measured Productivity Growth: United States Agriculture, 1940-1960." JOURNAL OF POLITICAL ECONOMY 71 (August 1963): 331-46.

> The author develops a model that attempts to explain technical change instead of deriving it as unexplained residual. Changes in output are attributed to changes in the quantity and quality of inputs and economies of scale.

359 Hansen, Alvin H. "The Effect of Price Fluctuations of Agriculture." JOURNAL OF POLITICAL ECONOMY 33 (April 1925): 196-216.

> Analyzing the effects of general price fluctuations over the last 130 years, the author considers specifically the effect on the purchasing power of farm products and the economic status of the farmer as a property owner. He then briefly surveys the outlook from that point in time.

360 Hibbard, B.A. A HISTORY OF THE PUBLIC LAND POLICIES. New York: Macmillan Co., 1924. 591 p.

> This study covers the acquisition and dispersion of the public domain from before the constitutional period. Discussion includes topics such as credit and cash sale systems, and various land acts and grants, with special emphasis on the Homestead Act and its modifications.

361 Higgs, Robert. "Race, Tenure, and Resource Allocation in Southern Agriculture, 1910." JOURNAL OF ECONOMIC HISTORY 33 (March 1973): 149-69.

> Concentrating on the distribution of farmers and land in 1910, Higgs attempts to discover what factors determine whether a farm rental contract is a share-rent or a fixed-rent contract and whether the tenant's race had any effect on the form of contract. Also, he analyzes whether race and/or the form of the contract have any effect on the size of the farm.

362 Hillard, Samuel Bowers. HOG MEAT AND HOECAKE, FOOD SUPPLY IN THE OLD SOUTH, 1840-1860. Carbondale and Edwardsville: Southern Illinois University Press; London and Amsterdam: Feffer and Simons, 1972. 361 p.

> This is a very thorough examination of agriculture production and methods in the growth of the Old South.

363 Irwin, H.S. "Seasonal Cycles in Aggregates of Wheat-Futures Contracts." JOURNAL OF POLITICAL ECONOMY 43 (February 1935): 34-49.

> Comparing the different cycles that can be traced out in futures contracts, the author attempts to explain seasonal variations.

The effect that farmers have on wheat prices through the futures market is also considered.

364 Johnson, A.N. "The Impact on Farm Machinery on the Farm Economy." AGRICULTURAL HISTORY 24 (January 1950): 58-61.

This is an analysis of the effect of mechanization on agricultural output and management and rural population.

365 Jorgenson, Lloyd P. "Agricultural Expansion into the Semiarid Lands of the West North Central States during the First World War." AGRICULTURAL HISTORY 23 (January 1949): 30-40.

Using selected census data for the period 1900-1919, the author attempts to analyze the increase in acreage tilled in North Dakota, South Dakota, Nebraska, and Kansas.

366 Klingman, David. "Food Surpluses and Deficits in American Colonies, 1768-1772." JOURNAL OF ECONOMIC HISTORY 31 (September 1971): 553-69.

An analysis of the self-sufficiency of the colonial economy and the degree of interregional coastal trade, the study casts some light on the degree of specialization and the changes in the standard of living.

367 _____. "The Significance of Grain in the Development of the Tobacco Colonies." JOURNAL OF ECONOMIC HISTORY 29 (June 1969): 268-78.

Dealing with the period prior to 1770, the author finds that grain production served as a supplemental income source during poor tobacco market years. Most of the analysis is concentrated on the Virginia colony.

368 Laird, William E., and Rinehart, James R. "Deflation, Agriculture, and Southern Development." AGRICULTURAL HISTORY 42 (April 1968): 115-24.

This is an examination of the monetary factors which may have affected the course of southern agriculture, and may have contributed to the persistence of an agrarian orientation. The limited extension of the National Banking system to the South was considered a factor contributing to the shortages of money and credit after the Civil War.

369 Lamar, Howard R. Land Policy in the Spanish Southwest, 1846-1891: A Study in Contrasts." JOURNAL OF ECONOMIC HISTORY 22 (December 1962): 498-522.

This study treats the issues that arose from the land grant policy and the willingness of businessmen to capitalize on this system as compared to the previously existing Spanish land grant system and the lifestyle it has generated.

370 LeDuc, Thomas. "The Disposal of the Public Domain of the Trans-Mississippi Plains: Some Opportunities for Investigation." AGRICULTURAL HISTORY 24 (October 1950): 199-204.

Analysis of different land types, occupancy and organization types, public land improvements, and settlement characteristics is necessary in order to ascertain the degree of success in the disposal of the public domain.

371 _____. "Public Policy, Private Investment, and Land Use in American Agriculture, 1825-1875." AGRICULTURAL HISTORY 37 (January 1963): 3-9.

This is an analysis of land policy which promoted settlement and land distribution after 1825.

372 Lerner, Eugene. "Southern Output and Agricultural Income, 1860-1880." AGRICULTURAL HISTORY 33 (July 1959): 117-25.

In an attempt to explain population movements and relative changes in agricultural income, the author's discussion encompasses the relatively quick recovery of manufacturing, the effect of labor disorganization, the lack of foreign markets, and farm prices.

373 Lindert, Peter H. "Land Scarcity and American Growth." JOURNAL OF ECONOMIC HISTORY 34 (December 1974): 851-81.

This is an analysis of the relationship between land rents and population and economic growth. Lindert asserts that a dichotomy exists, or existed, between the effects of population growth and economic growth.

374 Loehr, Rodney C. "Agricultural Frontiers in the United States: Moving Back from the Atlantic Seaboard." AGRICULTURAL HISTORY 17 (April 1943): 90-96.

Dealing primarily with the lifestyle of the typical settler, the article provides an account of the land policy and the movement of settlers inward from the Atlantic during and after the Revolution.

375 McGuire, Robert, and Higgs, Robert. "Cotton, Corn, and Risk in the Nineteenth Century: Another View." EXPLORATIONS IN ECONOMIC HISTORY 14 (April 1977): 167-82.

This is critique of an earlier paper by Wright and Kunreuther (see no. 431). The authors argue that the original approach was not very useful and an alternative explanation of the crop choice is proffered. This piece is followed by a reply by Wright and Kunreuther in this same issue of the journal.

376   Malin, James C.   "Mobility and History: Reflections on the Agricultural Policies of the United States in Relation to a Mechanized World."   AGRICULTURAL HISTORY   17 (October 1943): 177-91.

The author uses four categories for agricultural policies: (1) production policies; (2) general reform and third party movements; (3) rural social welfare; and (4) economies of agriculture. He then analyzes the effects of these four on agricultural policies which were enacted within the context of mobility and mechanization.

377   Mayhew, Anne.   "A Reappraisal of the Causes of Farm Protest in The United States, 1870-1900."   JOURNAL OF ECONOMIC HISTORY   32 (June 1972):   464-75.

Focusing only on the midwestern farmer's protests, an explanation is offered for why the farmers protested, even when the evidence indicates that the usual complaints were unfounded.

378   Morgan, James N.   "Consumer Substitutions between Butter and Margarine." ECONOMETRICA   19 (January 1951):   18-39.

Using data for retail stores of a chain in Rhode Island, this paper reports the results of a study of consumer response to price changes for butter and margarine.

379   National Bureau of Economic Research, ed.   OUTPUT, EMPLOYMENT, AND PRODUCTIVITY IN THE U.S. AFTER 1800.   Studies in Income and Wealth, no. 30.   New York: Columbia University Press, 1966.   660 p.

This is a collection of essays designed to provide extensive analysis of the quantitative economic activity.   Topics covered include consumption, investment, employment levels, output of final products, developments in minerals and fuels, development and adaption of power and machines, and sources of productivity change.

380   Osborn, George C.   "The Southern Agricultural Press and Some Significant Rural Problems, 1900-1940."   AGRICULTURAL HISTORY   29 (July 1955): 115-21.

Surveying the southern agricultural journals for the period, the major problems which were reported are discussed in this article, for example, single crop dependence, labor scarcity, soil exhaustion, race, and tenancy.

381 Passell, Peter, and Schmundt, Maria. "Pre-Civil War Land Policy and the Growth of Manufacturing." EXPLORATIONS IN ECONOMIC HISTORY 9 (Fall 1971): 35-48.

Using a two-sector general equilibrium model of the nineteenth-century economy, the land policy advocated by the various sectors of the economy was examined. Special interest was given to the effects of such policy on sectional growth.

382 Paxson, Frederic L. "The Agricultural Surplus: A Problem in History." AGRICULTURAL HISTORY 6 (April 1932): 51-68.

Examining the agricultural surplus of 1932 in particular, the production, composition, and allocation of this surplus are the topics discussed.

383 Peet, R. "Von Thunen Theory, and the Dynamics of Agricultural Expansion." EXPLORATIONS IN ECONOMIC HISTORY 8 (Winter 1970-71): 181-202.

Developing concentric agricultural zones, attention is focused upon the effects of rising urban export demand and transportation advances with respect to western agricultural development prior to the Civil War. This is an attempt to derive a theory of dynamic agricultural expansion using Von Thunen's model. Particular events such as the movement to the American interior of commercial farming are also considered.

384 Phillips, Edward Hake. "The Gulf Coast Rice Industry." AGRICULTURAL HISTORY 25 (April 1951): 91-95.

Analyzing improvements in cultivation methods, farm sizes, mechanization, and extensions to the upland prairie regions, the study provides a brief account of the Gulf Coast rice industry.

385 Primack, Martin L. "Farm Capital Formation as a Use of Farm Labor in the United States, 1850-1910." JOURNAL OF ECONOMIC HISTORY 26 (September 1966): 348-62.

Relating the size of the labor input in agricultural capital formation to the total labor force in agriculture, the author examines the various types of capital formation and the declining relative importance of labor in such things as land clearing. The increasing importance of irrigation is also discussed.

386 _____. "Farm Construction as a Use of Farm Labor in the United States, 1850-1910." JOURNAL OF ECONOMIC HISTORY 25 (March 1965): 114-25.

This is a study of the statewide patterns of this type of capital formation (construction and improvement of farm buildings), with special emphasis on the labor utilization for construction and

for agricultural output. The author considers factors in the
capital building decision such as the cost of capital rate of
interest and expected rate of depreciation. Included also is
an appendix discussing Tostlebee's study of agricultural capital formation "The Growth of Physical Capital in Agriculture."
STUDIES IN CAPITAL FORMATION AND FINANCING,
Occasional Paper 44. New York: National Bureau of
Economic Research, 1954. 146 p.

387 _____. "Land Clearing under Nineteenth-Century Techniques." JOUR-
NAL OF ECONOMIC HISTORY 22 (December 1962): 484-97.

Viewing the clearing and improving of land as capital improvement the author examines the techniques used and the relative
costs after 1850. The productivity increases for the land are
also considered in the various parts of the country.

388 Ransom, Roger, and Sutch, Richard. "The Impact of the Civil War and
of Emancipation on Southern Agriculture." EXPLORATIONS IN ECO-
NOMIC HISTORY 12 (January 1975): 1-28.

The argument contained in this study is that although the transportation and manufacturing sectors experienced growth during
the postbellum period, agriculture did not because of the voluntary reduction in the supply of labor. After emancipation
freedmen chose a different work-leisure trade-off than they
had as slaves.

389 Rasmussen, Wayne D. "The Civil War: A Catalyst of Agricultural Revolution." AGRICULTURAL HISTORY 39 (October 1965): 187-95.

Arguing that an agricultural revolution took place after the
Civil War, the author critically examines the views of other
economists. Wheat production, total acreage in cultivation,
wartime demand, and improvements in machinery are considered
for various states. One Wisconsin farm is used as a case study.

390 _____. "The Impact of Technological Change on American Agriculture,
1862-1962." JOURNAL OF ECONOMIC HISTORY 22 (December 1962):
578-91.

Tracing the shift from manpower to animal power and from
animal power to machine power, the author analyzes the effect
of such change on the rate of investment, effective demand,
and further advancements of technology.

391 _____, ed. GROWTH THROUGH AGRICULTURAL PROGRESS. Washington, D.C.: U.S. Department of Agriculture, 1961. 74 p.

A profile of the U.S.D.A. is provided along with discussions of the interrelationship between agriculture and various other areas of our economy.

392 _____. READINGS IN THE HISTORY OF AMERICAN AGRICULTURE. Urbana: University of Illinois Press, 1960. 340 p.

This work considers the development of agriculture from colonial times to the post–World War II period. Crops, fertilizers, technology, and breeds of animals are all discussed.

393 Reid, Joseph D., Jr. "Sharecropping as an Understandable Market Response--The Post-Bellum South." JOURNAL OF ECONOMIC HISTORY 33 (March 1973): 106-30.

Using a new theory of tenancy choice the author shows that tenancy should have increased productivity in southern agriculture, all other things remaining the same. The fall in the supplies of agricultural capital and labor emerge as the likely causal factors in explaining the fall in southern relative income between 1860 and 1880.

394 Rezneck, Samuel. "Coal and Oil in the American Economy." JOURNAL OF ECONOMIC HISTORY 7 (1947): supplement, 55-72.

These natural resources were viewed as important in 1947 and the author examines the expansion rates of the industries, as well as the qualitative factors that have affected this rate.

395 Robbins, Roy M. "Horace Greeley: Land Reform and Unemployment, 1837-1862." AGRICULTURAL HISTORY 7 (January 1933): 18-41.

Considering the Panic of 1837 and the general political environment, the economic reasons for H. Greeley's becoming a socialist are discussed. His position on land reform and its evolution are the primary subjects of this paper.

396 _____. "The Public Domain in the Era of Exploitation, 1862-1901." AGRICULTURAL HISTORY 13 (April 1939): 97-108.

Although primarily interested in the implication of the Homestead Act of 1862 for land distribution, the author also considers the impact of corporate interests on land distribution.

397 Rogin, Leo. THE INTRODUCTION OF FARM MACHINERY IN ITS RELATION TO THE PRODUCTIVITY OF LABOR IN THE AGRICULTURE OF THE UNITED STATES DURING THE NINETEENTH CENTURY. Berkeley: University of California Press, 1931. 260 p.

The discussion is directed primarily to the introduction of the plow, types of reaping machinery, and threshing machinery. A section also treats the manhour requirements in wheat production.

398   Rosenberg, Charles E.   "Science, Technology, and Economic Growth: The Case of the Agricultural Experiment Station Scientist 1875-1914." AGRICULTURAL HISTORY 45 (January 1971): 1-20.

> This is a study of scientists employed at the stations, the adverse conditions under which they worked, and the resulting experiments, in an attempt to cast light on the relation between science and technology and economic development.

399   Ross, Earle D.   "Agriculture in Our Economic History." AGRICULTURAL HISTORY 22 (April 1948): 65-68.

> This is a plea for a more general equilibrium approach to understanding the importance of agriculture in our economy.

400   Ruttan, Vernon W.   "The Contribution of Technological Progress to Farm Output: 1950-75." REVIEW OF ECONOMICS AND STATISTICS 38 (February 1956): 61-69.

> Using various models an attempt is made to measure the effect of alternative rates of technological change on different aggregate input categories. The analytical scheme used allows for the distinction between the contributions of technological change and increased nonlabor inputs.

401   Sachs, William S.   "Agricultural Conditions in the Northern Colonies before the Revolution." JOURNAL OF ECONOMIC HISTORY 13 (Summer 1953): 274-90.

> This is an investigation of the duration, intensity, and amplitude of economic fluctuation which may have precipitated the revolutionary war.

402   Saloutos, Theodore.   "The Agricultural Problem and Nineteenth Century Industrialism." AGRICULTURAL HISTORY 22 (July 1948): 156-74.

> This is a review of the agricultural transition that was necessary for the growth of the industrial economy during the nineteenth century.

403   _____.   "Land Policy and Its Relation to Agricultural Production and Distribution, 1862 to 1933." JOURNAL OF ECONOMIC HISTORY 22 (December 1962): 445-60.

> It is argued in this study that land "policy" was really a shortsighted, maladjusted turnover of land to farmers who were not accustomed to capitalistic market methods. It is further argued that it was this inability to adjust which produced the credit and other problems which arose during this period.

404 _____. "Southern Agriculture and the Problems of Readjustment: 1865-1877." AGRICULTURAL HISTORY 30 (April 1956): 58-76.

The situation of poor whites and emancipated blacks after the Civil War is considered with respect to the effects they may have had on output, land values, and land sales.

405 _____. "The Spring-Wheat Farmer in a Maturing Economy, 1870-1920." JOURNAL OF ECONOMIC HISTORY 6 (November 1946): 173-90.

Considering one aspect of agrarian unrest, the author examines the reasons for the suffering and disappointment. Farmers were said to have engaged in "anarchistic" competition while the merchants were more regulated. Changing socioeconomic conditions combined with the lack of scientific developments in farming were also considered factors that produced unrest.

406 Schmidt, Louis B. "The Agricultural Revolution in the Prairies and the Great Plains of the United States." AGRICULTURAL HISTORY 8 (October 1934): 169-95.

Looking at the second great settlement period, the author analyzes the people and the agriculture in order to (1) review the factors which allowed the prairies and the plains to produce the necessary food supplied to support the post-1850 industrial transformation; and (2) survey the present status and probable future of agriculture in this area.

407 Shannon, Fred A. THE FARMER'S LAST FRONTIER. New York: Farrar and Rinehart, 1945. 434 p.

Considering agricultural activity from the view of the farmer, Shannon examines the effects of commercialization, restricted migration, the disposition of public lands, and financing and marketing problems. The effects of government activity in agriculture are also discussed.

408 Shideler, James H. "The Development of the Parity Price Formula For Agriculture, 1919-1923." AGRICULTURAL HISTORY 27 (July 1953): 77-84.

Discussing the price movements, the sources of these movements, and the politically charged atmosphere, the author sets the concepts of the parity formula as a precise measurement of a agricultural price goal.

409 Stephenson, Wendell H. "Ante-Bellum New Orleans as an Agricultural Focus." AGRICULTURAL HISTORY 15 (October 1941): 161-74.

How important were agriculture commerce, the slave trade, and agricultural publications to the growth and prosperity of New Orleans? These questions are addressed in this study.

410 Street, James H. "Cotton Mechanization and Economic Development."
AMERICAN ECONOMIC REVIEW 45 (June 1955): 566-83.

> Classifying factors as either institutional, technological, or
> exogenous, an attempt was made to explain the prolonged re-
> tardation and sharp acceleration in the mechanization of cotton
> production in the United States.

411 Sutch, Richard, and Ransom, Roger. "The Ex-Slave in the Post-Bellum
South: A Study of the Economic Impact of Racism in a Market Environment." JOURNAL OF ECONOMIC HISTORY 33 (March 1973): 131-48.

> This is an attempt to explain the observed market structure and
> economic performance of the postbellum South. The analysis
> focuses on the costs of information in labor market decision
> making. They find that racism was a reason why freedmen
> were denied the opportunity to become independent farmers.
> Institutional change came very slowly.

412 Swierenga, Robert P. "Land Speculation and Frontier Tax Assessments."
AGRICULTURAL HISTORY 44 (July 1970): 253-66.

> The author examines the tax roles of Iowa for 1853-68, com-
> paring the assessed values of resident and nonresident lands in
> an attempt to determine whether the absentee land speculators
> were discriminated against.

413 _____. "Land Speculator 'Profits' Reconsidered: Central Iowa as a Test
Case." In his QUANTIFICATION IN AMERICAN HISTORY, pp. 317-46.
New York: Atheneum Press, 1970.

414 _____. "Land Speculator 'Profits' Reconsidered: Central Iowa as a Test
Case." JOURNAL OF ECONOMIC HISTORY 26 (March 1966): 1-28.

> A rigorous analysis of land speculation, this article contains
> calculations of rates of return realized by speculators who oper-
> ated in this twelve-million-acre area. A summary of the meth-
> odology used is also provided.

415 Taylor, George Rogers. "Agrarian Discontent in the Mississippi Valley
Preceding the War of 1812." JOURNAL OF POLITICAL ECONOMY 39
(August 1931): 471-505.

> Examining the western economic conditions, Taylor finds that
> the depression before the War of 1812 had important effects
> on the support given by the frontier to the Embargo and Non-
> intercourse Acts.

416 Taylor, H.C. "The Historical Approach to the Economic Problems of Agriculture." AGRICULTURAL HISTORY 11 (July 1937): 221-22.

417 Taylor, P.A.M., and Arrington, L.J. "Religion and Planning in the Far West: The First Generation of Mormons in Utah." ECONOMIC HISTORY REVIEW 11 (August 1958): 71-86.

This is an analysis of the Mormons' attempt to establish three hundred settlements in thirty years, studying the effect of their religious preoccupation and their organized immigration. All this was carried out in nearly complete isolation from the outside world.

418 Tennin, Peter. "The Causes of Cotton-Price Fluctuations in the 1830's." REVIEW OF ECONOMICS AND STATISTICS 49 (November 1967): 463-70.

Rejecting North's model where changing prices lead economic growth, the author reexamines aggregate fluctuations in the 1830s, with special attention to the roles of Biddle and Jackson.

419 _____. "The Post-Bellum Recovery of the South and the Cost of the Civil War." JOURNAL OF ECONOMIC HISTORY 36 (December 1976): 898-907.

This is an attempt to reconcile previous arguments over the causes of the South's failure to regain its pre-Civil War level of prosperity during the postbellum period. It is a reconciliation of the demand and supply arguments and an application of the results to a calculation of the cost of the Civil War.

420 Thompson, John G. "The Nature of Demand for Agricultural Products and Some Important Consequences." JOURNAL OF POLITICAL ECONOMY 24 (February 1916): 158-82.

This is an examination of the effects of the relatively inelastic demand for farm products on speculation, international trade, shortages and surpluses, and trends in migration.

421 Trumbower, Henry R. "The Incidence of Freight Charges on Agricultural Products." JOURNAL OF POLITICAL ECONOMY 33 (June 1925): 340-53.

This is an attempt to determine the distribution of the burden of transportation costs and the effects of a change in freight rates on producers, consumers, and agricultural conditions.

422 Waugh, F.V., and Ogren, K.E. "An Interpretation of Changes in Agricultural Manufacturing Costs." AMERICAN ECONOMIC REVIEW 51 (May 1961): 213-22.

Reviewing trends in food prices and marketing costs since 1913, the authors examine the cost-price squeeze of the 1950s with respect to the further expansion of the government's farm program. The effect of this expansion on farmers, consumers, and taxpayers is discussed.

423 Wells, O.V. "The Depression of 1873-79." AGRICULTURAL HISTORY 11 (July 1937): 237-54.

Wells compares agricultural conditions in the earlier depression with those which prevailed during the 1930s.

424 White, Gerald T. "Economic Recovery and the Wheat Crop of 1897." AGRICULTURAL HISTORY 13 (January 1939): 13-21.

Why the depression of 1897 occurred and the importance of the wheat crop in the economic recovery are main topics of this paper. The international market for the wheat crop is examined in this study.

425 Wiley, B.I. "Salient Changes in Southern Agriculture since the Civil War." AGRICULTURAL HISTORY 13 (April 1939): 65-76.

The subject of this article is the agricultural reorganization which took place as a result of the shift from slave to free labor and the eventual rise of tenancy. The expansion of the western lands and the over-cultivation of the South are also considered.

426 Williamson, Jeffrey G. "Late Nineteenth Century American Retardation: A Neoclassical Analysis." JOURNAL OF ECONOMIC HISTORY 33 (September 1973): 581-607.

This is an application of a simulation model to explain through the use of counterfactual analysis what the causes of retardation were in the U.S. economy. A great amount of the analysis is naturally concerned with agricultural activity.

427 Winters, Donald L. "Tenancy as an Economic Institution: The Growth and Distribution of Agricultural Tenancy in Iowa, 1850-1900." JOURNAL OF ECONOMIC HISTORY 37 (June 1977): 382-408.

This work is an attempt to explain the distribution of tenancy according to various economic factors, for example, the relation between the rate of return on land and the local interest rates.

428 Wright, Gavin. "Cotton Competition and the Post-Bellum Recovery of the American South." JOURNAL OF ECONOMIC HISTORY 34 (September 1974): 610-35.

This is an investigation of the quantitative significance of the "displaced market" and "exchange rate" hypotheses which have been proffered to explain the apparent stagnation of the southern economy. It is argued that the real reasons explaining this stagnation lie in the more traditional areas.

429 _____. "An Econometric Study of Cotton Production and Trade, 1830-1860." REVIEW OF ECONOMICS AND STATISTICS 53 (May 1971): 111-20.

Estimating the elasticities of demand and supply, the author attempts to test North's hypothesis regarding price changes and economic growth. He argues that Tennin's test (see no. 418) did not adequately specify the problem.

430 _____. "'Economic Democracy' and the Concentration of Agricultural Wealth in the Cotton South, 1850-1860." AGRICULTURAL HISTORY 44 (January 1970): 63-94.

The author presents new evidence regarding the concentration of agricultural wealth, and critiques the work of U.B. Phillips, Lewis C. Gray, and Frank and Harriet Owsley ("The Economic Basis of Society in the Late Antebellum South." JOURNAL OF SOUTHERN HISTORY 15 [March 1949]: 24-45). The concentration of improved acreage and other aspects are discussed.

431 Wright, Gavin, and Kunreuther, Howard. "Cotton, Corn, and Risk in the Nineteenth Century." JOURNAL OF ECONOMIC HISTORY 35 (September 1975): 526-51.

This is an attempt to explain the continued emphasis on cotton production during the postbellum period and the decline in the self-sufficient status of the antebellum South. According to the authors, risk conditions changed which altered the choices of economic agents. It was not cotton and corn prices or yields that were important, but rather the cotton yields, cotton prices, and food prices, which would ultimately set exchange conditions.

432 Zepp, Thomas M. "On Returns to Scale and Input Substitutability in Slave Agriculture." EXPLORATIONS IN ECONOMIC HISTORY 13 (April 1976): 165-78.

Using the 1860 data on the cotton South, the author attempts to test the significance of assuming that the elasticity of substitution between slaves and other factors was unitary. If factor proportions are not fixed, then some other explanation besides the lower supply of labor must be used to explain the slow recovery of the South after the Civil War.

433 Zusman, P. "An Investigation of the Dynamic Stability and Stationary States of the United States Potato Market, 1930-1958." ECONOMETRICA 30 (July 1962): 522-47.

> Using an econometric model of the U.S. potato market, the author attempts to analyze the static and dynamic properties of the model. Stability of the market is a major concern, and is examined with regard to both parameter changes and exogenous shocks.

3.2 GENERAL LISTINGS

434 Bidwell, P., and Falconer, J. HISTORY OF AGRICULTURE IN THE NORTHERN U.S., 1620-1860. Washington, D.C.: Carnegie Institution of Washington, 1925. 512 p.

435 Bogart, Ernest Ludlow. "Farm Ownership in the United States." JOURNAL OF POLITICAL ECONOMY 16 (April 1908): 201-11.

436 Boyle, James E. "The Farmers and the Grain Trade in the United States." ECONOMIC JOURNAL 35 (March 1925): 11-25.

437 Brown, Harry Gunnison. "Land Speculation and Land-Value Taxation." JOURNAL OF POLITICAL ECONOMY 35 (June 1927): 390-402.

438 Clements, Robert V. "British-Controlled Enterprise in the West between 1870 and 1900, and Some Agrarian Reactions." AGRICULTURAL HISTORY 27 (October 1953): 132-40.

439 Davenport, H.J. "Exhausted Farms and Exhausting Taxation." JOURNAL OF POLITICAL ECONOMY 17 (June 1909): 354-62.

440 Davis, Katharine Bement. "Tables Relating to the Price of Wheat and Other Farm Products." JOURNAL OF POLITICAL ECONOMY 6 (June 1898): 403-10.

441 DeCanio, Stephen. AGRICULTURE IN THE POST-BELLUM SOUTH: THE ECONOMICS OF PRODUCTION AND SUPPLY. Cambridge, Mass.: Prit Press, 1974. 335 p.

442 Grave, Erwin. "The Relationship of Business Activity to Agriculture." JOURNAL OF POLITICAL ECONOMY 38 (August 1930): 472-78.

443 Higgs, Robert. "Did Southern Farmers Discriminate?" AGRICULTURAL HISTORY 46 (April 1972): 325-28.

444   Hunt, Thomas F. THE CEREALS IN AMERICA. New York: Judd Co.,
       1908. 421 p.

445   Jacobstein, Meyer. THE TOBACCO INDUSTRY IN THE UNITED STATES.
       New York: Macmillan Co., 1907. 208 p.

446   Lemon, James T. "Household Consumption in Eighteenth-Century America
       and Its Relationship to Production and Trade: The Situation among Farmers
       in Southwestern Pennsylvania." AGRICULTURAL HISTORY 41 (January
       1967): 59-70.

447   Lurie, Jonathan. "Speculation, Risk, and Profits: The Ambivalent Agrarian
       in the Late Nineteenth Century." AGRICULTURAL HISTORY 46 (April
       1972): 269-78.

448   McVey, Frank L. "Cooperation by Farmers." JOURNAL OF POLITICAL
       ECONOMY 6 (June 1898): 401-3.

449   Nourse, E.G. "The Trend of Agricultural Exports." JOURNAL OF POLIT-
       ICAL ECONOMY 36 (June 1928): 330-52.

450   _____. "Will Agricultural Prices Fall?" JOURNAL OF POLITICAL ECON-
       OMY 28 (March 1920): 189-218.

451   Quaintance, W.H. THE INFLUENCE OF FARM MACHINERY ON PRO-
       DUCTION AND LABOR. New York: Macmillan Co., 1904. 106 p.

452   Rasmussen, Wayne D. A HISTORY OF THE EMERGENCY FARM LABOR
       SUPPLY PROGRAM 1943-47. Washington, D.C.: U.S. Department of
       Agriculture, 1951. 248 p.

453   Roberts, Peter. THE ANTHRACITE COAL INDUSTRY. New York: Mac-
       millan Co., 1901. 261 p.

454   Schmidt, L., and Ross, E. READINGS IN THE ECONOMIC HISTORY OF
       AMERICAN AGRICULTURE. New York: Johnson Reprint Corp., 1966.
       323 p.

455   Swierenga, Robert P. PIONEERS AND PROFITS: LAND SPECULATION
       ON THE IOWA FRONTIER. Ames: Iowa State University Press, 1968.
       260 p.

456   Taft, Oren, Jr. "Land Credit." JOURNAL OF POLITICAL ECONOMY
       6 (September 1898): 476-87.

457 Teele, R.P. "Notes on the Irrigation Situation." JOURNAL OF POLITI-
CAL ECONOMY 13 (December 1905): 237–45.

458 _____. "The Organization of Irrigation Companies." JOURNAL OF
POLITICAL ECONOMY 12 (March 1904): 161–78.

459 U.S. Department of Interior. PUBLIC LAND BIBLIOGRAPHY. Washington,
D.C.: Government Printing Office, 1962. 85 p.

460 Wik, Reynold M. "Henry Ford and the Agricultural Depression of 1920–
1923." AGRICULTURAL HISTORY 29 (January 1955): 15–21.

461 Wiser, Vivian, ed. TWO CENTURIES OF AMERICAN AGRICULTURE.
Washington, D.C.: Agricultural History Society, 1976. 315 p.

462 Wyse, R.C. "The Selling and Financing of the American Cotton Crop."
ECONOMIC JOURNAL 30 (December 1920): 473–83.

463 Zapoleon, L.B. "Farm Relief, Agricultural Prices, and Tariffs." JOUR-
NAL OF POLITICAL ECONOMY 40 (February 1932): 73–100.

Chapter 4
TECHNOLOGICAL CHANGE

The citations included in this chapter are, as usual, by no means inclusive of all the relevant literature. They are, however, a sampling of the more signifi- cant works that specifically treat technological change and productivity change. The emphasis has been to provide works from both the historical and the more rigorous economic literature. Many works that deal with technological change and growth, or other economic variables, will be cited in chapters that are specifically devoted to these other aspects, for example, agriculture and capi- tal accumulation. There are many modern theoretical economics studies which treat various aspects of technological change, but we have included only those studies which have particular historical applications.

Many historical (quasi-literary) accounts of technological change are not included due to the primary emphasis on the economic analysis of history that is maintained throughout this volume. The reader may also find it very helpful to consult par- ticular business histories for information regarding the evolution of production practices. Such works often illustrate how particular entrepreneurs took advan- tage of new techniques in order to increase the profitability of their enterprises.

The studies cited in this chapter are primarily concerned with changes in tech- nology on an aggregate basis, using individual firm or industry cases only for illustration when appropriate.

4.1 ANNOTATED LISTINGS

464 Abramovitz, Moses. "Resource and Output Trends in the United States since 1870." AMERICAN ECONOMIC REVIEW 40 (May 1956): 1-23.

> This is an analysis of changes in the rate of growth and pro- ductivity changes that are not part of the usual business cycle fluctuations.

465 Ames, Edward, and Rosenberg, Nathan. "Changing Technological Leader- ship and Industrial Growth." ECONOMIC JOURNAL 73 (March 1963): 13-31.

Dealing with the "late comer" thesis, the authors explore the thesis that innovative countries pay a penalty for their leadership position.

466 _____. "The Progressive Division and Specialization of Industries." JOURNAL OF DEVELOPMENT STUDIES 1 (July 1965): 363-83.

The authors maintain that there exists no theory of specialization which explains the observed behavior during the nineteenth and twentieth centuries in Britain. Such an explanation may hold much for the formation of development policy according to this study.

467 Asher, Ephraim. "Industrial Efficiency and Biased Technical Change in American and British Manufacturing: The Case of Textiles in the Nineteenth Century." JOURNAL OF ECONOMIC HISTORY 32 (June 1972): 431-42.

An assessment of the various labor scarcity arguments, this article measures factor-saving biases in technical change within the U.S. and British textile sectors.

468 Ashton, Herbert. "Some Considerations in the Measurement of Productivity of Railroad Workers." JOURNAL OF POLITICAL ECONOMY 46 (October 1938): 714-20.

This is an illustration of the problems which arise when one attempts to measure productivity change. A definition is used which nets out both the qualitative and quantitative effects of capital on labor productivity.

469 Ball, D.E., and Walton, Gary M. "Agricultural Productivity Change in Eighteenth-Century Pennsylvania." JOURNAL OF ECONOMIC HISTORY 36 (March 1976): 102-17.

Using a single county in Pennsylvania as a sample, tests are made to determine both total factor and labor productivity during the eighteenth century. The rates found were consistent with those found for the nineteenth-century United States. Various new ideas for research are provided by the authors.

470 Barzel, Yoram. "The Production Function and Technical Change in the Steam-Power Industry." JOURNAL OF POLITICAL ECONOMY 72 (April 1964): 133-50.

An attempt is made to discern whether the more sophisticated models yielded better information. Aspects considered were those such as the effects of changing amounts of inputs which were required as the fixed capital began to age. The effect on inputs of technological change and price index construction for capital are also discussed.

471 _____ . "Productivity in the Electric Power Industry, 1929-1955." RE-VIEW OF ECONOMICS AND STATISTICS 45 (November 1963): 395-408.

> After exploring the underlying assumptions of the technique of measuring productivity according to output per unit of input, the author applies this technique to the privately owned electric power industry. The results are compared with those obtained from the production function approach to measuring productivity.

472 Brady, Dorothy. "Relative Prices in the Nineteenth Century." JOURNAL OF ECONOMIC HISTORY 24 (June 1964): 145-203.

> Developing series of relative prices on the basis of the size and material of the functional products, an account is made for the variety of industrial output, the changing economy, changing demands, changing costs, innovations, expanding markets, as well as changing distributive methods.

473 Bright, Arthur A., Jr., and Madaurin, W. Rupert. "Economic Factors Influencing the Development and Introduction of the Fluorescent Lamp." JOURNAL OF POLITICAL ECONOMY 51 (October 1943): 429-50.

> The authors discuss the impact of the fluorescent lamp as well as the economic factors which influenced the rate of technical progress in the electric lamp industry. A short history is also provided of the competitive structure of the industry.

474 Brittain, James E. "The International Diffusion of Electrical Power Technology, 1870-1920." JOURNAL OF ECONOMIC HISTORY 34 (March 1974): 108-21.

> This article is one of a group in this issue of the journal which treat various aspects of diffusion of technology. This article discusses the transmission of information between Europe and the United States, citing the improvements that were made in each country. An attempt is also made to determine the effects of noneconomic forces on the rate of diffusion.

475 Brown, E[rnest].H[enry]. Phelps. "Levels and Movements of Industrial Productivity and Real Wages Internationally Compared, 1860-1970." ECONOMIC JOURNAL 83 (March 1973): 58-71.

> This is a reworking of the industrial productivity indexes for Germany, England, Sweden and the United States. The real wage data are compared among these four and France. Variables are included to account for structural change during the 1960s, and the methodology of constructing the indexes is explained.

476 Brown, Ernest Henry Phelps, and Hopkins, S.W. "The Course of Wage-
     Rates in Five Countries, 1860-1939." OXFORD ECONOMIC PAPERS 2
     (June 1950): 226-96.

     This is an extensive examination of wage rates, which con-
     siders the productivity changes that occurred as well.

477 Brown, Murray. ON THE THEORY AND MEASUREMENT OF TECHNO-
     LOGICAL CHANGE. Cambridge, Engl.: Cambridge University Press,
     1968. 214 p.

     The main purpose of this study is to provide ways in which
     one can measure the neutral and nonneutral components of
     technology. A theoretical framework is specified in the first
     six chapters, and the last three chapters deal with the mea-
     surement of the components of technology. There are four
     technical appendixes.

478 Bruchey, Stuart. "The Business Economy of Marketing Change, 1790-1840:
     A Study of Sources of Efficiency." AGRICULTURAL HISTORY 46 (Janu-
     ary 1972): 211-26.

     After dealing with the problems of defining marketing, degree
     of occupational differentiation, and efficiency, the author ex-
     amines the effects of specialization on the marketing of agri-
     cultural commodities.

479 Cavert, William L. "The Technological Revolution in Agriculture, 1910-
     1955." AGRICULTURAL HISTORY 30 (January 1956): 18-27.

     An account of changes in crop technology, irrigation, live-
     stock husbandry, management, specialization, and sources of
     power, this article also considers future trends.

480 Clague, Christopher. "An International Comparison of Industrial Efficiency:
     Peru and the United States." REVIEW OF ECONOMICS AND STATISTICS
     49 (November 1967): 487-93.

     Results of the relatively few studies in this area are summarized,
     including the difficulties encountered. Production functions are
     estimated for eleven manufacturing companies in both countries.
     The results of the estimates were used to determine the implica-
     tions that one could infer from the Heckscher-Ohlin theory of
     international trade. The policy issues resulting from such effi-
     ciency comparisons are also considered.

481 Cole, Arthur H. "An Approach to the Study of Entrepreneurship." JOUR-
     NAL OF ECONOMIC HISTORY 6 (1946): supplement, 1-15.

     Discussing the definition, activities, economic significance,
     and the historical development of entrepreneurship, the author

suggests possible methodologies which could be used in studying these topics.

482 _____. "Entrepreneurship as an Area of Research." JOURNAL OF ECONOMIC HISTORY 2 (December 1942): 118-25.

Without actually performing the test, a hypothesis is offered regarding the role of profits in guiding the entrepreneur in the efficient allocation of resources. In an attempt to establish the essential position of the entrepreneur in a private enterprise system, the author proffers a possible method for testing the hypothesis.

483 Comanor, William S. "Research and Technical Change in the Pharmaceutical Industry." REVIEW OF ECONOMICS AND STATISTICS 47 (May 1965): 182-90.

A study of the relationship between research expenditure and technical change, this study examines the effects of the size and character of research programs and economies of scale for the pharmaceutical industry between 1955 and 1960.

484 Conrad, Alfred H. "Productivity, Prices, and Income." REVIEW OF ECONOMICS AND STATISTICS 40 (May 1958): 169-72.

This is a review of PRODUCTIVITY, PRICES, AND INCOMES: MATERIALS PREPARED FOR THE JOINT ECONOMIC COMMITTEE (8th Cong., 1st sess.). Summaries of the investigations of price, output, and income trends for 1900 to 1947 are included. Various cost-price-income relationships are explored.

485 Dacy, Douglas C. "Productivity and Price Trends in Construction since 1947." REVIEW OF ECONOMICS AND STATISTICS 47 (November 1965): 406-11.

After presenting a summary of previous works, the author estimates productivity change for construction, using a model that avoids some of the weaknesses of the index cost approach.

486 Dalrymple, Dana G. "American Technology and Soviet Agricultural Development, 1924-1933." AGRICULTURAL HISTORY 40 (July 1966): 187-206.

Examining the Soviet use of U.S. technology, the author considers the organizational framework for obtaining technological change, the nature of the U.S. contribution, major problem areas, and the economic significance of the process.

487 David, Paul. "The 'Horndal Effect' in Lowell, 1834-1856: A Short Learning Curve for Integrated Cotton Textile Mills." EXPLORATIONS IN ECONOMIC HISTORY 10 (Winter 1973): 131-50.

This is an examination of the productivity growth that may be realized from a given physical plant through learning on the part of labor and/or management. Productivity growth resulting from the application of experience to the design and operation of production facilities is also examined.

488 _____. "Invention and Accumulation in America's Economic Growth: A Nineteenth-Century Parable." In CARNEGIE-ROCHESTER CONFERENCE SERIES ON PUBLIC POLICY, edited by Karl Brunner and Allan H. Meltzer, vol. 6, pp. 179-228. Amsterdam: North-Holland Publishing Co., 1977.

Through the use of macroeconomic growth models, the author attempts to relate his account of the growth of the U.S. economy. He emphasizes the role of technological change in such a growth process, along with the interaction of domestic and foreign financial intermediaries with respect to capital flows and formation.

489 _____. TECHNICAL CHOICE INNOVATION AND ECONOMIC GROWTH. Cambridge, Engl.: Cambridge University Press, 1975. 334 p.

Written by one of the leading analysts of technology and technological change, this work contains a group of essays previously published by the author. The first essay appears to print for the first time in this book. Each of these essays has been a seminal work with respect to its area of analysis.

490 _____. "Transport Innovation and Economic Growth: Professor Fogel On and Off the Rails." ECONOMIC HISTORY REVIEW 22 (September 1969): 506-25.

This is a very detailed critique of Robert W. Fogel's RAILROADS AND AMERICAN ECONOMIC GROWTH (Baltimore: Johns Hopkins Press, 1964. 296 p.). Through the construction of an alternative explanation about the impact of the railroad, David generates some questions with respect to Fogel's analysis.

491 Davis, Lance, and North, Douglas. "Institutional Change and American Economic Growth: A First Step towards a Theory of Institutional Innovation." JOURNAL OF ECONOMIC HISTORY 30 (March 1970): 131-49.

After developing a model to explain the formation and change of U.S. economic institutions, the authors make some effort to predict future changes. As a result, a theory of institutional innovation is proffered and used to study the public-private mix in the economy.

492 Day, H. Richard. "The Economics of Technological Change and the Demise of the Sharecropper." AMERICAN ECONOMICS REVIEW 57 (June 1967): 427-49.

After presenting a nontechnical description of the problem, a recursive programming model was used to examine trends in output, technology, and productivity. The effects on labor and population were also examined for the Mississippi Delta region.

493 Destler, Chester McArthur. "Entrepreneurial Leadership among the 'Robber Barons': A Trial Balance." JOURNAL OF ECONOMIC HISTORY 6 (1946): supplement, 28-49.

In an attempt to analyze the growth and contraction of the power of these semipractical entrepreneurs the author examines the origins, training, incentives, and risks associated with these men.

494 DuBoff, Richard B. "The Introduction of Electric Power in American Manufacturing." ECONOMIC HISTORY REVIEW 20 (December 1967): 509-18.

Both the long- and short-run aspects of electrification are examined, with emphasis on the economic rationale for electrification and the processes that are transformed by the process.

495 East, Robert A. "The Business Entrepreneur in a Changing Colonial Economy, 1763-1795." JOURNAL OF ECONOMIC HISTORY 6 (1946): supplement, 16-27.

This is an examination of the activities of entrepreneurs in this prerevolutionary period. The effect of the Revolution on their activities is also considered.

496 Evans, G. Herberton, Jr. "Business Entrepreneurs, Their Major Functions and Related Tenets." JOURNAL OF ECONOMIC HISTORY 19 (June 1959): 250-70.

After demonstrating the general importance of the entrepreneur, the author tests the proposition that an entrepreneur is the person or group who determines the type of business the firm should undertake against alternative hypotheses regarding the role of the entrepreneur, for example, that the entrepreneur is the risk bearer, innovator, or manager.

497 _____. "A Theory of Entrepreneurship." JOURNAL OF ECONOMIC HISTORY 2 (December 1942): 142-46.

In this piece the hypothesis that the entrepreneur is an economic opportunist is tested, using the author's definition of an entrepreneur.

498 Fay, C.R. "North Carolina and the New Industrial Revolution." ECONOMIC JOURNAL 35 (June 1925): 200-213.

Based on a geographical and economic description of North Carolina, the author discusses the forces constraining the move towards becoming an industrial state.

499   Feller, Irwin. "The Draper Loom in New England Textiles, 1894-1914: A Study of Diffusion of an Innovation." JOURNAL OF ECONOMIC HISTORY 26 (September 1966): 320-47.

Comparing the northeastern and southern responses to this loom, the author attempts to determine why the South responded differently from the Northeast. Such issues as profitability and other factors affecting adoption are also examined. A comment by Lars G. Sandberg appears in the JOURNAL OF ECONOMIC HISTORY 28 (December 1968): 624-27 and is directly followed by a reply from Feller.

500   Ferguson, C.E. "Time-Series Production Functions and Technological Progress in American Manufacturing Industry." JOURNAL OF POLITICAL ECONOMY 73 (April 1965): 135-47.

Using a constant elasticity of substitution (CES) production function, an attempt is made to measure the extent of neutral and biased technical change in two-digit industries between 1949 and 1961.

501   Flueckiger, Gerald. "Observation and Measurement of Technical Change." EXPLORATIONS IN ECONOMIC HISTORY 9 (Winter 1971-72): 145-78.

Presenting a qualitative characterization of production, this paper characterizes technical change as a directly observable qualitative phenomenon, and demonstrates how individual technological changes can be related to production processes so that measures of technical change can be constructed.

502   Fogel, Robert W. "The Specification Problem in Economic History." JOURNAL OF ECONOMIC HISTORY 27 (September 1967): 283-308.

Cited previously, this article also discusses various problems in the area of technology as well as the related area of labor scarcity, all in the context of a methodological critique. A minor correction may be found in JOURNAL OF ECONOMIC HISTORY 28 (March 1968): 126.

503   Fowler, Loretta. "The Arapahoe Ranch: An Experiment in Cultural Change and Economic Development." ECONOMIC DEVELOPMENT AND CULTURAL CHANGE 21 (April 1973): 446-64.

This study examines the interaction of a particular set of socio-cultural traditions and a particular set of economic forces, and considers the factors which make the enterprise (ranch) a success. It is a study of organizational effects.

504   Goodrich, Carter. "The Revulsion against Internal Improvements." JOUR-
NAL OF ECONOMIC HISTORY 10 (November 1950): 145-69.

This is an examination of the withdrawl of government support
for the development of canals and railways during the nineteenth century. The effects of availability of funds, failure
of state programs, restrictive policy, and the business cycle
are considered with respect to development of these industries.

505   Griliches, Zvi. "Research Costs and Social Returns: Hybrid Corn and
Related Innovations." JOURNAL OF POLITICAL ECONOMY 66 (October
1958): 419-31.

Deriving estimates of the social returns on investment in hybrid
corn and sorghum, the implications of these estimates are reviewed. The return on total agricultural research is also discussed.

506   _____ . "The Sources of Measured Productivity Growth: United States
Agriculture, 1940-60." JOURNAL OF POLITICAL ECONOMY 71 (August
1963): 331-46.

Criticizing the usual production function approach to measuring
productivity, an alternative method is proposed where economic
growth is attributed to changes in the quantities and qualities
of inputs and economies of scale. The results of this study
are compared with those from previous studies.

507   Habakkuk, H.J. AMERICAN AND BRITISH TECHNOLOGY IN THE NINE-
TEENTH CENTURY. Cambridge, Engl.: Cambridge University Press,
1962. 222 p.

This is a very extensive comparative analysis of the nineteenth-
century technology levels in the United States and the United
Kingdom. It is one of the earlier works dealing with the concepts of labor-saving technology in the United States and the
United Kingdom at this time. It has been the seedbed of much
further research.

508   Haites, Erik R., and Mak, James. "Economies of Scale in Western River
Steamboating." JOURNAL OF ECONOMIC HISTORY 36 (September 1976):
689-703.

This attempt to identify the presence of economies of scale
during the antebellum period utilizes evidence which was previously unknown. The results do not indicate that economies
of scale were present. It is a very useful application of cost
functions for testing this hypothesis.

509   Hall, Lady, and Knapp, J. "Numbers of Shops and Productivity in Retail Distribution in Great Britain, the United States, and Canada." ECO-
NOMIC JOURNAL 65 (March 1955): 72-88.

A comparison was made of the composition of shops and the factors causing this composition, as well as the structure and productivity of the three distributive systems. Variations in the volume of merchandise sold at the various shops were examined in an attempt to determine the extent of large-scale organization in retailing.

510 Harley, C.K. "On the Persistence of Old Techniques: The Case of North American Wooden Shipbuilding." JOURNAL OF ECONOMIC HISTORY 33 (June 1973): 372-98.

A competing explanation for the persistence of old techniques in the presence of new methods is presented as a substitute for the usual Schumpeterian view of the process. It is an interesting application of market analysis to a historical observation, useful to economists and historians.

511 Intriligator, Michael D. "Embodied Technical Change and Productivity in the United States, 1929-1958." REVIEW OF ECONOMICS AND STATISTICS 47 (February 1965): 65-70.

Both embodied and disembodied technical change are estimated, using the production function approach. Results are compared with those of other investigators. A comment by Edward F. Denison appears in REVIEW OF ECONOMICS AND STATISTICS 50 (May 1968): 291.

512 Jewkes, J., et al. THE SOURCES OF INVENTION. New York: W.W. Norton, 1969. 428 p.

Twentieth- and nineteenth-century conditions for industrial innovation are compared and an attempt is made to define innovation, invention development, and research. Part 1 of the book deals primarily with inventions and their effect on industry while part 2 presents numerous case histories.

513 Kendrick, John W. "Productivity Trends: Capital and Labor." REVIEW OF ECONOMICS AND STATISTICS 38 (August 1956): 248-57.

Productivity trends for major segments and industries during the period 1899-1953 are provided and analyzed with respect to the information they provide about past increased earnings and future projections.

514 _____. PRODUCTIVITY TRENDS IN THE UNITED STATES. Princeton, N.J.: Princeton University Press, 1961. 630 p.

One of several studies done for the National Bureau of Economic Research on long-run trends in productivity and wages, this work entails an analysis of the significance, measurement, and extent of productivity change both on an aggregate and an industry basis. Extensive appendixes are provided indicating format used for measurement and the empirical results.

515 Knight, Frank H. "Profit and Entrepreneurial Functions." JOURNAL OF ECONOMIC HISTORY 2 (December 1942): 126-31.

By defining the functions of the entrepreneur, an attempt is made to determine the existence of pure profits in entrepreneurial income. That is, does the entrepreneur receive payment in excess of the normal wages and interest for his services.

516 Lebergott, Stanley. "Comments on Measuring Agricultural Change." AGRICULTURAL HISTORY 46 (January 1972): 227-34.

This is a comment on three papers by William Parker and J.L. Klein, Robert Gallman, and Stuart Bruchey on the evaluation of efficiency and agricultural change. These articles are cited elsewhere in this book (see nos. 528, 349, and 478).

517 Lorant, John H. "Technological Change in American Manufacturing during the 1920's." JOURNAL OF ECONOMIC HISTORY 27 (June 1967): 243-46.

This is an investigation of the relationship between the increase in average productivity and the accelerated application of scientific information during the period 1919-29. Statistical evidence is presented to substantiate the position.

518 MacDougall, G.D.A. "Does Productivity Rise Faster in the United States?" REVIEW OF ECONOMICS AND STATISTICS 38 (May 1956): 155-76.

Examining productivity growth rates in raw materials, foodstuffs, and manufactures for the United States, Russia, China, and East Europe, the author attempts to determine relative rates of growth. The differential effects of per capita income and saving are also examined.

519 Machlup, Fritz, and Penrose, Edith. "The Patent Controversy in the Nineteenth Century." JOURNAL OF ECONOMIC HISTORY 10 (May 1950): 1-29.

The patent system prior to 1850, the rise of the antipatent movement, and the defeat of this movement are examined in light of prevailing economic theory and the concept of natural property rights. The concept of just reward to the inventor and the role of incentives are also discussed.

520 MacLaurin, W. Rupert. "Technological Progress in Some American Industries." AMERICAN ECONOMIC REVIEW 44 (May 1954): 178-89.

Comparing thirteen different industries over time, the author attempts to assess the effect of corporate size on technical progress. General causal factors for technical progress are also examined.

521   Maddala, G.S. "Productivity and Technological Change in the Bituminous Coal Industry, 1919-1954." JOURNAL OF POLITICAL ECONOMY 73 (August 1965): 352-65.

Using a disaggregated aggregate production function approach, the author examines the contributions made to the economic growth of the bituminous coal industry by economies of scale, improvements in the quality of inputs, improvement in the organization of production, and pure technical change.

522   Mansfield, Edwin. THE ECONOMICS OF TECHNOLOGICAL CHANGE. New York: W.W. Norton & Co., 1968. 257 p.

This work deals primarily with the twentieth-century experience of the United States and discusses the effects of an the diffusion of technology. The article includes discussion of the problems of automation and labor displacement, government expenditures on research and development, and general public policy toward technical change.

523   Mantoux, Paul. THE INDUSTRIAL REVOLUTION IN THE EIGHTEENTH CENTURY. London: J. Cape, 1976. 528 p.

A comprehensive survey which includes an introduction to the functions of the "modern" factory system, its effects on centralization and the division of labor, and its causes. An examination is made of the structure of industrial capitalism before the transformation into the factory system, as well as the organizational changes and the labor-capital conflict after the transformation. The social and economic effects of land distribution are also discussed along with impact of the factory system on population, cities, labor, and capital classes. It is truly a classic piece of historiography.

524   Massell, Benton F. "Capital Formation and Technological Changes in United States Manufacturing." REVIEW OF ECONOMICS AND STATISTICS 42 (May 1960): 182-88.

Analyzing the annual increase in output per man hour from 1919 to 1955 in the manufacturing sector, the author attempts to allocate the appropriate amounts of the gains to the particular contributing factors, such as technology, capital, and management. It is an effort to determine which areas should receive the greatest amount of resources.

525 Mesthene, Emmanuel G. TECHNOLOGICAL CHANGE: ITS IMPACT ON MAN AND SOCIETY. Cambridge, Mass.: Harvard University Press, 1970. 127 p.

> Concentrating on the social effects of technological change, the author explores the possible effects on social change, values, and possible alterations in the economic and political organization which may result. An annotated bibliography is included at the end of the book.

526 Mills, C. Wright. "The American Business Elite: A Collective Portrait." JOURNAL OF ECONOMIC HISTORY 5 (December 1945): 20-44.

> Using bibliographical information, the following characteristics of the business elite were examined: (1) effect of westward migration on upward mobility; (2) class levels of parents for each generation; (3) education levels; and (4) participation in politics.

527 Olmstead, Alan L. "The Mechanization of Reaping and Mowing in American Agriculture, 1833-1870." JOURNAL OF ECONOMIC HISTORY 35 (June 1975): 327-52.

> This is a very thorough reexamination of a problem for which the explanation had become accepted as fact rather than conjecture. By more completely specifying the model, the author is able to consider cases which were previously neglected. It is a very useful article for understanding the diffusion process and the modification effects on productivity and the rate of diffusion.

528 Parker, William N., and Klein, J.L. "Productivity Growth in Grain Production in the United States, 1840-1860 and 1900-1910." In OUTPUT EMPLOYMENT AND PRODUCTIVITY IN THE UNITED STATES AFTER 1800. Edited by National Bureau of Economic Research, pp. 523-79. Studies in Income and Wealth, no. 30. New York: Columbia University Press, 1966.

> Productivity increased and westward expansion occurred along with technological change. This study attempts to assess the relative importance of the factors that produced the productivity increase. Over thirty pages of technical appendixes provide background for the authors' conclusions.

529 Person, H.S. "The Rural Electrification Administration in Perspective." AGRICULTURAL HISTORY 24 (April 1950): 70-88.

> The role of the REA as a stimulator of employment is discussed, and its wartime and postwar activities are also examined. Labor was used to produce electric lines and supporting materials.

530   Rasmussen, Wayne D. "Technological Change in Western Sugar Beet Production." AGRICULTURAL HISTORY 41 (January 1967): 31-36.

Concentrating on the period after 1946, the author examines the economic incentives motivating the mechanization process.

531   Rosenberg, Nathan. "Anglo-American Wage Differences in 1820's." JOURNAL OF ECONOMIC HISTORY 27 (June 1967): 221-29.

See no. 217 for description.

532   _____. "Capital Goods, Technology, and Economic Growth." OXFORD ECONOMIC PAPERS 15 (November 1963): 217-27.

This study attempts to determine why the United States generated labor-saving technology due to its relative scarcity of labor, while other countries with abundant labor supplies have not generated capital-saving technology.

533   _____. "Factors Affecting the Diffusion of Technology." EXPLORATIONS IN ECONOMIC HISTORY 10 (Fall 1972): 3-34.

The hypothesis tested is that the "rate at which new technologies replace old ones will depend upon the speed with which it is possible to overcome an array of supply side problems." The author is trying to bridge the gap between the technical and economic realms of discourse.

534   _____. PERSPECTIVES ON TECHNOLOGY. Cambridge, Engl.: Cambridge University Press, 1976. 353 p.

Starting with an analysis of two particular industries, the author then discusses the generation and diffusion of technologies. The interaction of changing technology and environmental factors are the topics of the last section, with much attention given to the importance of natural resources in the growth process.

535   _____. "Technological Change in the Machine Tool Industry, 1840-1910." JOURNAL OF ECONOMIC HISTORY 23 (December 1963): 414-46.

In an attempt to explain why certain firms, industries, regions or countries are more ready for technological innovations at different points in time, the major causes of technological change are examined. The analysis is carried out using a case study of the machine tool industry, which played a crucial role in the development process.

536   _____. TECHNOLOGY AND AMERICAN ECONOMIC GROWTH. New York: Harper & Row, 1972. 211 p.

In an attempt to examine the relationship between technological

change and long-term economic growth, the author provides
an extensive historical view of technology and productivity
change. The relationships among various economic factors
are examined to determine the forces at work in the economy.
The various developmental stages of the United States during
the nineteenth and twentieth centuries and the effect of technology on social options are considered in this book.

537   , ed. THE ECONOMICS OF TECHNOLOGICAL CHANGE: SELEC-
TED READINGS. Middlesex, Engl.: Penguin Books, 1971. 509 p.

Incorporating economic reasoning to analyze technological
change, the readings in this book cover five major areas:
(1) the nature and process of technological change; (2) the
determinants of technological change; (3) the diffusion of new
technology; (4) the long-term consequences of technological
change; and (5) international aspects of technological change.
Each of the twenty-two articles is written by a well-known
economist.

538   Ross, Earle D. "Retardation in Farm Technology before the Power Age."
AGRICULTURAL HISTORY 30 (January 1956): 11-17.

This is an account of the reasons for the relatively slow development of farm technology before power machinery became
available.

539   Rostas, L. "Productivity of Labour in the Cotton Industry." ECONOMIC
JOURNAL 55 (June 1945): 192-205.

Discussing the methods used to measure the differences of per
capita output in the United States and Great Britain, the
author analyzes the different methods of production used in
the cotton industry in 1944 with respect to factors causing
discrepancies between the two methods.

540   Rothbarth, E. "Causes of the Superior Efficiency of U.S.A. Industry as
Compared to British Industry." ECONOMIC JOURNAL 56 (September
1946): 383-90.

This is primarily a study of aggregate productivity differences,
but factors contributing to industry differences are examined as
well.

541   Sahota, G.S. "The Sources of Measured Productivity Growth: United
States Fertilizer Mineral Industries, 1936-1960." REVIEW OF ECONOMICS
AND STATISTICS 48 (May 1966): 193-204.

In this study intrafirm technical progress in the state of the
arts is separated from scale economics and productivity changes

due to interfirm shifts of resources. The technique used was
to fit production functions and to apply covariance analysis.

542 Salter, W.E.G. PRODUCTIVITY AND TECHNICAL CHANGE. 2d ed.
Cambridge, Engl.: Cambridge University Press, 1966. 200 p.

This is an attempt to analyze productivity within a specific
model and to use empirical information to test the hypotheses
developed from this model. Interindustry analyses are also
undertaken, and technical appendixes provide information about
data and the techniques used in testing procedures.

543 Saul, S.B., ed. TECHNOLOGICAL CHANGE: THE UNITED STATES
AND BRITAIN IN THE NINETEENTH CENTURY. London: Methuen &
Co., 1970. 198 p.

This collection of essays brings together the various ideas of
authors in order that a more complete understanding may be
had of the technology leadership switch which took place in
the last half of the nineteenth century. There are six essays
dealing with particular aspects of this changing situation.

544 Schmookler, Jacob. "The Changing Efficiency of the American Economy:
1869-1938." REVIEW OF ECONOMICS AND STATISTICS 34 (August
1952): 214-31.

A classic work in this area, this report presents an index of
total inputs on a per unit basis, and produces an aggregate
efficiency index for analyzing the magnitude and pattern of
technical change. This index is compared with alternative indexes that have been developed.

545 _____. "Economic Sources of Inventive Activity." JOURNAL OF ECO-
NOMIC HISTORY 22 (March 1962): 1-20.

By examining the total research and development of all firms
producing products in a certain class, and comparing this against
the sales of products in this class, the author concludes that
inventive activities are a consequence of economic conditions.
They have not been the independent cause of socioeconomic
change over time.

546 Schultz, Theodore W. TRANSFORMING TRADITIONAL AGRICULTURE.
New Haven, Conn.: Yale University Press, 1964. 212 p.

Dealing primarily with the problems of developing countries,
Schultz discusses the benefits of technological change as well
as the inappropriateness of such advances for certain countries.
It is an excellent work that anyone wishing to consider agricultural development should read.

547 Shen, T.Y. "Innovation, Diffusion, and Productivity Changes." REVIEW OF ECONOMICS AND STATISTICS 42 (May 1961): 175-81.

Using cross-section plant data, the weaknesses of time series data are overcome and a set of initial conditions are now available from which innovations and the diffusion of change can be studied. Forecasts of productivity, inputs, and outputs are evaluated for New England manufacturing firms, according to their two digit codes (SIC).

548 Smith, Vernon L. "Engineering Data and Statistical Techniques in the Analysis of Production and Technological Change: Fuel Requirements in the Trucking Industry." ECONOMETRICA 25 (April 1957): 281-301.

Deriving the input requirements from the microeconomic foundations of a multidimensional firm, aggregation of the process functions for the industry was achieved through knowledge of the joint frequency distributions of the output dimensions of the processes. Certain relationships were found for the industry between average load, average length of haul, and number of hauls on the one hand, and aggregate ton-miles, vehicle-miles, and tons on the other hand.

549 Temin, Peter. "Labor Scarcity and the Problem of American Industrial Efficiency in the 1850's." JOURNAL OF ECONOMIC HISTORY 26 (September 1966): 277-98.

This is an attempt to reexamine the observed higher cost of labor in the United States, in comparison to Great Britain, as the rationale for supposed different technologies. Were the technologies different and if so was this because of relative labor scarcity in the United States? I. Drummond has a comment in JOURNAL OF ECONOMIC HISTORY 27 (September 1967): 383-90, and P. Temin has a reply in JOURNAL OF ECONOMIC HISTORY 28 (March 1968): 124-25.

550 Thompson, George V. "Intercompany Technical Standardization in the Early American Automobile Industry." JOURNAL OF ECONOMIC HISTORY 14 (March 1954): 1-20.

Using the automobile industry as an example, the author attempts to illustrate the influence of changing business conditions on standardizations and mechanical technology.

550a Uselding, Paul [J]. "Henry Burden and the Question of Anglo-American Technological Transfer in the Nineteenth Century." JOURNAL OF ECONOMIC HISTORY 30 (June 1970): 312-37.

This case study is used to illustrate the large impact of technological transfer in the form of immigrant skills. The study illustrates well the importance of human capital to a developing economy.

551 _____. "Technical Progress at the Springfield Armory, 1820-1850." EXPLORATIONS IN ECONOMIC HISTORY 9 (Spring 1972): 291-316.

By using conventional theoretical and empirical analysis, sources of technical changes are examined for a high-volume metalworking establishment. Estimates of factor-saving technical bias and values of elasticities of substitution are presented. The Ames-Rosenberg hypothesis regarding a "material" factor in the production function is also discussed.

552 Uselding, Paul [J.], and Juba, Bruce. "Biased Technical Progress in American Manufacturing." EXPLORATIONS IN ECONOMIC HISTORY 11 (Fall 1973): 55-72.

The authors give estimates of factor-saving bias in nineteenth-century manufacturing which provide a foundation for the labor scarcity hypothesis of Rothbarth (no. 540) and Habakkuk (no. 507). The article also reviews the cyclic nature of growth in the manufacturing sector.

553 Usher, A. A HISTORY OF MECHANICAL INVENTION. Cambridge, Mass.: Harvard University Press, 1954. 526 p.

Devoted primarily to the early history of the mechanical sciences, things such as the development of water wheels and windmills, water and mechanical clocks, printing, and precision clocks and watches are discussed. The production and application of power machine tools and the production and distribution of power since 1832 are explored.

554 You, Jong Kean. "Embodied and Disembodied Technical Progress in the United States, 1829-1968." REVIEW OF ECONOMICS AND STATISTICS 58 (February 1976): 123-27.

The author attempts to produce an estimate of the relative importance of embodied versus disembodied technical change over the period. His findings are that disembodied technical change was identifiable but that embodied technical change was insignificant.

4.2 GENERAL LISTINGS

554a Allen, Robert C. "The Peculiar Productivity History of American Blast Furnaces, 1840-1913." JOURNAL OF ECONOMIC HISTORY 37 (September 1977): 605-33.

555 Arrow, Kenneth J. "Classificatory Notes on the Production and Transmission of Technological Knowledge." AMERICAN ECONOMIC REVIEW 59 (May 1969): 29-35.

556 _____. "The Economic Implications of Learning by Doing." REVIEW OF ECONOMIC STUDIES 29 (June 1962): 155-73.

557 Atkinson, Anthony B., and Stiglitz, Joseph E. "A New View of Technological Change." ECONOMIC JOURNAL 79 (September 1969): 632-47.

558 Bruni, L. "Internal Economics of Scale with a Given Technique." JOURNAL OF INDUSTRIAL ECONOMICS 12 (July 1964): 175-90.

559 David, Paul A., and van de Klundert, Th. "Biased Efficiency Growth and Capital-Labor Substitution in the U.S., 1899-1960." AMERICAN ECONOMIC REVIEW 55 (June 1965): 357-94.

560 Fellner, William. "Does the Market Direct the Relative Factor-Saving Effects of Technological Progress?" In THE RATE AND DIRECTION OF INVENTIVE ACTIVITY, edited by Universities--National Bureau Committee for Economic Research, pp. 171-90. Princeton, N.J.: Princeton University Press, 1962.

561 _____. "Two Propositions in the Theory of Induced Innovations." ECONOMIC JOURNAL 71 (June 1961): 305-8.

562 Fisher, Franklin M. "Embodied Technical Change and the Existence of an Aggregate Capital Stock." REVIEW OF ECONOMIC STUDIES 32 (October 1965): 263-88.

563 Fishlow, Albert. "Productivity and Technological Change in the Railroad Sector, 1840-1910." In OUTPUT, EMPLOYMENT AND PRODUCTIVITY IN THE UNITED STATES AFTER 1800. Edited by National Bureau of Economic Research, pp. 584-645. Studies in Income and Wealth, no. 30. New York: Columbia University Press, 1966.

564 Hollander, Samuel. THE SOURCES OF INCREASED EFFICIENCY. Cambridge: MIT Press, 1965. 228 p.

565 Jerome, Harry. MECHANIZATION IN INDUSTRY. New York: National Bureau of Economic Research, 1934. 484 p.

566 Jorgenson, Dale W., and Griliches, Zvi. "The Explanation of Productivity Change." REVIEW OF ECONOMIC STUDIES 34 (July 1967): 249-83.

567 National Commission on Technology, Automation, and Economic Progress. TECHNOLOGY AND THE AMERICAN ECONOMY. 12 vols. Washington, D.C.: Government Printing Office, 1966.

568 Nelson, R.; Peck, M.; and Kalachek, E. TECHNOLOGY, ECONOMIC GROWTH, AND PUBLIC POLICY. Washington, D.C.: Brookings Institution, 1967. 238 p.

569 Rogin, Leo. THE INTRODUCTION OF FARM MACHINERY IN ITS RELATION TO THE PRODUCTIVITY OF LABOR IN THE AGRICULTURE OF THE UNITED STATES DURING THE NINETEENTH CENTURY. Berkley and Los Angeles: University of California Press, 1931. 260 p.

570 Rosenberg, Nathan, ed. THE AMERICAN SYSTEM OF MANUFACTURES. Edinburgh: Edinburgh University Press, 1969. 440 p.

571 Schmookler, Jacob. INVENTION AND ECONOMIC GROWTH. Cambridge, Mass.: Harvard University Press, 1966. 332 p.

572 Schumpeter, Joseph A. THE THEORY OF ECONOMIC DEVELOPMENT. Cambridge, Mass.: Harvard University Press, 1934. 255 p.

573 Solow, Robert M. "Investment and Technical Change." In MATHEMATICAL METHODS IN THE SOCIAL SCIENCES, edited by Kenneth J. Arrow, S. Karlin, and P. Suppes, pp. 84-104. Stanford, Calif.: Stanford University Press, 1960.

574 Stigler, George J. "Economic Problems in Measuring Changes in Productivity." In OUTPUT, INPUT, AND PRODUCTIVITY MEASUREMENT, pp. 47-63. Princeton, N.J.: Princeton University Press, 1961.

575 Strassman, W. Paul. "Interrelated Industries and the Rate of Technological Change." REVIEW OF ECONOMIC STUDIES 27 (October 1959): 16-22.

576 _____. RISK AND TECHNOLOGICAL INNOVATION. Ithaca, N.Y.: Cornell University Press, 1959. 249 p.

577 Universities--National Bureau Committee for Economic Research, ed. THE RATE AND DIRECTION OF INVENTIVE ACTIVITY. Princeton, N.J.: Princeton University Press, 1961. 635 p.

578 Williams, B.R., ed. SCIENCE AND TECHNOLOGY IN ECONOMIC GROWTH. New York: John Wiley & Sons, 1973. 446 p.

579 Young, Allyn. "Increasing Returns and Economic Progress." ECONOMIC JOURNAL 38 (December 1928): 527-42.

Chapter 5

INDUSTRIAL GROWTH AND STRUCTURE

This chapter contains citations for a subject that has been more widely covered by historians and historical novelists than any other in this grouping of chapters. It is an area about which an individual can write a great deal while possessing little technical expertise.

The works cited below are a collection of what I consider to be good historical studies of a particular industry or group of industries, and industrial growth in general. A wide variety of works are included, ranging from some very theoretical and rigorous studies to virtual narrative descriptions of some aspect(s) of the industrial growth process, during the period from colonial times to the 1960s.

Undoubtedly, many well-written business or industry histories have been omitted and we apologize for this. It was, however, not possible to include all such works, and many from both the historical and the more theoretical economics sides have been left out. Many of these may be found in the references of the included works and, in some instances, in other chapters of this book.

The main data source of research in this area is the various censuses of manufacturing that have been compiled by the U.S. government. Some businesses have excellent records which, under special conditions, they sometimes will allow researchers to study. Data, in general, are very difficult to obtain in this area, especially prior to 1929.

5.1 ANNOTATED LISTINGS

580   Adams, Walter. "The American Case: Legal Victory--Economic Defeat."
      AMERICAN ECONOMIC REVIEW 41 (December 1951): 915-22.

> Using the ALCOA case to illustrate his point, the author argues that the legal victories of the government have not been successful in bringing relief from monopoly power.

581   American Economic Association. READINGS IN INDUSTRIAL ORGANIZA-

TION AND PUBLIC POLICY. Homewood, Ill.: Richard D. Irwin, 1958. 426 p.

This is a collection of papers on industrial structure and market behavior, industrial organization and economic theory, and monopoly and competition and public policy. It was compiled with both the nonspecialist and the graduate student in mind.

582 Ames, Edward. "Trends, Cycles, and Stagnation in U.S. Manufacturing Since 1860." OXFORD ECONOMIC PAPERS 11 (October 1959): 270-81.

Developing a series for manufacturing production from 1860 to 1955, the author is able to examine the various rates of growth and changes in the rate of growth over time. Periods of relative retardation are of great interest during this period.

583 Ames, Edward, and Rosenburg, Nathan. "The Progressive Division and Specialization of Industries." JOURNAL OF DEVELOPMENT STUDIES 1 (July 1965): 363-83.

The authors argue that economic theory cannot cope with the capital goods industries because of special characteristics. A particular maximization and specialization theory is developed to handle these unique firms.

584 Arden, Robert S., and Shaw, Lawrence H. "Output Effects of a Changing Composition of Industry, 1947-1965." REVIEW OF ECONOMICS AND STATISTICS 50 (February 1968): 134-36.

Using the measure of output per man-hour an attempt is made to indicate changes both in individual sectors and in sectoral shifts in the composition of output. The causative factors affecting each are discussed.

585 Aubrey, Henry G. "Industrial Investment Decisions: A Comparative Analysis." JOURNAL OF ECONOMIC HISTORY 15 (December 1955): 335-59.

Although this article emphasizes the situation in Pakistan, the general discussion of industrial investment decisions in developing countries has a broad application. A comment by Benjamin Higgins and a rejoinder by Aubrey appear in JOURNAL OF ECONOMIC HISTORY 16 (September 1956): 350-55.

586 Bain, Joe S. "Changes in Concentration in Manufacturing Industries in the United States, 1954-1966: Trends and Relationships to the Levels of 1954 Concentration." REVIEW OF ECONOMIC AND STATISTICS 52 (November 1970): 411-16.

This article contains an analysis of changes in concentration ratios over the period as well as a comparison of these changes with the particular 1954 concentration ratios.

587 Barth, Harry A. "Co-operation in the Blue-Grass." JOURNAL OF PO-
LITICAL ECONOMY 33 (August 1925): 455-65.

> The essential factors of a successful tobacco cooperative are
> outlined and the conditions necessary to set price above cost
> are also given. The Burley Tobacco Growers Co-Operative
> Association is the one discussed.

588 Berle, A., and Means, G. THE MODERN CORPORATION AND PRIVATE
PROPERTY. New York: Macmillan Co., 1933. 396 p.

> This is a classic work which studies trends in corporate develop-
> ment by examining its effect on property, workers, and con-
> sumers. The general focus is on the effects of the separation
> of ownership and control and the effects of the corporate system
> on the fundamental economic concepts.

589 Bishop, J.L. HISTORY OF AMERICAN MANUFACTURES FROM 1608 TO
1860. 3 vols. Philadelphia: E. Young and Co., 1868. 584, 522, 465 p.

> The progressive steps as well as those which retarded growth
> are discussed both in general and for specific industries during
> this period.

590 Blyth, Conrad A. "The United States Cycle in Private Fixed Investment
1946-50." REVIEW OF ECONOMICS AND STATISTICS 38 (February 1956):
41-49.

> By breaking down the official investment statistics by sector
> and industry, it becomes possible to examine the turning points
> and the various cyclical patterns in private fixed investment.

591 Bolch, Ben; Fels, Rendig; and McMahon, Marshall. "Housing Surplus in
the 1920's?" EXPLORATIONS IN ECONOMIC HISTORY 8 (Spring 1971):
259-84.

> This is an extensive analysis of the housing market during the
> period between World War I and 1930. Various other arguments
> are considered and compared with the finding of these authors.

592 Brownlee, W. Elliot. "Income Taxation and Capital Formation in Wisconsin,
1911-1929." EXPLORATIONS IN ECONOMIC HISTORY 8 (Fall 1970):
77-102.

> This is an analysis of the effect of taxes on the rate of capi-
> tal accumulation and regional growth in general.

593 Buchanan, Norman S. "The Origins and Development of the Public Utility
Holding Company." JOURNAL OF POLITICAL ECONOMY 44 (February
1936): 31-53.

This is an examination of a particular corporate form which has been widely adopted by utilities as well as other industries.

594 Bunting, David. "The Truth about 'The Truth about the Trusts'." JOURNAL OF ECONOMIC HISTORY 31 (September 1971): 664-71.

This is a critical analysis of previous work with respect to the quality of the data and the contribution of the analyses.

595 Carter, Anne P. "Changes in the Structure of the American Economy, 1947 to 1958 and 1962." REVIEW OF ECONOMICS AND STATISTICS 49 (May 1967): 209-24.

Using an input-output approach, the author examines technical change in the aggregate as well as changes in the patterns of specialization. The tendency toward diversification of materials usage through the rise of such inputs as fuels and services is also discussed.

596 Chandler, Alfred D., Jr., and Galambos, Louis. "The Development of Large-Scale Economic Organizations in Modern America." JOURNAL OF ECONOMIC HISTORY 30 (March 1970): 201-17.

Focusing on the periods 1870-1930 and 1930-50 and four types of formal organizations--corporations, unions, trade associations, and governmental agencies--the authors present the process by which our large-scaled industrial complex evolved.

597 Cobb, Charles W. "Production in Massachusetts Manufacturing, 1890-1928." JOURNAL OF POLITICAL ECONOMY 38 (December 1930): 705-7.

These data are used to test the Cobb-Douglas production function. Trends and relations among production, labor, and capital are also produced.

598 Cochran, T.C.; Marburg, T.F.; Clark, T.D.; and Dennison, H.S. "Historical Aspects of Imperfect Competition: Theory and History." JOURNAL OF ECONOMIC HISTORY 3 (December 1943): 27-50.

Using brass manufacturing in the 1930s, the southern retail trade after 1865, and the Dennison Manufacturing Company as historical data, these authors have attempted to make the theory of imperfect competition explicit.

599 Collins, Norman R., and Preston, Lee G. "The Size Structure of The Largest Industrial Firms, 1909-1958." AMERICAN ECONOMIC REVIEW 51 (December 1961): 986-1011.

Using the one hundred largest firms, the authors analyze changes in the size and structure, the distribution of assets among them, movements in the distribution, and the sources of size changes.

They are attempting to determine whether business organizations are rigid or flexible.

600 Coman, Katharine. INDUSTRIAL HISTORY OF THE UNITED STATES. New York: Macmillan Co., 1910. 461 p.

The period covered spans from the colonial period until the first decade of the 1900s. Topics include the business aspects of colonization, industrial development under British control, industrial aspects of the Revolution and the War of 1812, territorial expansion and the revenue tariffs, economic aspects of the Civil War, government regulation, labor organizations, business monopolies, immigration, and conservation.

601 Daly, Patricia; Olson, Ernest; and Douglas, Paul H. "The Production Function for Manufacturing in the United States, 1904." JOURNAL OF POLITICAL ECONOMY 51 (February 1943): 61-65.

This is a study using cross-section and time series data to estimate production functions for Australia, the United States, and Canada.

602 Daniels, Bruce C. "Long Range Trends of Wealth Distribution in Eighteenth Century New England." EXPLORATIONS IN ECONOMIC HISTORY 11 (Winter 1973-74): 123-36.

Tracing various New England areas through the period 1700-1776, the author analyzes the changing trends in wealth distribution.

603 David, Paul A. "The Growth of Real Product in the United States before 1840: New Evidence, Controlled Conjectures." JOURNAL OF ECONOMIC HISTORY 27 (June 1967): 151-97.

Providing new estimates of real product, the author rejects the hypothesis that there was a significant acceleration of the secular trend in real GNP.

604 David, Paul A., and van De Klundert, Th. "Biased Efficiency Growth and Capital-Labor Substitution in the U.S. 1899-1960." AMERICAN ECONOMIC REVIEW 55 (June 1965): 357-94.

Exploring aggregate production function relationships, the author examines the form of factor efficiency growth in the United States, but the sources are not identified. The possibility that growth of efficiency of the individual inputs may not be neutral was allowed for in the analysis.

605 Davis, John P. CORPORATIONS--A STUDY OF THE ORIGIN OF GREAT COMBINATIONS. 2 vols. New York: G.P. Putnam's Sons, 1905. 295, 318 p.

Although it is not intended to be an exhaustive work, it is an interpretation of existing and accessible historical materials, which purports to provide a clear conception of the technical and legal nature of the corporation. A myriad of corporation types is considered.

606   Degler, Carl N. THE AGE OF THE ECONOMIC REVOLUTION, 1876-1900. Glenview, Ill.: Scott, Foresman and Co., 1976. 197 p.

Each chapter addresses the question: "How did the coming of the factory and the city alter the United States?" The analysis includes internal experiences as well as comparisons with the experience of other countries that had similar situations. The interaction of various noneconomic events with economic events is discussed at some length.

607   Dixson, Frank Haigh. "The Economic Significance of Interlocking Directorates in Railway Finance." JOURNAL OF POLITICAL ECONOMY 22 (December 1914): 937-54.

Interlocking directorates are examined for railroads where the purposes are (1) obtaining credit; (2) industrial and commercial purchases of supplies; (3) railway construction and operation; and (4) restraining competition.

608   Einhorn, Henry A. "Competition in American Industry, 1939-1958." JOURNAL OF POLITICAL ECONOMY 74 (October 1966): 506-11.

Like the work done for earlier periods, this study substantiates the argument that competition has not significantly changed. An appendix is included which explains the methodology.

609   Evans, G. Herberton, Jr. "Geographical Differences in the Use of the Corporation in American Manufacturing in 1899." JOURNAL OF ECONOMIC HISTORY 14 (June 1954): 113-25.

The data in the 1900 U.S. Census volumes revealed that the corporate form of business was widely used in Arizona, Nevada, Washington, and California, but to a much smaller degree in the East and Midwest. The reasons for this are analyzed along with the forces for change.

610   _____. "A Sketch of American Business Organization, 1832-1900." JOURNAL OF POLITICAL ECONOMY 60 (December 1952): 475-87.

Using state and city directories, the author attempts to estimate the importance of the corporate form of business with respect to size and number.

611   Fabricant, Solomon. "Is Monopoly Increasing?" JOURNAL OF ECONOMIC HISTORY 13 (Winter 1953): 89-93.

A preliminary investigation into the share of monopoly power over time, this is an attempt to measure the degree of monopolistic competition to each industry. Various suggestions for further research are given.

612 Fisher, Franklin M.; Griliches, Zvi; and Kaysen, Carl. "The Costs of Automobile Model Changes since 1949." AMERICAN ECONOMIC REVIEW 52 (May 1963): 259-62.

This is an examination of the cost of resources that would have been saved if the specifications of 1949 had been maintained into 1950. This accounts for technological change in the industry.

613 Fogel, Robert W., and Engerman, Stanley L. "A Model for the Explanation of Industrial Expansion during the Nineteenth Century: With an Application to the American Iron Industry." JOURNAL OF POLITICAL ECONOMY 77 (March-April 1969): 306-28.

This paper is useful as an example of how a model may be formulated to obtain the most from scarce data. Using this model the growth of the iron industry is examined in order to more fully understand the industrial revolution.

614 Frank, Lawrence K. "The Significance of Industrial Integration." JOURNAL OF POLITICAL ECONOMY 33 (April 1925): 179-95.

Vertical integration is the topic and the economic impact of industrial unification is discussed, especially the effects on competition, planning, raw materials, and so forth.

615 Frickey, Edwin. PRODUCTION IN THE U.S., 1860-1914. Cambridge, Mass.: Harvard University Press, 1947. 266 p.

The methods and processes of constructing the indexes of manufacturing are discussed in detail and then applied to the transportation and communication industry and to industrial and commercial production. Data tables and charts are included.

616 Friedland, Seymour. "Turnover and Growth of the Largest Industrial Firms, 1906-1950." REVIEW OF ECONOMICS AND STATISTICS 39 (February 1957): 79-83.

The relationship between the absolute rate of growth of the firms and the rate of growth of demand for their industries is examined, along with the relative degree of stability of the largest firms.

617 Fucho, Victor R. "The Determinants of the Redistribution of Manufacturing in the United States since 1929." REVIEW OF ECONOMICS AND STATISTICS 44 (May 1962): 167-77.

Rejecting the idea that regional shifts in demand or markets
were the major determinants of locational changes, an attempt
is made to explain these shifts and differential regional growth
rates.

618 Gilfillan, S.C. "Invention as a Factor in Economic History." JOURNAL
OF ECONOMIC HISTORY 5 (December 1945): 66-85.

Using the fall of Rome, discovery of the United States, and
World War II as examples, the author examines the contention
that inventions are the key to understanding these historical
events. The function and nature of inventions are defined.

619 Glover, John George, and Cornell, William Bouck, eds. THE DEVELOP-
MENT OF AMERICAN INDUSTRIES: THEIR ECONOMIC SIGNIFICANCE.
3d ed. New York: Prentice-Hall, 1951. 1,121 p.

This work contains a rather detailed description of approximately
thirty-six different industries from very early stages up to its
position in 1950. The many aspects covered included geographic
location, raw materials used, manufacturing methods, valuable
products and by-products, number and types of people employed,
and methods of financing and capital invested.

620 Goodrich, Carter. "American Development Policy: The Case of Internal
Improvements." JOURNAL OF ECONOMIC HISTORY 16 (December 1956):
449-60.

Analyzing the role of government in the internal development
of railroads and canals, weaknesses in the American policy are
discussed and international comparisons are made. A plan for
developing countries is recommended on the basis of this analysis.

621 _____. "Internal Improvements Reconsidered." JOURNAL OF ECONOMIC
HISTORY 30 (June 1970): 289-311.

This is a review of the literature on internal improvements in
order to identify the direction of current research, as well as
the existing accomplishments.

622 Gordon, Robert J. "A New View of Real Investment in Structures, 1919-
1966." REVIEW OF ECONOMICS AND STATISTICS 50 (November 1968):
417-28.

Deriving new and improved price indexes of contract construction, the finding was that since World War II, productivity increases have been rapid whereas in the prewar period, efficiency
was stagnated.

623 Gottlieb, Manuel. "New Measures of Value of Nonfarm Building for the United States Annually, 1850-1939." REVIEW OF ECONOMICS AND STATISTICS 47 (November 1965): 412-19.

> Using data from Ohio, the author attempts to produce a new measure of nonfarm building.

624 Gunn, Grace T., and Douglas, Paul H. "The Production Function for American Manufacturing for 1914." JOURNAL OF POLITICAL ECONOMY 50 (August 1942): 595-602.

> Using census data, the authors attempt to determine the effect of changes in the quantities of labor and capital on the quantity of product.

625 Hagen, Everett E. "The Internal Functioning of Capitalistic Organizations." JOURNAL OF ECONOMIC HISTORY 30 (March 1970): 222-36.

> The motives, functions, management organization, and the corporation men who dominate the large corporations are the subject of this study. The information is taken from interviews conducted by Hagen with senior business executives.

626 Handlin, Oscar, and Handlin, Mary F. "Origins of the American Business Corporation." JOURNAL OF ECONOMIC HISTORY 5 (May 1945): 1-23.

> The topic entails an analysis of the quick popularity of large business operations in the late 1700s and the rate at which charters of incorporation were granted.

627 Haney, Lewis H. BUSINESS ORGANIZATION AND COMBINATION. New York: Macmillan Co., 1913. 483 p.

> After considering the various types of business organization, the corporate form is studied in some detail. The negative aspects are enumerated and public policy is discussed.

628 Harberger, Arnold. "Monopoly and Resource Allocation." AMERICAN ECONOMIC REVIEW 44 (May 1954): 77-87.

> Arguing that the long-run allocation of resources in the United States should produce constant returns to scale, the author attempts to derive quantitative notions of the allocation and welfare effects of monopoly.

629 Harbeson, Robert W. "The Clayton Act: Sleeping Giant of Antitrust." AMERICAN ECONOMIC REVIEW 48 (March 1958): 92-104.

> A review of the economic significance of the court decisions against DuPont when it bought 23 percent of General Motors, the analysis also discusses the effects of this case on the later

cellophane case and how this expanded the seventh section of
the Clayton Act to include vertical and horizontal acquisitions
in stock. A new set of guidelines for determining monopolistic
characteristics is also discussed.

630 Henrich, F.K.; Handlin, O.; Hartz L.; and Heath, M.S. "The Develop-
     ment of American Laissez-Faire." JOURNAL OF ECONOMIC HISTORY
     3 (December 1943): 51-100.

     This is an account of the pervasive thought regarding laissez-
     faire as it appeared in pamphlets and public documents.

631 Hidy, Ralph. A HISTORY OF STANDARD OIL. New York: Harper and
     Brothers, 1955. 839 p.

     By focusing on one company, an attempt is made to analyze
     the role played by businesses, especially the multinational type,
     in the economy from 1927 to 1950. The specific changes in
     operations, organization, personnel, products, and obligations
     are reviewed.

632 _____. "The Standard Oil Company (New Jersey)." JOURNAL OF
     ECONOMIC HISTORY 12 (Fall 1952): 411-24.

     Studying the evolution of management concepts, organizational
     patterns, and policies before 1911, the author examines the
     development of this so-called monopoly firm. The creators
     of the company were largely the same men who administered
     it at this time.

633 Houghton, Harrison F. "The Growth of Big Business." AMERICAN ECO-
     NOMIC REVIEW 38 (May 1948): 72-94.

     A comparison of the existence of monopoly power in England
     and the United States, this study examines the post-World War
     II era, focusing on the degree of control in ownership and the
     organization of industry.

634 Hughes, Jonathan R.T. THE VITAL FEW. London: Oxford University
     Press, 1965. 504 p.

     This is an account of the role played by the great business
     organizers of the late nineteenth century in the development,
     growth and ultimate structure of the U.S. economy.

635 Jenks, J.W. THE TRUST PROBLEM. New York: McClure, Phillips and
     Co., 1903. 362 p.

     This is a brief compendium of industrial conditions and the
     manner in which they affect industrial combinations, the fac-

tors influencing them, and their future trends. It is not a
highly theoretical work.

636   Jones, Alice Hanson. "Wealth Estimates for the American Middle Colonies,
1774." ECONOMIC DEVELOPMENT AND CULTURAL CHANGE 18 (July
1970): 1-166.

What are the forces that induce technical change and how have
they affected industrializing countries over the past two centuries?
These questions are considered along with the existing technological level itself, discipline of the labor force, and effects of
war as a study of the industrialization process.

637   _____. "Wealth Estimates for the New England Colonies about 1770."
JOURNAL OF ECONOMIC HISTORY 32 (March 1972): 98-127.

Total and per capita wealth estimates for the thirteen colonies
in the early 1770s are presented and analyzed with respect to
composition, distribution. A comparison of these data with
those for 1966 was made, and growth rates were inferred. Size
and age distributions are investigated, as well as inequality
comparisons over time and regions.

638   Jorgenson, Dale W., and Stephenson, James A. "Investment Behavior in
U.S. Manufacturing, 1947-1960." ECONOMETRICA 35 (April 1967):
169-220.

Using neoclassical theory, the authors derive investment functions for fifteen subindustries of manufacturing, and group these
under three headings. The results point up the importance of
the cost of capital in investment decisions. A review of neoclassical theory is included.

639   _____. "The Time Structure of Investment Behavior in U.S. Manufacturing, 1947-1960." REVIEW OF ECONOMICS AND STATISTICS 49 (February 1967): 16-27.

This is an analysis of the underlying time structure of the underlying determinants or investment. Quarterly data are used to
test the model for the behavior of manufacturing firms.

640   Kendrick, John W. THE FORMATION AND STOCKS OF TOTAL CAPI-
TAL. New York: National Bureau of Economic Research, 1976. 265 p.

Although particular works have attempted to provide estimates
of the quantities of various types of capital, no one has previously compiled these estimates with newly derived ones to
form a series for total capital. This stock includes estimates
of both tangible and intangible capital. The period covered
is from 1929 to 1969 in general, with comparisons with previous
years of two particular subperiods--1966-69 and 1969-73.

641   Kessler, William C.   "Incorporation in New England: A Statistical Study,
      1800-1875."   JOURNAL OF ECONOMIC HISTORY   8 (May 1948):   43-
      62.

      This is a study of the path and the timing of the incorporation
      movement.   The legal procedures of the New England states
      are investigated and statistical data are compared with previous
      works.

642   Kirkland, Edward Chase.   INDUSTRY COMES OF AGE: BUSINESS,
      LABOR AND PUBLIC POLICY, 1860-1897.   New York: Holt, Rinehart
      and Winston, 1961.   445 p.

      This is an attempt to write a history of economic policy, both
      public and private, from the point of view of the contemporar-
      ies.   All of the various aspects of economic activity, both
      domestic and international, are covered in this work.

643   Laffer, Arthur B.   "Vertical Integration by Corporations, 1929-1965."
      REVIEW OF ECONOMICS AND STATISTICS   51 (February 1969):   91-93.

      Deriving a measure of vertical integration, the author analyzes
      the belief that it has increased over the postwar period.   The
      finding is that vertical integration in fact has decreased.

644   Larner, Robert J.   "Ownership and Control in the 200 Largest Nonfinan-
      cial Corporation, 1929 and 1963."   AMERICAN ECONOMIC REVIEW   56
      (September 1966):   777-87.

      This is an attempt to measure the extent to which management
      control actually existed in 1963.   The results are compared
      with those from the Berle-Means study (see no. 588) conducted
      for 1929.

645   Leontief, Wassily W.   THE STRUCTURE OF AMERICAN ECONOMY, 1919-
      1939:   AN EMPIRICAL APPLICATION OF EQUILIBRIUM ANALYSIS.   2d
      ed.   New York: Oxford University Press, 1951.   264 p.

      This is a very detailed theoretical and empirical analysis of
      the American economy, in which the author sets out his input-
      output approach to the analysis of economic performance.   The
      first half of the book is a detailed discussion of the structure
      and relevant condition of the various industries, and the second
      half is devoted to the theoretical and empirical work.

646   Lewis, Cleona.   "The Trend of Savings, 1900-1929."   JOURNAL OF
      POLITICAL ECONOMY   43 (August 1935):   530-47.

      This is a reanalysis of Warburton's data (see no. 689) and
      methodology, which argues that both are suspect.

647 Lippincott, I. "Pioneer Industry in the West." JOURNAL OF POLITICAL ECONOMY 18 (April 1910): 269-93.

The author examines the West's isolation and the development of its pioneer industry and investigates the effects of settlement and transportation improvements.

648 McGee, J. "Predatory Price Cutting: The Standard Oil (N.J.) Case." JOURNAL OF LAW AND ECONOMICS 1 (October 1958): 137-69.

This is a reexamination of the Standard Oil Company's pre-dissolution price behavior in an attempt at determining whether it did actually use such practices to maintain its monopoly power.

649 Main, Jackson Turner. "Trends in Wealth Concentration before 1860." JOURNAL OF ECONOMIC HISTORY 31 (June 1971): 445-47.

This is one explanation for the rapid accumulation of wealth by 10 per cent of the population during the sixty years following the Revolution.

650 Maisel, Sherman J. "A Theory of Fluctuations in Residential Construction Starts." AMERICAN ECONOMIC REVIEW 53 (June 1963): 359-83.

Offering a model of the housing market, the authors analyze the results of movements of final demand, net removals from available housing, movements of housing inventory, and changes in inventories under construction.

651 Martin, David Dale. "The Brown Shoe Case and the New Antimerger Policy." AMERICAN ECONOMIC REVIEW 53 (June 1963): 340-58.

By examining the court's treatment of the issues along with the criteria used for defining "relevant lines of commerce" and sections of the country, the author analyzes the verticle and horizontal effects of mergers and the significance of the new antimerger law with respect to the development of antimerger policy and future corporate concentration.

652 Mason, Edward S. ECONOMIC CONCENTRATION AND THE MONOPOLY PROBLEM. Cambridge, Mass.: Harvard University Press, 1957. 411 p.

This analysis of what turns out to be primarily twentieth-century industrial development attempts to explain the performance of firms and groups of firms in a broader sense than just price-quantity relationships, for example, cost-price relations, capacity-output relations, role of product variation and selling outlays, and profit rates.

653 Mayor, Thomas H. "The Decline in the United States Capital: Output Ratio." ECONOMIC DEVELOPMENT AND CULTURAL CHANGE 16 (July 1968): 495-516.

It is argued in this piece that the decline in the capital-output ratio was not due to biased technological change or inadequate savings. It was due to such factors as the relative price of capital goods, depreciation rates, and tax rates.

654 Melman, Seymour. "The Rise of Administrative Overhead in the Manufacturing Industries of the U.S., 1899-1947." OXFORD ECONOMIC PAPERS 3 (February 1951): 62-112.

This is an attempt to explain the rising fixed costs of administrative overhead and the rigidity of costs and prices along with the disproportionate growth of administrative personnel as opposed to production personnel.

655 Mercer, Lloyd J., and Morgan, W. Douglas. "Housing Surplus in the 1920's? Another Evaluation." EXPLORATIONS IN ECONOMIC HISTORY 10 (Spring 1973): 295-304.

Reformulating the Bolch-Fels-McMahon model (no. 591), the authors present an alternative measure of overbuilding in the housing market, from both a static and a dynamic view.

656 Mitchell, Broadus. THE RISE OF COTTON MILLS IN THE SOUTH. Baltimore: John Hopkins Press, 1921. 281 p.

A brief survey of the industrial and economic background from which the industry was born is provided along with the effect on southern labor and capital formation. It is solely a history of the birth of the industry.

657 Moore, John Hebron. "The Textile Industry of the Old South." JOURNAL OF ECONOMIC HISTORY 16 (June 1956): 200-205.

This is a reprint of a letter by the president of the Mississippi Manufacturing Company (1858) which describes the organization, management, and methods of production and distribution in the antebellum southern textile industry.

658 National Bureau of Economic Research, ed. OUTPUT, EMPLOYMENT AND PRODUCTIVITY IN THE U.S. AFTER 1800. Studies in Income and Wealth, no. 30. New York: Columbia University Press, 1966. 660 p.

This is a collection of papers dealing with various aspects of production for particular industries such as manufacturing, cereal grains, machine tools, and cotton textiles. A price series is also the topic of one study.

659 Nelson, Ralph. MERGER MOVEMENTS IN AMERICAN INDUSTRY, 1895-1965. Princeton, N.J.: Princeton University Press, 1959. 177 p.

In addition to providing a complete record for the entire period, this work considers three specific questions dealing with the period 1898 to 1920: (1) did mergers retard industrial growth during this period; (2) was competition sharpened due to the development of a national transportation system; and (3) how did the merger movement affect the growth of the securities market?

660 Nicholls, William H. "Price Flexibility and Concentration in the Agricultural Processing Industries." JOURNAL OF POLITICAL ECONOMY 48 (December 1940): 883-88.

This is an analysis of price flexibility and concentration of control in agricultural industries, and a comparison with manufacturing industries.

661 Nixon, H.C. "The Rise of the American Cottonseed Oil Industry." JOURNAL OF POLITICAL ECONOMY 38 (February 1930): 73-85.

This is an examination of both the antebellum and postbellum development of the industry, including discussion of the innovations.

662 North, Douglas C. THE ECONOMIC GROWTH OF THE U.S., 1790-1860. Englewood Cliffs, N.J.: Prentice-Hall, 1961. 304 p.

The author provides a model to explain the growth of the economy which is based upon the export-led type of growth analysis and the accompanying institutional changes. He offers conjectures regarding the development of particular sectors of the economy.

663 North, Douglas C., and Thomas, Robert Paul. "An Economic Theory of the Growth of the Western World." ECONOMIC HISTORY REVIEW 23 (April 1970): 1-17.

This is a presentation of a rather new explanation of the way in which the world developed. It is an argument that stresses the effects of changes in relative prices in producing incentives that lead toward productivity-increasing activity.

664 Oakland, William H. "Corporate Earnings and Tax Shifting in U.S. Manufacturing, 1930-1968." REVIEW OF ECONOMICS AND STATISTICS 54 (August 1972): 436-43.

Using a model based on standard competitive behavior, an attempt has been made to explain corporate earnings over time. The model attempts to isolate contributions to profits by technological change, capital intensity, and aggregate demand. The effect of the corporate income tax is also examined.

665 Oshima, Harry. "The Price System and National Income and Product." REVIEW OF ECONOMICS AND STATISTICS 23 (August 1951): 248-54.

Problems associated with the use of compositional national income data are discussed with respect to use in analyzing the national price system, commodity movements and prices, labor mobility, and specialization for backward countries.

666 Passer, Harold C. "Electrical Manufacturing around 1900." JOURNAL OF ECONOMIC HISTORY 12 (Fall 1952): 378-95.

Using internal operations information from General Electric and Westinghouse, the author studies and compares the innovations in management which accompanied the drastic changes in scale.

667 Perloff, Harvey S. "Interrelations of State Income and Industrial Structure." REVIEW OF ECONOMICS AND STATISTICS 39 (May 1957): 162-71.

Investigating the reasons for differences by state in per capita income, the author examines the relation of industrial employment patterns and shifts in the labor force to the level of income.

668 Poulson, Barry W. "Estimates of the Value of Manufacturing Output in the Early Nineteenth Century." JOURNAL OF ECONOMIC HISTORY 29 (September 1969): 521-25.

Two values of manufacturing output are computed for the years 1809-39, each using a different basis for estimating. A detailed explanation of the estimation process is included, along with a summary of relative changes in such industries as textiles, transportation equipment, metals, and foods and spirits.

669 Refsell, Oscar N. "The Farmers' Elevator Movement, Parts 1 & 2." JOURNAL OF POLITICAL ECONOMY 22 (November 1914): 872-95; (December 1914): 969-91.

After a discussion of the importance of elevators to grain shippers, the main events in the rise of the farmers' elevator movement against the large line elevator companies are discussed.

670 Ripley, William Z. TRUSTS, POOLS, AND CORPORATIONS. New York: Ginn and Co., 1916. 872 p.

Tracing the development of the trust problem in the United States, the author reviews specific cases to illustrate trends and legislative advancements. The effects on certain industries and a survey of the literature on trusts are also provided.

671   Sands, Saul S.   "Changes in Scale of Production in U.S. Manufacturing Industry, 1904-1947."   REVIEW OF ECONOMICS AND STATISTICS   43 (November 1961):   365-68.

Measuring the scale of a plant by the output per establishment, the author examines the long-term movements in scale with respect to changes in optimal plant size and optimal ranges of output.   The effects of technical change and changes in demand are discussed.

672   Scoville, Warren C.   "Growth of the American Glass Industry to 1880, Parts I & II."   JOURNAL OF POLITICAL ECONOMY   52 (September 1944):   193-216; (December 1944):   340-55.

The study focuses on the effect of fuel and material sources on industry location, the demand for and price of glassware, government policy, wars and depressions.   The industry's organization and the extent of competition are also examined.

673   Sharp, Paul F.   "The War of the Substitutes: The Reaction of the Forest Industries to the Competition of Wood Substitutes."   AGRICULTURAL HISTORY   23 (October 1949):   274-78.

Presenting a brief historical survey of the forest products industry, the twentieth-century market for wood and wood substitutes is analyzed.

674   Shepherd, William G.   "Trends of Concentration in American Manufacturing Industries, 1947-1958."   REVIEW OF ECONOMICS AND STATISTICS   46 (May 1964):   200-212.

Using data points for comparison, an attempt is made to investigate changes in concentration over time, and the relationships of these changes to factors such as growth and oligopoly.   An attempt is also made to test Bain's and Stigler's theories concerning oligopolistic behavior.

675   Simonson, G.R.   "The Demand for Aircraft and the Aircraft Industry 1907-1958."   JOURNAL OF ECONOMIC HISTORY   20 (September 1960):   361-82.

This study of the growth of demand for aircraft examines the effects of wars and legislations on the growth of the industry.

676   Soltow, Lee C.   "Evidence on Income Inequality in the United States, 1866-1965."   JOURNAL OF ECONOMIC HISTORY   29 (June 1969):   279-86.

A comparison of income distributions after the Civil War until 1912 and from 1912 to 1965, this study concludes that inequality among upper income groups did not increase during the postbellum period.

677   Stigler, George J. "The Division of Labor is Limited by the Extent of the Market." JOURNAL OF POLITICAL ECONOMY 59 (June 1951): 185-93.

This Smithian dictum is applied to the analysis of vertical integration. Wider implications regarding size, location, geographical structure, and competition are derived.

678   Stocking, George W., and Mueller, William F. "The Cellophane Case and the New Competition." AMERICAN ECONOMIC REVIEW 45 (May 1955): 29-63.

The authors attempt to establish criteria for measuring degrees of monopolization. They use the duPont case as an example.

679   Stopler, Wolfgang F. "The Schumpeterian System." JOURNAL OF ECONOMIC HISTORY 11 (Summer 1951): 272-76.

This work deals with important and unique aspects of Schumpeter's stationary model.

680   Strassmann, W. Paul. "Creative Destruction and Partial Obsolescence in American Economic Development." JOURNAL OF ECONOMIC HISTORY 19 (September 1959): 335-49.

This is an examination of the evolution of production process in the United States between 1850 and 1914. The persistence of obsolete methods is explained and the "creative destruction" hypothesis is shown not to be an adequate explanation for the evolution of production.

681   Suits, Daniel B. "The Demand for New Automobiles in The United States, 1929-1956." REVIEW OF ECONOMICS AND STATISTICS 40 (August 1958): 273-80.

Examining the effects of credit conditions and the accumulation of a stock of cars on the demand for new cars, Suits formulates a demand function which he estimates and compares with earlier works.

682   Swanson, Joseph A., and Williamson, Samuel H. "Estimates of National Product and Income for the United States Economy, 1919-1941." EXPLORATIONS IN ECONOMIC HISTORY 10 (Fall 1972): 53-74.

This study contains the new series of U.S. national income which is totally compatible with the Department of Commerce series which begins in 1941. This extends the data base for more than twenty extra years. A note by Robert R. Keller, commenting on this study, appears in EXPLORATIONS IN ECONOMIC HISTORY 11 (Fall 1973): 87-88.

683   Tarbell, Ida M.   HISTORY OF THE STANDARD OIL COMPANY.   New York: McClure, Phillips, and Co., 1904. 406 p.

This is a history of the birth and early growth of Standard Oil Company up through and including the destruction of the trust. The various aspects of the rise to power of Standard Oil Company are also discussed, for example, the oil war of 1872, the beginning of the secret combination, and the fight for the seaboard pipeline.

684   Temin, Peter.   "Composition of Iron and Steel Products, 1869-1909." JOURNAL OF ECONOMIC HISTORY 23 (December 1963): 447-76.

The composition of the output is used to reveal the demand curve through an estimation of what the products were used for during the period. The second revolution in the production of iron and steel, which occurred after 1870, is discussed on the supply side examination.

685   _____.   IRON AND STEEL IN NINETEENTH-CENTURY AMERICA.   Cambridge: MIT Press, 1964. 304 p.

An account of the progress of iron and steel manufacture which discusses the economic forces that produced change.

686   _____.   "A New Look at Hunter's Hypotheses about the Antebellum Iron Industry."   AMERICAN ECONOMIC REVIEW 54 (May 1964): 344-51.

Hunter's thesis is countered by the argument that the slow adaptation of the U.S. iron industry to the use of coke was a supply problem.

687   Valter, Harold G.   THE DRIVE TO INDUSTRIAL MATURITY: THE U.S. ECONOMY 1860-1914.   Westport, Conn.: Greenwood Press, 1976. 368 p.

This is a general survey of the events and developments of the period which attempts "to integrate the best in the heritage of the old narrative history with the more analytical and quantitative approach of the new. . . . " Supply factors are more heavily emphasized than demand factors, except when explaining the causes of industrialization.

688   Veblen, Thorstein.   ABSENTEE OWNERSHIP AND BUSINESS ENTERPRISE IN RECENT TIMES.   New York: B.W. Huebsch, 1923. 445 p.

Veblen assails the industrial system of the twentieth century, specifically the industrial arts, the institution of absentee ownership, and the use of credit. A brief discussion of the nineteenth-century situation in both the United States and England is provided as background.

689 Warburton, Clark. "The Trend of Savings, 1900-1929." JOURNAL OF POLITICAL ECONOMY 43 (February 1935): 84-101.

This study contains the evidence for an opposing view to the one proffered by the Brookings Institution, regarding the saving behavior of the upper classes vis-a-vis the lower income levels as an explanation of higher aggregate saving.

690 Williamson, Harold F., et al. THE AMERICAN PETROLEUM INDUSTRY. 2 vols. Evanston, Ill.: Northwestern University Press, 1959. 864, 928 p.

This is an account of the growth of the industry from the early medicinal uses of petroleum to the birth of the modern industry and the reaction to foreign competition. It is an excellent work for anyone interested in industrial growth and development in general, as well as the petroleum industry in particular.

691 Williamson, Jeffrey G. "Optimal Replacement of Capital Goods: The Early New England and British Textile Firm." JOURNAL OF POLITICAL ECONOMY 79 (November-December 1971): 1320-34.

Two models of replacement behavior are developed: one with neutral and one with labor-saving technical change. They are used to examine the effects of technological parameters, wages, interest rates, capital goods prices, and output prices on replacement decisions. Tariffs were said to have significantly affected replacement behavior, and helped explain the different experiences of these two economics.

692 Wooster, Harvey A. "Manufacturer and Artisan, 1790-1840." JOURNAL OF POLITICAL ECONOMY 34 (February 1926): 61-77.

This is an investigation of merchant manufacture in southern New England to determine whether manufacturers were primarily craftsmen or opportunists. A brief historical survey of the beginning of the factory system is also included.

693 Yoodon, Wesley J., Jr. "Industrial Concentration and Price Flexibility in Inflation: Price Response Rates in Fourteen Industries, 1947-1958." REVIEW OF ECONOMICS AND STATISTICS 43 (August 1961): 287-94.

Using fourteen industries, the author attempts to measure the different rates at which inflation is transmitted through indus-

tries of varying degrees of concentration. The relative responses of prices to demand and cost changes are also considered.

694 Young, James Harvey. "Patent Medicines: An Early Example of Competitive Marketing." JOURNAL OF ECONOMIC HISTORY 20 (December
1960): 648-56.

This is an analysis of the ingenuity and nature of the marketing techniques employed by the patent medicine peddlers.

695 Zevin, Robert Brooke. THE GROWTH OF MANUFACTURING IN EARLY
NINETEENTH CENTURY NEW ENGLAND. New York: Arno Press, 1975.
120 p.

This book contains three essays on manufacturing: one on
general manufacturing; one on cotton textiles; and one on
long-run learning in the Massachusetts cotton textile industry.

5.2 GENERAL LISTINGS

696 Alexandersson, Gunnar. INDUSTRIAL STRUCTURE OF AMERICAN CITIES.
London: University of Nebraska Press, 1956. 133 p.

697 Burns, Arthur. PRODUCTION TRENDS IN THE U.S. SINCE 1870. New
York: National Bureau of Economic Research, 1934. 363 p.

698 Clark, Victor. HISTORY OF MANUFACTURING IN THE UNITED STATES.
3 vols. New York: McGraw-Hill, 1929. 607, 566, 466 p.

699 Clemen, Rudolf. THE AMERICAN LIVESTOCK AND MEAT INDUSTRY.
New York: Ronald P. Co., 1923. 872 p.

700 Cole, Arthur. THE AMERICAN WOOL MANUFACTURE. Cambridge,
Mass.: Harvard University Press, 1926. 314 p.

701 Coons, Arthur G. "Investment Activity in the Period 1910-25." JOUR-
NAL OF POLITICAL ECONOMY 35 (August 1927): 480-500.

702 Copeland, Melvin T. THE COTTON MANUFACTURING INDUSTRY OF
THE UNITED STATES. Cambridge, Mass.: Harvard University Press, 1912.
415 p.

703 Ely, Richard T. MONOPOLIES AND TRUSTS. New York: Macmillan
Co., 1900. 278 p.

704 Gallman, Robert E. "Estimates of American National Produce Made before the Civil War." ECONOMIC DEVELOPMENT AND CULTURAL CHANGE 8 (April 1961): 397-412.

705 Hughes, J.R.T. INDUSTRIALIZATION AND ECONOMIC HISTORY: THESES AND CONJECTURES. New York: McGraw-Hill, 1970. 336 p.

706 Kuznets, Simon. "Quantitative Aspects of the Economic Growth of Nations, Industrial Distribution of National Product and Labor Force." ECONOMIC DEVELOPMENT AND CULTURAL CHANGE 5 (July 1957): 3-111.

707 _____. "Quantitative Aspects of the Economic Growth of Nations: Long-Term Trends in Capital Formation Proportions." ECONOMIC DEVELOPMENT AND CULTURAL CHANGE 8 (July 1961): 3-124.

708 Laughlin, J.L. INDUSTRIAL AMERICA. New York: C. Scribner's Sons, 1906. 261 p.

709 Moore, J.R.H. AN INDUSTRIAL HISTORY OF THE AMERICAN PEOPLE. New York: Macmillan Co., 1913. 496 p.

710 Myrdal, Gunnar. RICH LANDS AND POOR LANDS. New York: Harper, 1958. 168 p.

711 North, Douglas C. "Early National Income Estimates of the U.S." ECONOMIC DEVELOPMENT AND CULTURAL CHANGE 8 (April 1961): 387-96.

712 Notz, William. "International Private Agreements in the Form of Cartels, Syndicates, and Other Combinations." JOURNAL OF POLITICAL ECONOMY 28 (October 1920): 658-79.

713 Nutter, G. Warren. THE EXTENT OF ENTERPRISE MONOPOLY IN THE U.S. Chicago: University of Chicago Press, 1951. 169 p.

714 Putnam, George E. "Joint Cost in the Packing Industry." JOURNAL OF POLITICAL ECONOMY 29 (April 1921): 293-303.

715 U.S. Senate. Temporary National Economic Committee. THE DISTRIBUTION OF OWNERSHIP IN THE 200 LARGEST NONFINANCIAL CORPORATIONS. Monograph 29 of Investigation of Concentration of Economic Power. Washington, D.C.: Government Printing Office, 1940. 183 p.

716 Waltersdorf, M.C. "The Holding Company in American Public Utility Development." ECONOMIC JOURNAL 36 (December 1926): 586-97.

717 Ware, Caroline. THE EARLY NEW ENGLAND COTTON MANUFACTURE. New York: Houghton Mifflin Co., 1931. 349 p.

718 Weseen, Maurice H. "The Co-operation Movement in Nebraska." JOURNAL OF POLITICAL ECONOMY 28 (June 1920): 477-98.

719 Zon, Raphael. "Reconstruction and Natural Resources." JOURNAL OF POLITICAL ECONOMY 27 (April 1919): 280-99.

Chapter 6

TRANSPORTATION AND SPATIAL LOCATION

The works cited below relate to the problems and difficulties which developed while the U.S. economy was growing and maturing during the nineteenth and early twentieth centuries. Many aspects of transportation, such as the financing, regulation, and construction of various types of transportation facilities, are covered. Many of the works assess the relationship transport growth had with economic growth, as well as the relative contributions of the types of transportation.

The works concerned with spatial location examine the general historical trends and the economic rationales for why people choose particular areas or cities for settlement. Some of the works which appear in chapter 8 on interregional growth are also related to the problems of spatial location. Both transportation and regional growth are concerned with some of the same basic issues, for example, least-cost location for the maximum benefit to the producer and consequently to the consumer.

A further aspect of the transport literature which tends to affect location decisions is the role played by government in the development of a transport system. Sometimes outright grants of land were given to railroads and canals for construction or to offset the cost of construction. This role of government is examined for nearly every possible period of time, beginning with the colonial period.

6.1 ANNOTATED LISTINGS

720 Allen, W.H. "The Charter Tax of the Illinois Central Railway." JOURNAL OF POLITICAL ECONOMY 6 (June 1898): 353-67.

>   The article discusses the question, what was the direct financial return to the state of Illinois as donor of 2,595,000 acres of land, vis-a-vis the gains from the work of railroad construction on this land?

721 Allport, W.H. "American Railway Relief Funds, I and II." JOURNAL OF POLITICAL ECONOMY 20 (January 1912): 49-78; (February 1912): 191-34.

This is an analysis of the social and economic aspects of hospital and relief departments organized by the railroads for sick and/or injured employees. Coverage includes the nature of the programs, offerings, funds available and their sources, and identification of gainers and losers.

722 Arrington, Leonard J. "The Desert Telegraph--A Church-owned Public Utility." JOURNAL OF ECONOMIC HISTORY 11 (Spring 1951): 117-39.

This is an account of development, organization, and financing of the line and its eventual confiscation by the U.S. government and its sale to Western Union.

723 Benton, E.J. THE WABASH TRADE ROUTE. Baltimore: Johns Hopkins Press, 1903. 112 p.

This is an attempt to analyze the influence of the Wabash route on resource development, western expansion, settlement creation, and commerce. A history of the organization, administration, and improvements of the Wabash and Erie Canal is included.

724 Bogart, Ernest L. "Economic and Social Effects of the Interurban Electric Railway in Ohio." JOURNAL OF POLITICAL ECONOMY 14 (December 1906): 585-601.

Examining the social and economic effects of the developmental interurban electric railways in Ohio, the author compares them with steam roads.

725 Borts, George H. "Increasing Returns in the Railway Industry." JOURNAL OF POLITICAL ECONOMY 62 (August 1954): 316-33.

A review of the literature is conducted to check the internal consistency and the empirical consistency of the theory. The assumptions regarding railway cost behavior made by regulatory agencies is also examined and compared with the behavior of railway costs.

726 _____. "Production Relations in the Railway Industry." ECONOMETRICA 20 (January 1952): 71-79.

Given that one should know whether increasing or decreasing costs prevail in order to evaluate questions concerning freight-rate discrimination, nonrail competition, and regulation of transportation, the author estimates production functions from cross-sectional data for two processes in railway technology.

727 Carman, Ernest C. "How to Avoid Government Ownership of the Railroads." JOURNAL OF POLITICAL ECONOMY 25 (April 1917): 374-84.

This is a discussion of various suggestions of how the railroad could provide adequate rail transport facilities and avoid government ownership.

728 Cavanagh, J.R. "The Pooling of Railway Freight Cars." JOURNAL OF POLITICAL ECONOMY 8 (June 1900): 347-53.

This cost study examines the costs of moving traffic and maintenance of the railways as well as attempts to reduce costs, such as pooling of freight cars.

729 Clark, Andrew H. "Geographical Change: A Theme for Economic History." JOURNAL OF ECONOMIC HISTORY 20 (December 1960): 607-16.

This is an attempt by a geographer to illustrate how historical geography is related to economic history.

730 Cootner, Paul H. "The Role of the Railroads in United States Economic Growth." JOURNAL OF ECONOMIC HISTORY 23 (December 1963): 477-528.

The argument here is that railroads were the result and not the cause of economic growth. The innovational and social overhead capital theories of economic growth were investigated, as well as the secondary impact of the railroad on other industries.

731 Daggett, Stuart. "The Panama Canal and Transcontinental Railroad Rates." JOURNAL OF POLITICAL ECONOMY 23 (December 1915): 953-60.

This is a relative impact study of what happened to the transcontinental railways when the Panama Canal opened. A survey of the determination of rail rates is also included.

732 David, Paul A. "Transport Innovation and Economic Growth: Professor Fogel on and off the Rails." ECONOMIC HISTORY REVIEW 22 (December 1969): 505-25.

This is a review of Fogel's book (see no. 750) in which the methodology used to examine the "axiom of indispensability" is discussed. The justification for some of the statistical methods used by Fogel is questioned.

733 Day, Clive. HISTORY OF COMMERCE. New York: Longman, Green, and Co., 1923. 676 p.

This is a history of commerce, not only for the United States but from ancient times to the early twentieth century. A recommended bibliography of the history of commerce is included.

734 Deimel, Henry L., Jr. "U.S. Shipping Policy and International Economic Relations." AMERICAN ECONOMIC REVIEW 36 (May 1946): 547-60.

This is an examination of the extension of the merchant marine beyond the level yielded by competition. The position upon emerging from World War II is examined along with the effects of additional wartime international shipping regulations and national shipping policies.

735 Dewey, Ralph L. "Transportation Act of 1940." AMERICAN ECONOMIC REVIEW 31 (March 1941): 15-26.

This is an examination of the technical aspects of the act, which explains the underlying policy motives as well as some of the effects on the transportation industry.

736 Dick, Trevor T.O. "United States Railroad Inventions' Investment since 1870." EXPLORATIONS IN ECONOMIC HISTORY 11 (Spring 1974): 249-70.

The author attributes the lack of research on the technological change which accompanied railroad investment to measurement problems and the belief that such changes were exogenous. He analyzes patents with respect to the inventions' investment behavior for different groups of patents and various subperiods.

737 Dunn, Samuel O. "Railway Discrimination." JOURNAL OF POLITICAL ECONOMY 20 (May 1912): 437-61.

An examination of cases heard by the Interstate Commerce Commission, this is an investigation of rate discrimination by large corporations who own their own switching or industrial lines.

738 _____. "Railway Efficiency in Its Relation to an Advance in Freight Rates." JOURNAL OF POLITICAL ECONOMY 23 (February 1915): 128-43.

Analyzing the efficiency of the railways, the author also compares them to railways in other countries. The analysis entails wages, rates, costs, and management.

739 _____. "Shall Railway Profits Be Limited?" JOURNAL OF POLITICAL ECONOMY 18 (October 1910): 593-609.

This is an examination of how finance and transportation would be affected if railway rates were limited. The extent of regulation necessary to impose profit limitations is also considered.

740 _____. "Valuation of Railways, with Especial Reference to the Physical Valuation in Minnesota." JOURNAL OF POLITICAL ECONOMY 17 (April 1909): 189-205.

> Rate-setting regulation requires that the regulating board know the value of the enterprise, and this study examines valuation methods and results used in Minnesota.

741 Ekelund, Robert B., Jr. "Economic Empiricism in the Writing of Early Railway Engineers." EXPLORATIONS IN ECONOMIC HISTORY 9 (Winter 1971-72): 179-96.

> Through a comparative study of the writings of English, French, and U.S. engineers, the author attempts to illustrate how these writers approached problems dealing with railway pricing. The development of economic theory, as well as the pricing problems that prevailed are examined.

742 Engerman, Stanley L. "Some Economic Issues Relating to Railroad Subsidies and the Evaluation of Land Grants." JOURNAL OF ECONOMIC HISTORY 32 (June 1972): 443-63.

> The reasons for and the appropriate form of land grant subsidies, the size of the optimum subsidy to encourage private investment, and the social desirability of land grant policy are considered in this article.

743 Esterbrook, W.T. "Problems in the Relationship of Communication and Economic History." JOURNAL OF ECONOMIC HISTORY 20 (December 1960): 559-65.

> Using both the "media approach" and the "information approach," the author attempts to link media research to periods of economic history.

744 Evans, Robert, Jr. "'Without Regard for Cost': The Returns on Clipper Ships." JOURNAL OF POLITICAL ECONOMY 72 (February 1964): 32-43.

> Outlining the use of clipper ships and reestimating the profitability of these vessels, the author is able to demonstrate that investment in these vessels was not for nonpecuniary benefit.

745 Feller, Irwin. "The Urban Location of United States Invention, 1860-1910." EXPLORATIONS IN ECONOMIC HISTORY 8 (Spring 1971): 285-304.

> As part of an attempt to determine the role which cities play in economic development, the major factors which account for the urban concentration of inventive activity are examined, for example, population and employment differences.

746　Fisher, Walter L.　"Waterways: Their Place in Our Transportation System."
JOURNAL OF POLITICAL ECONOMY 23 (July 1915): 641-62.

This analysis of the failure of waterways in America casts
doubt on their feasibility in competition with railroads.

747　Fishlow, Albert.　AMERICAN RAILROADS AND THE TRANSFORMATION
OF THE ANTE-BELLUM ECONOMY.　Cambridge, Mass.:　Harvard University Press, 1965.　452 p.

A quantitative study of the contribution of railroads, this work
is also an economic history of the period 1830 to 1860.　It is
an excellent analysis of the contribution of an industry to overall growth.　A selected bibliography is included.

748　Fleisig, Heywood.　"The Union Pacific Railroad and the Railroad Land
Grant Controversy."　EXPLORATIONS IN ECONOMIC HISTORY　11
(Winter 1973-74):　155-72.

This is an investigation of the rate of return earned by promoters on the land grant lands.　It concludes that the subsidies were excessive.　The implications for wealth distribution
and the risk loss are also discussed.

749　Fogel, Robert W.　"A Quantitative Approach to the Study of Railroads
in American Economic Growth:　A Report of Some Preliminary Findings."
JOURNAL OF ECONOMIC HISTORY　22 (June 1962):　163-97.

Asserting that previous research has only established an association between railroads and economic growth, the author sets up
a model to test whether there was a causal relation.

750　_____.　RAILROADS AND AMERICAN ECONOMIC GROWTH.　ESSAYS
IN ECONOMETRIC HISTORY.　Baltimore:　Johns Hopkins Press, 1964.
296 p.

This work is a compilation of work dealing with the idea of
the indispensability of railroads to economic growth.　An attempt is made to determine the saving realized from the development of the railroad, with respect to foregone product.
It is an application of economic theory and quantitative methods to a very complex problem.

751　_____.　"Railroads as an Analogy to the Space Effort:　Some Economic
Aspects."　ECONOMIC JOURNAL　76 (March 1966):　16-43.

This is an example of how analysis developed for a historical
example may well have modern-day applications.　He assesses
the marginal contributions and marginal losses assigned to these
types of investments.

753 _____ . THE UNION PACIFIC RAILROAD: A CASE IN PREMATURE
ENTERPRISE. Baltimore: Johns Hopkins Press, 1960. 129 p.

This is a new study of the Union Pacific railroad that suggests
that legislation was a result of the difficulty Congress held
in breaking away from government enterprise schemes. New
data are used to estimate the social rate of return on the
railroad.

754 Fowke, Vernon C. "National Policy and Western Development in North
America." JOURNAL OF ECONOMIC HISTORY 16 (December 1956):
461-81.

Reviewing various historical accounts of development of the
West, underdevelopment is recognized as an undesirable condition. This undesirability is the basis of humanitarian goals
to uplift less fortunate people, the search for profitable investment, and the drive for defense. The author concentrates
on the latter two.

755 Frederick, John H. "Federal Regulation of Railway Securities under the
Transportation Act of 1920." JOURNAL OF POLITICAL ECONOMY 37
(April 1929): 175-202.

Reviewing aspects of the Transportation Act of 1920, this work
includes an examination of the nature and effect of federal
regulation of railway securities on railroad financing.

756 Goldin, H.H. "Government Policy and the Domestic Telegraph Industry."
JOURNAL OF ECONOMIC HISTORY 7 (May 1947): 53-68.

This is an investigation of some weaknesses in the telegraph
industry, such as obsolete plants and equipment, inadequate
rate structure, deteriorating service quality, high unit labor
costs, and considerable competition. Governmental policy is
also discussed.

757 Goodrich, Carter, ed. CANALS AND AMERICAN ECONOMIC DEVELOP-
MENT. New York: Columbia University Press, 1961. 303 p.

This is a compilation of three dissertations related to canals
and economic growth, and a chapter is included comparing
the various state laws for New York, Pennsylvania, and New
Jersey. The political decisions, the financing, and the nature
of the improvements are enumerated.

758 Greeley, Horace. AN OVERLAND JOURNEY FROM NEW YORK TO
SAN FRANCISCO IN THE SUMMER OF 1859. New York: C.M. Saxton,
Barker and Co., 1860. 386 p.

This is an account of the author's travels and a definite advertisement for the Union Pacific Railroad. It is a roughly written piece that does describe the methods of transportation available at that time.

759 Greever, William S. "A Comparison of Railroad Land-Grant Policies." AGRICULTURAL HISTORY 25 (April 1951): 83-90.

This is a comparative study of Canadian and U.S. land grant policies and their effects on the railroad.

760 Haites, Erik F., and Mak, James. "The Decline of Steamboating on the Ante-Bellum Western Rivers: Some New Evidence and an Alternative Hypothesis." EXPLORATIONS IN ECONOMIC HISTORY 11 (Fall 1973): 25-36.

Using new evidence on steamboat tonnage between 1811 and 1860, it is inferred that steamboating did not decline absolutely during the antebellum period. Factors producing movements in the new estimates are also analyzed.

761 _____. "Ohio and Mississippi River Transportation, 1810-1860." EXPLORATIONS IN ECONOMIC HISTORY 8 (Winter 1970-71): 153-80.

This is a comparative study of keelboating, flatboating, and steamboating on the Louisville to New Orleans route. Profitability on each of these is compared with the others.

762 Hammond, Seth. "Location Theory and the Cotton Industry." JOURNAL OF ECONOMIC HISTORY 2 (December 1942): 101-17.

Using the Weber school's location theory, the antebellum location of the cotton industry is examined. The model must be adapted for historical data and for purposes of historical inquiry.

763 Haney, Lewis H. "Railway Regulation in Texas." JOURNAL OF POLITICAL ECONOMY 19 (June 1911): 437-55.

An account of railroad regulation in Texas, the legislative hassles, the rate system, the nature of the commission, and railways' organization and control over capitalization are all examined.

764 Harbeson, Robert W. "Railroads and Regulation 1877-1916: Conspiracy or Public Interest?" JOURNAL OF ECONOMIC HISTORY 27 (June 1967): 230-42.

This is an analysis of previous work on the view of the railroad toward regulation. This work argues that others have made numerous errors in their arguments that the railroad favored regulation as a means of producing profit stability.

765   Hayter, Earl W. "The Fencing of Western Railways." AGRICULTURAL HISTORY 19 (July 1945): 163-66.

Both the actual and legislative problems which arose from livestock being killed by the trains are discussed. The effects of fencing and its costs are considered.

766   Healy, Kent T. "The Merger Movement in Transportation." AMERICAN ECONOMIC REVIEW 52 (May 1962): 436-44.

Healy analyzes common carriers in railroads, trucking, and air transport, and characteristics of the three industries, such as competitive classification, size, institutional factors, pricing, and overall economic performance. Various social and economic development issues are also discussed.

767   _____. "Transportation as a Factor in Economic Growth." JOURNAL OF ECONOMIC HISTORY 7 (1947): supplement, 72-88.

This is a survey of the innovations and technological changes that have occurred during the nineteenth and twentieth centuries. The author asks what the relationship is between general technical change and that specifically related to transportation and whether transportation innovations contributed to innovation in general.

768   Heath, Milton S., and Cochran, Thomas C. "The Development of the North American Railroads." JOURNAL OF ECONOMIC HISTORY 10 (1950): supplement, 40-67.

Consideration is primarily with the relationship between public and private railroads, for example, public railroads in relation to private enterprise in general, public policy in relation to private enterprise within the field of rail transportation, and the influence of the public railroad movement upon the evolution of the forms of private business organization.

769   Heilman, Ralph E. "The Chicago Subway Problem." JOURNAL OF POLITICAL ECONOMY 22 (December 1914): 992-1005.

This is an investigation of the struggle between the City of Chicago and the traction companies, and an outline of inadequate street railway system. The implications of the "Settlement Ordinances" adopted to relieve problems of the subway system are also examined.

770   Higgs, Robert. "Railroad Rates and the Populist Uprising." AGRICULTURAL HISTORY 44 (July 1970): 291-98.

Arguing that freight rates did not decline steeply during the period 1867-96, the author demonstrates that farmers were not benefitting from lower transportation costs.

771 Hill, Forest G. "Government Engineering Aid to Railroads before the Civil War." JOURNAL OF ECONOMIC HISTORY 11 (Summer 1951): 235-46.

> During the antebellum period, the government aided railroad development by providing engineering services. This is a study of the effect on railroading of government promotion of engineering and science.

772 Hill, William. "Changes in Railway Transportation Rates." JOURNAL OF POLITICAL ECONOMY 2 (March 1894): 282-84.

> The changes in railway freight rates are analyzed from statistics compiled by the Senate Finance Committee.

773 Hoagland, H.E. "Early Transportation on the Mississippi." JOURNAL OF POLITICAL ECONOMY 19 (February 1911): 111-23.

> Examining the presteamboat era, this article looks at the types of transportation and the trades in which they were engaged.

774 Hoover, Edgar M. THE LOCATION OF ECONOMIC ACTIVITY. New York: McGraw-Hill, 1948. 387 p.

> A preliminary investigation, this book examines the location decisions of the shoe and leather industries, in order to illustrate the methodology to be used. Such problems as market imperfections and overhead and joint costs are not considered, but it remains a classic work.

775 Horowitz, Morris A. "Wage Guarantees of Road Service Employees of American Railroads." AMERICAN ECONOMIC REVIEW 45 (December 1955): 853-66.

> This is an examination of the dual system under which employees were many times paid for work they did not perform. Such payments, for work done outside the scope of regular time or duties, and other payments added greatly to the variable cost of the railroads.

776 Hunt, E.H. "Railroad Social Saving in Nineteenth-Century America." AMERICAN ECONOMIC REVIEW 57 (December 1967): 909-10.

> This critique of the model used by Fogel (see no. 750) reviews the social saving argument. Many of Fogel's assumptions are too unrealistic. Comments by P.R.P. Coehlo, R.P. Thomas and D.D. Shetler and a reply by E.H. Hunt appear in AMERICAN ECONOMIC REVIEW 58 (March 1968): 184-89.

777 Hutchins, John G.B. "The Effect of the Civil War and the Two World

Wars on American Transportation." AMERICAN ECONOMIC REVIEW 2 (May 1952): 626-38.

>This is an analysis of the effects of public policy on capacity and the nature of the physical plant, especially the changes in attitude from laissez-faire to the more regulated and military self-sufficiency oriented economy.

778 Isard, Walter, and Capron, William M. "The Future Locational Pattern of Iron and Steel Production in the United States." JOURNAL OF POLITICAL ECONOMY 57 (April 1949): 118-33.

>Building upon the findings in the following Isard article (see no. 779), the authors consider the future location of iron and steel plants on the basis of costs, current experimentation, future market expectations, and the institutional structure of the American economy.

779 _____. "Some Locational Factors in the Iron and Steel Industry since the Early Nineteenth Century." JOURNAL OF POLITICAL ECONOMY 56 (June 1948): 203-17.

>This argument is based on evidence from various nations, and purports that the location of coal deposits has not, for many decades, determined the location or the extent of the development of the iron and steel plants.

780 Jenks, Leland H. "Britain and American Railway Development." JOURNAL OF ECONOMIC HISTORY 11 (Fall 1951): 375-88.

>This is an examination of the role of British investors, financiers, engineers, contractors, and financial groups involved with the railways in the development in the Western Hemisphere.

781 _____. "Railroads as an Economic Force in American Development." JOURNAL OF ECONOMIC HISTORY 4 (May 1944): 1-20.

>Using Schumpeter's theory of innovations, the author examines the railroad (1) as an idea; (2) as a constructive enterprise; and (3) as a producer of transportation services.

782 Kelso, Harold. "Waterways versus Railways." AMERICAN ECONOMIC REVIEW 31 (September 1941): 537-44.

>This considers the improved waterways in the United States in 1938, for which the net registered tonnage of large or light-draft motorboats exceeded the net registered tonnage of ocean or lake vessels. The total cost of light-draft waterway transportation is compared with the total cost of equivalent service by railroads. The effects of waterway competition and federal aid to waterways are also considered.

783 Kementa, Jan, and Williamson, Jeffrey G. "Determinants of Investment Behavior: United States Railroads 1872-1941." REVIEW OF ECONOMICS AND STATISTICS 48 (May 1966): 172-81.

Examining the historical background of railway development during the years 1872-1941 and modeling investment behavior, the authors argue that investment behavior depends upon the industry's phase in its life cycle.

784 Leavitt, Charles T. "Transportation and the Livestock Industry of the Middle West to 1860." AGRICULTURAL HISTORY 8 (January 1934): 20-33.

This is an analysis of the effect of steamboats, canals, and railroads on livestock growing in the Middle West before 1860. A comparison is made between the effect on grain and the effect on livestock.

785 Lebergott, Stanley. "United States Transport Advance and Externalities." JOURNAL OF ECONOMIC HISTORY 26 (December 1966): 437-61.

Arguing that some of the measures used to assess the social saving of the railroad do not fully capture the value of the externalities, the case is made that railroads advanced the effectiveness of the U.S. transport system. Thomas Weiss has a comment and Lebergott a reply in JOURNAL OF ECONOMIC HISTORY 28 (December 1968): 631-35.

786 Leonard, W.N. "The Decline of Railroad Consolidation." JOURNAL OF ECONOMIC HISTORY 9 (May 1949): 1-24.

Concentrating on the years 1893-1908, the author considers the factors contributing to the consolidation movement, for example, changing public attitude, public policy, and legislation. A revision of the statutes to enable machinery to be established to accomplish consolidation is also included.

787 Lorenz, M.O. "Railway Rates as Protective Tariffs--Another View." JOURNAL OF POLITICAL ECONOMY 14 (March 1906): 170-76.

It is argued that railway rates are not "protective" tariffs, but rather, characteristic of free trade if "protective" takes on an international trade definition. Railway rates do not protect the railroads from competition, allowing them to change higher prices. They are the result of free trade and are sufficiently low as to prevent the loss of business.

788 McClelland, Peter D. "Railroads, American Growth, and the New Economic History: A Critique." JOURNAL OF ECONOMIC HISTORY 28 (March 1968): 102-23.

This is a simplified approach to the analysis of R. Fogel's and A. Fishlow's work on calculating the contribution of the railroad to economic growth. It is claimed that their methodology does not allow them to measure what they said they measured.

789 _____. "Social Rates to Return on American Railroads in the Nineteenth Century." ECONOMIC HISTORY REVIEW 25 (August 1972): 471-88.

After attacking the common usage of social rates of return, the author elaborates the formula for deriving such a rate. The difficulties involved with moving from average to marginal social rates of return are also considered.

790 McCusker, John J. "Colonial Tonnage Measurement: Five Philadelphia Merchant Ships as a Sample." JOURNAL OF ECONOMIC HISTORY 27 (March 1967): 82-91.

This is a study of the hypothesis that North American vessels were consistently registered at two-thirds of actual tonnage. Eighteenth-century examples are used to support this hypothesis. Gary M. Walton, in a comment in JOURNAL OF ECONOMIC HISTORY 27 (September 1967): 392-97, has discussed McClusker's work, arguing that one must be especially careful to be consistent with specifying tonnage of a ship, because there is more than one type.

791 McLuhan, Marshall. "Effects of the Improvements of Communication Media." JOURNAL OF ECONOMIC HISTORY 20 (December 1960): 566-75.

This is a discussion of the impact on decision making made by advancements. A sociological history of communications is offered.

792 McManus, John. "An Economic Analysis of Indian Behavior in the North American Fur Trade." JOURNAL OF ECONOMIC HISTORY 32 (March 1972): 36-53.

This is an attempt via use of the fur trade to illustrate how economic analysis of institutions can be used to develop an approach to studying economic history.

793 McPherson, Logan G. "City Competition in Railroad Rate Making." JOURNAL OF POLITICAL ECONOMY 16 (April 1908): 227-29.

This study of Kansas City merchants attempts to measure the actual effect on freight rates of railroads on the commerce of the United States. Competition between the merchants of large cities was found to be a potent rate-making force and a source of many complaints against the railroad.

794 McVey, Frank L. "Shipping Subsidies." JOURNAL OF POLITICAL ECON-
OMY 9 (December 1900): 24-46.

In order to more fully understand the future implications of
subsidizing, the author presents a historical examination of
the decline in American shipping.

795 Mak, James, and Walton, Gary M. "Steamboats and the Great Productivity Surge in River Transportation." JOURNAL OF ECONOMIC HIS-
TORY 32 (September 1972): 619-40.

The rate of change in total factor productivity is measured
and the cost determinants are examined to find the sources of
improvement. Improvement was made because of a marked
productivity change during the antebellum period, but attri-
butable to the sources of trial and error or learning by doing.

796 Mercer, Lloyd J. "Building Ahead of Demand: Some Evidence for the
Land-Grant Railroads." JOURNAL OF ECONOMIC HISTORY 34 (June
1974): 492-500.

This deals with the hypotheses regarding profitability of railroads built after the Civil War. It asks, for example, whether
profit rate positively correlated with age of firm, and if the
profit rate of new firms was below that of alternative investments.

797 _____. "Rates of Return for Land-Grant Railroads: The Central Pacific
System." JOURNAL OF ECONOMIC HISTORY 30 (September 1970):
602-26.

Concentrating upon the transfer of ownership of land in the
public domain to pioneer railroads in order to aid their construction, the author produces estimates of the social and private rates of return to analyze the benefits of the program.

798 Milton, John W. "State Aid to Railroads in Missouri." JOURNAL OF
POLITICAL ECONOMY 3 (December 1894): 73-97.

Missouri attempted to enter into the construction of public
works and this article is an investigation of such experiments
in internal improvements in Missouri and other states.

799 Montague, Gilbert Holland. "The Transportation Phase of the Oil Industry." JOURNAL OF POLITICAL ECONOMY 15 (October 1907): 449-69.

The tendency for combination in transportation is examined
along with the relationship between Standard Oil and its various transportation agencies.

800 Moulton, H.G. "The Cost of the Erie Barge Canal." JOURNAL OF POLITICAL ECONOMY 23 (May 1915): 490-500.

This is an analysis of the progress made on the New York Barge Canal and the probable eventual cost.

801 _____. "The Illinois Water-Power Scheme." JOURNAL OF POLITICAL ECONOMY 18 (May 1910): 381-87.

Extant doubt concerning the feasibility of canal transportation in the United States prompted this study in which estimates of the value of the waterway indicate that the costs were greatly underestimated.

802 Neal, Larry. "Investment Behavior by American Railroads." REVIEW OF ECONOMICS AND STATISTICS 51 (May 1969): 126-35.

Analyzing the period 1897-1914, the author attempts to explain railroad investment behavior as a result of changes in the methods of railroad financing, namely, use of external funds. This is a critique of the Kementa and Williamson paper cited above (no. 783). W. Douglas Morgan has a comment and Neal a reply in REVIEW OF ECONOMICS AND STATISTICS 53 (August 1971): 294-300.

803 Nerlove, Mark. "Railroads and American Economic Growth." JOURNAL OF ECONOMIC HISTORY 26 (March 1966): 107-15.

It is argued that unless capital markets permitted a gross misallocation of investment, Fogel's calculations for the contribution of railroads are incorrect.

804 Newcomb, H.T. "The Decline in Railway Rates: Some of Its Causes and Results." JOURNAL OF POLITICAL ECONOMY 6 (September 1898): 457-75.

Using general averages for data, the author examines freight charges, decline in prices and rates, prices and uses of steel rail efficiency, and the unification of the railway system.

805 Niemi, Albert W., Jr. "A Further Look at Interregional Canals and Economic Specialization: 1820-1840." EXPLORATIONS IN ECONOMIC HISTORY 7 (Summer 1970): 499-520.

This article is a challenge to the traditional view of the role of internal improvements in the regional specialization and development. It is argued that the West did not specialize in agriculture but rather maintained a growing manufacturing sector.

806 North, Douglas C. "Ocean Freight Rates and Economic Development, 1750-1913." JOURNAL CF ECONOMIC HISTORY 18 (December 1958): 537-55.

Focusing on the period 1750-1913, the author provides an examination of the costs of ocean transportation and the implications of their decline.

807 _____. "Sources of Productivity Change in Ocean Shipping, 1600-1850." JOURNAL OF POLITICAL ECONOMY 77 (September-October 1968): 953-70.

This is an attempt to attribute the productivity increase to something other than "technological change." The primary sources of the increase were found to be a reduction in piracy and improved economic organization.

808 Northrup, Herbert R. "The Railway Labor Act and Railway Labor Disputes in Wartime." AMERICAN ECONOMIC REVIEW 36 (June 1946): 327-43.

Analyzing the period 1941-45 with respect to the labor dispute cases, the author assumes that the period is a good test period because of the emergency situation of World War II. It could serve to illustrate a model for legislation during normal times.

809 Pollard, Sidney. "British and World Shipbuilding, 1890-1914: A Study in Comparative Costs." JOURNAL OF ECONOMIC HISTORY 17 (September 1957): 426-44.

Although the general emphasis is on the industry in Britain, shipbuilding in competing countries is also examined.

810 Putnam, J.W. "An Economic History of the Illinois and Michigan Canal." JOURNAL OF POLITICAL ECONOMY 17 (May 1909): 272-95; (June 1909): 337; and (July 1909): 413-33.

This is a historical survey of the economic factors considered in the construction of this canal.

811 Rae, John Bell. "Federal Land Grants in Aid of Canals." JOURNAL OF ECONOMIC HISTORY 4 (November 1944): 167-77.

This is an examination of the forces behind land grants and the economic and political influences of them, as well as their nature during the eighteenth century.

812 _____. "The Great Northern's Land Grant." JOURNAL OF ECONOMIC HISTORY 12 (Spring 1953): 140-45.

This is a study of the efficiency of the land subsidy policies with respect to economic growth, entrepreneurship, induced investment, and territorial development.

813 Ransom, Roger L. "Canals and Development: A Discussion of the Issue." AMERICAN ECONOMIC REVIEW 54 (May 1964): 365-76.

On the basis of the contribution of the canal system, the author examines the case for regional specialization, to the degree permitted by the extent of the market. Railroads were held to have been the most important contributors to the developmental process.

814 _____. "A Closer Look at Canals and Western Manufacturing in the Canal Era." EXPLORATIONS IN ECONOMIC HISTORY 8 (Summer 1971): 501-10.

This is a response to the article by A. Niemi cited above (no. 805). Niemi had challenged the traditional view that the West specialized in agriculture while the East specialized in manufacturing as a response to internal improvements. Ransom analyzes these opposing views and concludes that the traditional view was correct. A reply and a rebuttal appear in EXPLORATIONS IN ECONOMIC HISTORY 9 (Summer 1972): 423-26.

815 Ransom, Roger L., and Sutch, Richard. "Debt Peonage in the Cotton South after the Civil War." JOURNAL OF ECONOMIC HISTORY 32 (September 1972): 641-69.

The authors examine the hypothesis that the South was unable to reestablish a system of commercial banks due to the readjustment of agriculture and the legal difficulties. Supposedly, the local merchant was the supplier of credit and this was said to have introduced the market.

816 _____. "Interregional Lands and Economic Specialization in the Ante-Bellum U.S." EXPLORATIONS IN ECONOMIC HISTORY 5 (Fall 1967): 12-35.

This is an examination of the impact of investment by state governments on canals and the effect of these canals on interregional trade. Focusing on the years 1835-50, the traffic along the canal routes and the cost of gaining increased specialization and improvements are considered.

817 _____. "Social Returns from Public Transport Investment: A Case Study of the Ohio Canal." JOURNAL OF POLITICAL ECONOMY 78 (September-October 1970): 1041-60.

This study examines population growth, valuation changes of adjacent property, and industry and commercial activity as measures of benefits from the canal as well as the railroad.

818 Ripley, William Z. RAILROADS, FINANCE, AND ORGANIZATION. New York: Longmans, Green, and Co., 1915. 638 p.

Railway construction finance, capital and capitalization, securities, speculation, stock watering, market prices, reorganization, railroad combinations and pooling are all discussed, along with the impact of the antitrust laws and interrailway agreements.

819 _____. RAILROADS, RATES AND REGULATIONS. New York: Longmans, Green, and Co., 1912. 659 p.

This is an examination of how the government regulates prices and rate-setting techniques, as well as the interrailroad relations and combinations. The problems of routing and rate discrimination are discussed.

820 _____. RAILWAY PROBLEMS. New York: Ginn and Co., 1913. 830 p.

By utilizing technical information, the author analyzes the historical conditions of the railroad, problems in rate setting, government regulation, costs of railroads, and railroad associations. A short comparison with French and German railway systems is provided.

821 Rivet, Felix. "American Technique and Steam Navigation on the Soane and the Rhone, 1827-1850." JOURNAL OF ECONOMIC HISTORY 16 (March 1956): 18-33.

This is an examination of the effect of the American technique and steam navigation on French waterways. The channels of cooperation between the two countries are also explored.

822 Royd, J. Hayden, and Walton, Gary M. "The Social Savings from Nineteenth-Century Rail Passenger Services." EXPLORATIONS IN ECONOMIC HISTORY 9 (Spring 1972): 233-54.

Complementing Fogel's study (see no. 750) for railroad social savings with regard to agricultural freight, this study refines the measurement of historical benefits from technological innovations by including value of time saved along with better estimates of the demand elasticity for transportation.

823 Schaefer, Donald, and Weiss, Thomas. "The Use of Simulation Techniques in Historical Analysis: Railroads versus Canals." JOURNAL OF ECONOMIC HISTORY 31 (December 1971): 854-84.

Using the technique of generating probability distributions for particular unknown variables, the authors estimate the returns "likely" to be available for nineteenth-century railroads and canals.

824 Shaw, John A. "Railroads, Irrigation, and Economic Growth: The San Joaquin Valley of California." EXPLORATIONS IN ECONOMIC HISTORY 10 (Winter 1973): 211-28.

Although it is not an attempt to critique Fogel's book (see no. 750), this author does criticize Fogel for misrepresenting the situation in the San Joaquin Valley by ignoring the effects of irrigation.

825 Shepherd, James F., and Walton, Gary F. SHIPPING MARITIME GRADE AND THE ECONOMIC DEVELOPMENT OF COLONIAL NORTH AMERICA. Cambridge, Engl.: Cambridge University Press, 1972. 255 p.

This book treats the economic development of the colonies with regard to the effect of colonial shipping. Some of the trade was international but much was coastal shipping. An excellent and analytically sound work.

826 _____. "Trade Distribution, and Economic Growth in Colonial America." JOURNAL OF ECONOMIC HISTORY 32 (March 1972): 128-45.

Using the period 1768-72, the authors argue that overseas trade was important to the colonies, and the growth of the market sector spurred the growth of productivity. A balance of payments analysis is presented, and long-term trends in output and population are examined.

827 Smith, J. Russell. "Ocean Freight Rates and Their Control by Line Carriers." JOURNAL OF POLITICAL ECONOMY 14 (November 1906): 525-41.

This comparison of ocean freight rates and the degree of control exercised by line carriers also examines the agreements between carriers.

828 Smolensky, E., and Ratajczak, D. "The Conception of Cities." EXPLORATIONS IN ECONOMIC HISTORY 2 (Winter 1965): 90-131.

An investigation of the determinants of city location and size, this article also analyzes the magnitude and timing of population and economic growth, along with the required amounts of overhead capital. San Diego is the city used to test the three-stage theory proffered in this article.

829 Taff, Charles A. "The Competition of Long-Distance Motor Trucking:

Farm and Industrial Products and Supplies." AMERICAN ECONOMIC REVIEW 46 (May 1956): 508-20.

This is an analysis of the competition against railroads and the regulations imposed on different types of carriers. The findings of the Presidential Advisory Committee on Transport Policy and Organization are also reviewed.

830 Taylor, George Rogers. "American Urban Growth Preceding the Railway Age." JOURNAL OF ECONOMIC HISTORY 27 (September 1967): 309-39.

Using the period 1775 to 1840, statistics on urban population changes are analyzed in an effort to evaluate the contributions by four different city groups in these changes.

831 _____. THE TRANSPORTATION REVOLUTION, 1815-1860. New York: Harper & Row, 1968. 490 p.

A classic work in the field of transportation, the book analyzes all of the various types of transportation. The major factors and institutions that influenced the development of the transportation system are also discussed.

832 Teele, Ray P. "Present Status of Rights to Interstate Streams." JOURNAL OF POLITICAL ECONOMY 11 (March 1903): 273-79.

In order to establish the status of rights of states to interstate waterways, judicial action up to the time when states began to interfere in the rights of others is reviewed. The several cases pending at the time of this article are also discussed.

833 Temin, Peter. "Steam and Waterpower in the Early Nineteenth Century." JOURNAL OF ECONOMIC HISTORY 26 (June 1966): 187-205.

This is an analysis of the utilization of stationary steam engines in the United States, with respect to both demand and supply. The situation for steam engines and waterpower is discussed for various countries.

834 Tunell, George G. "Charge for Railway Mail Carriage." JOURNAL OF POLITICAL ECONOMY 7 (March 1879): 145-60.

Considering the railway mail carriage, the author also reviews and discusses cost and rates of mail coverage.

835 _____. "The Diversion of the Flour and Grain Traffic from the Great Lakes to the Railroads." JOURNAL OF POLITICAL ECONOMY 5 (June 1897): 340-75.

The waterway of the Great Lakes served as a major route for

flour and grain for many years, and this article analyzes the reasons for the diversion of this trade to the railroads.

836 _____. "The Growth and Character of the Commerce on the Great Lakes." JOURNAL OF POLITICAL ECONOMY 4 (March 1896): 243-45.

Using traffic statistics and tonnage, the author analyzes the nature of growth and the character of commerce on the Great Lakes.

837 _____. "Lake Transportation and the Iron-Ore Industries." JOURNAL OF POLITICAL ECONOMY 5 (December 1896): 23-39.

This analysis of the effect of the iron ore output of the Lake Superior region on other regions also includes a geographical survey of iron ore regions.

838 Walton, Gary M. "A Measure of Productivity Change in American Colonial Shipping." ECONOMIC HISTORY REVIEW 21 (August 1968): 268-82.

This analysis attempts to measure the rate of productivity gain produced by various measures, and arrives at a figure of about 1.35 percent per year over the period 1675-1775.

839 _____. "Obstacles to Technical Diffusion in Ocean Shipping, 1675-1775." EXPLORATIONS IN ECONOMIC HISTORY 8 (Winter 1970-71): 123-40.

In the exploration of technological change for ocean shipping, the differences between acquired technical change and the existing methods are discussed. Primary interest was in the colonial wires shipping news.

840 _____. "Productivity Change in Ocean Shipping after 1870." JOURNAL TO ECONOMIC HISTORY 30 (June 1970): 435-41.

This article contains a new measure of productivity for ocean shipping, that is, it is a measure of total factor productivity rather than just labor productivity.

841 _____. "Sources of Productivity Change in American Colonial Shipping, 1675-1775." ECONOMIC HISTORY REVIEW 20 (April 1967): 67-78.

Most of the gains were found to have resulted from organizational changes and reduced uncertainties, for example, rates and privateerism. Freight rate indexes for a sample of commodity rates were used in lieu of input-output analysis, because of the lack of necessary data.

842 White, Henry K. "Pacific Railway Debts." JOURNAL OF POLITICAL ECONOMY 2 (June 1894): 424-52.

>   The government made a loan to Pacific Railways and this article examines the terms of the loan and the debt paying ability and financial status of the railway.

843 Williams, Ernest W., Jr. "Railroad Traffic and Costs." AMERICAN ECONOMIC REVIEW 33 (June 1943): 360-65.

>   This article reviews the effect of competition on the process of rate making used by railroad management, and the changes in their methods of cost accounting.

844 Williamson, Jeffrey, and Swanson, Joseph A. "The Growth of Cities in the American Northeast, 1820-1870." EXPLORATIONS IN ECONOMIC HISTORY 4 (Fall 1966): 1-101.

>   This is a very extensive and rigorous study of the location and growth of urban centers during the nineteenth century.

6.2 GENERAL LISTINGS

845 Acworth, W.M. "The American Railway Situation." ECONOMIC JOURNAL 30 (June 1920): 177-95.

846 Adams, H. CHAPTERS FROM THE EARLY HISTORY OF THE ERIE RAILWAY. New Haven, Conn.: Yale University Press, 1929. 410 p.

847 Armroyd, George. A CONNECTED VIEW OF THE WHOLE INTERNAL NAVIGATION OF THE UNITED STATES. Philadelphia: Lydia R. Bailey, 1830. 617 p.

848 Bates, William W. AMERICAN NAVIGATION. New York: Houghton Mifflin and Co., 1906. 466 p.

849 Clarke, T.C. THE AMERICAN RAILWAY. New York: C. Scribner's Sons, 1897. 456 p.

850 Davis, John P. THE UNION PACIFIC RAILWAY. Chicago: S.C. Griggs and Co., 1894. 247 p.

851 Dean, Robert D.; Leahy, W.H.; and McKee, Danid L. SPATIAL ECONOMIC THEORY. New York: Free Press, 1970. 365 p.

852 Gates, Paul W. "The Railroad Land-Grant Legend." JOURNAL OF ECONOMIC HISTORY 14 (June 1954): 143-45.

853   Gee, Joshua.   THE TRADE AND NAVIGATION OF GREAT BRITAIN
      CONSIDERED.   New York: A.M. Kelley, 1969.   239 p.

854   Hadley, A.T.   RAILROAD TRANSPORTATION, ITS HISTORY AND ITS
      LAWS.   New York: G.P. Putnam's Sons, 1900.   269 p.

855   Harmon, Daniel Williams.   A JOURNAL OF VOYAGES AND TRAVELS
      IN THE INTERIOR OF NORTH AMERICA, 1800.   Andover, Mass.: Flagg
      and Gould, 1820.   432 p.

857   Hewett, D.   THE AMERICAN TRAVELLER.   Washington, D.C.: Davis and
      Force, 1825.   440 p.

858   Hughes, J., and Reiter, S.   "The First 1,945 British Steamships."   JOUR-
      NAL OF AMERICAN STATISTICAL ASSOCIATION 53 (June 1958):   360-
      81.

859   Inman, Henry.   THE GREAT SALT LAKE TRAIL.   Topeka: Crane and Co.,
      1914.   529 p.

860   _____.   THE OLD SANTA FE TRAIL.   Topeka: Crane and Co., 1912.
      493 p.

861   Isard, Walter.   LOCATION AND SPACE-ECONOMY.   Cambridge: MIT
      Press, 1956.   350 p.

862   Johnson, Emory R.   AMERICAN RAILWAY TRANSPORTATION.   New York:
      D. Appleton and Co., 1910.   434 p.

863   Krzyzanowski, Witold.   "Review of the Literature of the Location of In-
      dustries."   JOURNAL OF POLITICAL ECONOMY 34 (April 1927):   278-
      91.

864   Meeker, Royal.   HISTORY OF SHIPPING SUBSIDIES.   New York: Mac-
      millan Co., 1905.   234 p.

865   Meyer, B.H.   RAILWAY LEGISLATION IN THE UNITED STATES.   New
      York: Macmillan Co., 1909.   329 p.

866   Morrison, John H.   HISTORY OF AMERICAN STEAM NAVIGATION.   New
      York: Stephen Days Press, 1958.   630 p.

867   Moses, Leon N.   "A General Equilibrium Model of Production, Interre-
      gional Trade and Location of Industry."   REVIEW OF ECONOMICS AND
      STATISTICS 42 (November 1960):   373-97.

868 Moulton, H.G. WATERWAYS VERSUS RAILWAYS. New York: Houghton Mifflin and Co., 1912. 469 p.

869 Orton, W.A. "Valuation Theory as Applied to United States Railroads." ECONOMIC JOURNAL 39 (June 1929): 226-36.

870 Pitkin, Timothy. STATISTICAL VIEW OF THE COMMERCE OF THE UNITED STATES. New York: Eastburn, 1817. 445 p.

871 Poor, H.V. MANUAL OF RAILROADS IN THE UNITED STATES: 1868-1924. New York: H.V. and H.W. Poor, 1868-1924. 632 p.

Chapter 7

MONETARY AND FINANCIAL DEVELOPMENT

The works cited and annotated in this chapter reflect a wide range of topics and methods of analysis. Much of the literature on capital accumulation was included in chapter 4 and chapter 5. The citations in this chapter that refer to capital formation do so with respect to the financial aspects of capital formation.

Most of the studies deal with money, the monetary system, banking, interest rates, and/or prices. The time span for analysis ranges from the colonial period to the 1950s. Analyses of gold standard issues necessarily include some analysis of international trade and relative prices, especially when one is considering capital flows.

The range of methodology is from traditional history to the rigorous econometric approach by some of the new economic historians. Although there are quite a few books that may warrant inclusion but which are not included, I think the user will usually find references to these other works in the notes of the works that are cited below.

There are various U.S. government publications that include data on prices, monetary variables, and institutional data. These are not cited because of their general use by most authors and their availability at nearly any library that has a government documents section. Prior to 1914 these data were produced primarily by the U.S. Treasury, but since then the Federal Reserve System has produced an increasingly larger proportion of these data. The researcher would be well advised to search both categories, because the Federal Reserve has produced some historical work as well as contemporary data recordings. That is, analysis of earlier time periods should include research in Federal Reserve publications.

7.1 ANNOTATED LISTINGS

872   Adams, Donald R., Jr. "The Bank of Stephen Girard, 1812-1831." JOURNAL OF ECONOMIC HISTORY 32 (December 1972): 841-68.

Besides being a detailed study of the Girard bank, this article is also an examination of the financial climate of Philadelphia.

873 _____. FINANCE AND ENTERPRISE IN EARLY AMERICA: A STUDY OF STEPHEN GIRARD'S BANK, 1812-1831. Philadelphia: University of Philadelphia Press, 1978. 163 p.

This is a comparison of European and U.S. banking structure and procedures, with the Girard bank serving as a point of reference in the United States. The sources and uses of capital fund are of primary concern.

874 Alhadeff, David A., and Alhadeff, Charlotte. "A Growth of Large Banks, 1930-1960." REVIEW OF ECONOMICS AND STATISTICS 46 (November 1964): 356-63.

Starting with the secular trend of few but larger banks the authors attempt to measure relative rates of growth among banks of different sizes.

875 Anderson, Frank F. "Fundamental Factors in War Finance." JOURNAL OF POLITICAL ECONOMY 25 (November 1917): 857-87.

This article considers the sources of war financing, the extent to which these resources can be used, the methods of war finance, and the U.S. share of the expense.

876 Axilrod, Stephen H. "Yield on U.S. Foreign Investment, 1920-1953." REVIEW OF ECONOMICS AND STATISTICS 38 (August 1956): 331-34.

Using his calculated yields on existing foreign investment, the author compares these with the existing series on domestic rates for similar risk category.

877 Benner, Claude L. "Credit Aspects of the Agricultural Depression, 1920-21, Parts I and II." JOURNAL OF POLITICAL ECONOMY 33 (February 1925): 94-106; (April 1925): 217-33.

This is an examination of the role of country banks, city correspondent banks, and the Federal Reserve in credit deflation of the farmers, which in part caused the agriculture depression of 1920-21. Part 2 analyzes the causes which led to the cessation of credit expansion in 1919, and to the discount policy of the Federal Reserve banks in 1920.

878 Bernstein, Edward M. "The Adequacy of U.S. Gold Reserves." AMERICAN ECONOMIC REVIEW 51 (May 1961): 439-46.

Observing that U.S. gold reserves fell by seven billion dollars between 1949 and 1960, the author assesses the reserve position in 1961 and expresses his concern about the reserves needed for the future.

879 Bogue, Allan. MONEY AT INTEREST. Ithaca, N.Y.: Cornell University Press, 1955. 293 p.

The status of the late nineteenth century agricultural credit market is thoroughly examined, including the reasons why farmers borrowed, as well as the sources of the funds.

880 Brady, Dorothy. "Relative Prices in the Nineteenth Century." JOURNAL OF ECONOMIC HISTORY 24 (June 1964): 145-203.

Relative price comparisons over time are examined within the context of progressive improvements in standardization, production, construction, labor, and changes in costs.

881 Bratter, Herbert M. "The Silver Episode, I and II." JOURNAL OF POLITICAL ECONOMY 46 (October 1938): 609-52; (December 1938): 802-37.

In the aftermath of the depression of the early 1930s, there was an increased interest in the use of silver as money, and this article is an analysis of the international and governmental effects on the price of silver. Part 2 examines the Silver Agreement of 1933, its impact on the U.S. monetary system, and the impact of subsequent ammendments to the agreement.

882 Brown, Kenneth L. "Stephen Girard, Promoter of the Second Bank of the United States." JOURNAL OF ECONOMIC HISTORY 2 (November 1942): 125-48.

This is an attempt to illustrate that Girard was not solely a heavy investor in the stock of the bank. He was in fact heavily involved in its establishment and functioning until 1818.

883 Brown, William Adams, Jr. "Gold as a Monetary Standard, 1914-1949." JOURNAL OF ECONOMIC HISTORY 9 (September 1949): supplement, 39-49.

After reviewing the reasons for the gold standard, the author illustrates why the gold standard has been gradually displaced since 1914.

884 Brunner, Karl, and Meltzer, Alan. "What Did We Learn from the Monetary Experience of the U.S. during the Great Depression?" CANADIAN JOURNAL OF ECONOMICS 1 (May 1968): 334-48.

This is a follow-up to Wicker's article (see no. 1039), in which the authors show that the Federal Reserve's policy was con-

sistent when one uses the Riefler–Burgess doctrine as the basis
for judgment. One does not need to resort to the inclusion
of international factors to consistently explain the Federal Reserve's behavior.

885 Burton, Theodore E. "Probable Financial and Industrial Effects after the
War." JOURNAL OF POLITICAL ECONOMY 24 (January 1916): 1-13.

On the basis of the experience of other countries in the aftermath of war, the author predicts the probable financial and
industrial effects of World War I on the United States. Effects
considered are capital accumulation, production, interest rates,
and unemployment.

886 Cagan, Phillip. DETERMINANTS AND EFFECTS OF CHANGES IN THE
MONEY STOCK, 1875-1960. New York: Columbia University Press,
1965. 380 p.

This is a very extensive treatment of the velocity and other
aspects of the money stock in its various definitions.

887 Cagan, Phillip, and Schwartz, Anna J. "Has the Growth of Money Substitutes Hindered Monetary Policy?" JOURNAL OF MONEY CREDIT AND
BANKING 7 (May 1975): 137-60.

This is an analysis of monetary behavior from 1921 to 1971,
excluding the years 1942-53, in an attempt to discern whether
the short-run interest elasticity of the demand for money has
declined. Concluding that it has declined, the authors offer
some implications for policy.

888 Carlile, William Warrand. "Historical Changes in the Monetary Standard."
JOURNAL OF POLITICAL ECONOMY 7 (June 1899): 352-66.

This is a comparative analysis of the transition from the silver
to the gold standard in England during the eighteenth century
with other historical monetary changes in the world.

889 Carson, Deane, ed. BANKING AND MONETARY STUDIES. Homewood,
Ill.: Richard D. Irwin, 1963. 441 p.

The first six articles included in this book deal with economic
history of banking and/or monetary policy in one form or another. The authors include such people as Bray Hammond,
Phillip Cagan, Raymond P. Kent, Allan Sproal, George Horwich,
and Hyman P. Minsky.

890 Catterall, Ralph C.H. THE SECOND BANK OF THE UNITED STATES.
Chicago: University of Chicago Press, 1903. 538 p.

A history of the Second Bank of the United States, which emphasizes political relations and its operations as a commercial bank, this book also includes a detailed appendix concerning bank data.

891 Chandler, Lester. BENJAMIN STRONG, CENTRAL BANKER. Washington, D.C.: Brookings Institution, 1958. 495 p.

This is a biography of the man who was president of the New York City Federal Reserve Bank until 1928. It concentrates on his contributions to central banking.

892 _____. "Monopolistic Elements in Commercial Banking." JOURNAL OF POLITICAL ECONOMY 46 (February 1938): 1-22.

The author argues that monopoly power exists in the banking industry despite the lack of open collusion. He illustrates this through an examination of interest rate setting policy for the banks.

893 Christ, Carl F. "Monetary and Fiscal Influences on U.S. Money Income 1891-1970." JOURNAL OF MONEY CREDIT AND BANKING 5 (February 1973): part 2, 279-300.

This is an examination of the relative impacts and speeds of impact for monetary and fiscal policy using annual data. The lags and longer-term effects of such policy are also discussed, using many subperiods as well as the complete period. A series of comments by other economists follow this article.

894 Clarke, Stephen V.O. CENTRAL BANK COOPERATION, 1924-31. New York: Federal Reserve Bank of New York, 1967. 234 p.

This is an examination of the role played by central bank when attempting to provide stability to both domestic and international money markets. Most countries were only readjusting to World War I encrouchments upon freedom when the Great Depression began. This work analyzes the response to the various central banks to the shocks of the period.

895 Copeland, Morris A. "Tracing Money Flows through the U.S. Economy." AMERICAN ECONOMIC REVIEW 37 (March 1947): 30-49.

An attempt is made to construct a picture of money flows from accounting reports, and to show how these can be used in economic analysis.

896 Currie, Lauchlin. "The Failure of Monetary Policy to Prevent the Depression of 1929-32." JOURNAL OF POLITICAL ECONOMY 42 (April 1934): 145-77.

The author's analysis suggests that the depression might have been avoided if the appropriate policy had been followed.

897   Cutler, Ward A. "Insolvent National Banks in City and Country." JOURNAL OF POLITICAL ECONOMY 7 (June 1899): 367-79.

This is a study of the relative risk of insolvency for city and country banks. Particular developments in operations, responses to crises, and the relative means to advance business interest are all considered.

898   Davis, Lance E. "Capital Immobilities and Finance Capitalism." EXPLORATIONS IN ECONOMIC HISTORY 1 (Fall 1963): 88-105.

An argument which shows that certain interregional and inter-industry capital immobilities are more useful in explaining U.S. development and understanding risk than the classical model. The lives of Rockefeller and Morgan are used to illustrate the increase in the availability of capital by the decrease in their importance.

899   _____. "The Investment Market 1870-1914: The Evolution of a National Market." JOURNAL OF ECONOMIC HISTORY 25 (September 1965): 355-99.

This is one of the first treatments of the problem of mobilizing capital from old to new industries and from one region to another. Some interregional barriers to capital mobility are examined.

900   _____. "The New England Textile Mills and the Capital Markets: A Study of Industrial Borrowing, 1840-1860." JOURNAL OF ECONOMIC HISTORY 20 (March 1960): 1-30.

Using financial data, Davis provides new information on the conditions and structure of the Boston credit market. New information on suppliers of finance and monthly interest rates is included.

901   Dorfman, Joseph. "A Note on the Interpretation of Anglo-American Finance, 1837-1841." JOURNAL OF ECONOMIC HISTORY 11 (Spring 1951): 140-47.

This is an investigation of the charges that U.S. financiers deceived European bankers and investors after the panic in 1837. He bases his analysis on newly found transactions records.

902   Dudley, Dean A. "Bank Born of Revelation: The Kirtland Safety Society Anti-Banking Company." JOURNAL OF ECONOMIC HISTORY 30 (December 1970): 848-53.

This is an examination of the activities of the Mormon Church and how it affected this society and the subsequent activities of the society.

903 Durand, E. Dana. "Taxation versus Bond Issues for Financing the War." JOURNAL OF POLITICAL ECONOMY 25 (November 1917): 888-916.

Through clarification of the places from which funds may be drawn for war expenditures, the author attempts to reduce some of the argument between those who favor bonds and those who favor taxation.

904 Edelstein, Michael. "The Determinants of U.K. Investment Abroad, 1870-1913." JOURNAL OF ECONOMIC HISTORY 34 (December 1974): 980-1007.

This is an examination of the flows and the forces behind those flows of capital which predominately came to the United States during this period. In general it was found that the funds were pushed out of the United Kingdom because of rising wealth and the lack of suitable alternatives to the U.S. opportunities.

905 Edit, L.D. "Gold Economies and Stable Prices." JOURNAL OF POLITICAL ECONOMY 37 (February 1929): 1-30.

This is an evaluation of the situations of the various gold-using economies to see if they are adequately stable to support an expansion of bank reserves, bank notes, and bank deposits to maintain a stable price level over the long run.

906 _____. "The 1928 Hearings on the Strong Bill." JOURNAL OF POLITICAL ECONOMY 37 (June 1929): 340-54.

The indecisiveness of the monetary authorities is underscored by pointing out the confusion in the various testimonies on this bill, which was intended to produce stability.

907 Engerman, Stanley L. "A Note on the Economic Consequences of the Second Bank of the United States." JOURNAL OF POLITICAL ECONOMY 78 (July-August 1970): 725-28.

This is a comment on the Temin article (see no. 1022), and points out some implications contained in Temin's monetary estimates that provide additional information on the cyclical and secular role of the Second Bank and its destruction.

908 Fenstermaker, J. Van. "The Statistics of American Commercial Banking, 1782-1818." JOURNAL OF ECONOMIC HISTORY 25 (September 1965): 400-413.

Variables examined in this study include the number of commercial banks, the size of their capital stock, the size of their monetary reserves, and the relative importance of banknote money to demand deposits.

909 Fishlow, Albert. "The Trustee Savings Bank, 1817-1860." JOURNAL OF ECONOMIC HISTORY 21 (March 1961): 27-40.

In order to determine the efficacy of using banks as instruments of policy, the author examines the growth of savings banks and their ability to attract funds from the poor.

910 Frass, Arthur. "The Second Bank of the United States: An Instrument for an Interregional Monetary Union." JOURNAL OF ECONOMIC HISTORY 34 (June 1974): 447-67.

The Second Bank of the United States was charged with the responsibility of creating a uniform national currency, and this paper attempts to analyze its success. The analysis centers around the issue of replacing a flexible exchange rate system with a fixed exchange rate system among the regions.

911 Frederiksen, D.M. "Mortgage Banking in America." JOURNAL OF POLITICAL ECONOMY 2 (March 1894): 203-34.

Using U.S. Census data from 1879 and 1890, the nature and amount of indebtedness is examined with special emphasis given to those who were the borrowers and those who were the lenders. A short account of U.S. mortgage banking is also provided.

912 French, D.R. "The Significance of Time Deposits in the Expansion of Bank Credit, 1922-28." JOURNAL OF POLITICAL ECONOMY 39 (December 1931): 759-82.

This is an analysis of the extent to which deposits listed as commercial shifted from demand to time deposits during the period. Interviews with bankers and businessmen are combined with official banking statistics to perform the analysis.

913 Friedman, Milton. "Price, Income, and Monetary Changes in Three Wartime Periods." AMERICAN ECONOMIC REVIEW 42 (May 1952): 612-25.

These three wars--the Civil War, and World Wars I and II-- provide a near perfect test case for an examination of these variables and their interrelationships. Conditions were sufficiently similar among them that the effects of the variables could be examined.

914 Friedman, Milton, and Schwartz, Anna J. A MONETARY HISTORY OF THE U.S. Princeton, N.J.: Princeton University Press, 1963. 860 p.

Covering the money stock from 1867 to 1960, this book is a superb analysis of the movements in the money stock and changes in the rate of economic growth. It is the most thorough treatment of this particular topic.

915   . MONETARY STATISTICS OF THE UNITED STATES. New York: Columbia University Press, 1970. 629 p.

This is the third of five books written or proposed by the authors and Phillip Cagan (see no. 886). This book contains a detailed description of sources, methods of estimation, supplementary tables, an examination of the definition of money, and a survey of earlier estimates.

916 Gilman, Theodore. "The Clearing House System." JOURNAL OF POLITICAL ECONOMY 2 (March 1904): 208-24.

In order to ascertain the historical importance of the clearing house system, the author examines the relations between the banks and the debtors.

917 Goldsmith, Raymond. FINANCIAL INTERMEDIARIES IN THE AMERICAN ECONOMY. Princeton, N.J.: Princeton University Press, 1958. 415 p.

This work provides a distinctive picture of the set of institutions that constitutes a distinctive component of modern economic organizations. It is about the long-term growth of those institutions that receive and distribute funds of ultimate savers to those who need these funds. An attempt is made to analyze all the quantifiable information and account for trends in market shares as well as other aspects.

918   . A STUDY OF SAVINGS IN THE U.S. 3 vols. Princeton, N.J.: Princeton University Press, 1955. 1138, 632, 476 p.

A detailed analysis of savings behavior during the first half of the twentieth century, volume 1 is a summary of the main findings and volume 2 is a discussion of the measurement techniques used and the accompanying difficulties. Volume 3 is a supplement of data to volume 1 and an analysis of household expenditure studies and estate tax returns. The first objective was to increase factual knowledge of the saving process, the second was to subject these elements to analysis.

919 Gramm, William P. "The Real-Balance Effect in the Great Depression." JOURNAL OF ECONOMIC HISTORY 32 (June 1972): 499-519.

This is an examination of the endogenous determinants of the deposit ratios during the severe downturn and their relation to cyclical changes in the price level. Changes in business activity, which are subjected in all price levels, affect the stock of demand deposits, bank reserves, and thus the stock of bonds held by the banks.

920 Gurley, John G., and Shaw, E.S. "The Growth of Debt and Money in the United States, 1800-1950: A Suggested Interpretation." REVIEW OF ECONOMIC AND STATISTICS 39 (August 1957): 250-62.

Using their model of financial development, the authors attempt to determine the optimal and warranged growth of the monetary system. The model is sensitive to both real and monetary factors of growth and can be used prospectively as well as retrospectively.

921 Hamilton, Earl J. "Prices and Progress." JOURNAL OF ECONOMIC HISTORY 12 (Fall 1952): 325-49.

Evidence is presented to support the hypothesis that rising prices and wages which may harm salaried people tend to benefit society in the long run. Short-run benefits from price and wage declines are shown to have disadvantages.

922 _____. "Use and Misues of Price History." JOURNAL OF ECONOMIC HISTORY 4 (December 1944): 47-60.

This is a demonstration of the difficulties that may be encountered even under the most carefully devised statistical techniques when one attempts to use price series or indexes.

923 Hammond, Bray. BANKS AND POLITICS IN AMERICA. Princeton, N.J.: Princeton University Press, 1957. 771 p.

From the vantage point of banking, the author surveys the general surroundings of industrial commerce, agriculture, and their competition for influence over banking, 1790-1860. In an attempt to make the study comparative, the parallel history of Canada is also reported. A rather extensive list of the works cited appears just prior to the index.

924 _____. "Jackson, Biddle, and the Bank of the United States." JOURNAL OF ECONOMIC HISTORY 7 (May 1947): 1-23.

This article is an attempt to correct the generally conceived purpose of the Second Bank, and further analyzes the failure of the Pennsylvania successor vis-a-vis the Jackson-Biddle battle.

925 Harding, William F. "The State Bank of Indiana." JOURNAL OF POLITICAL ECONOMY 4 (December 1895): 1-36.

A detailed discussion of the 1834 charter the state bank is provided along with an examination of relations between the state and state banks, state bank restrictions and extensions of power, and the nature of state bank bonds.

926 Harris, S.E. "American Gold Policy and Allied War Economics." ECONOMIC JOURNAL 50 (June 1940): 224-30.

This is a study that analyzes British and U.S. gold policy during 1938-39, British capital outflows, and balance of payments.

927 _____. "Dollar Scarcity: Some Remarks Inspired by Lord Keynes' Last Article." ECONOMIC JOURNAL 57 (June 1947): 165-78.

Harris cites the three points which troubled Keynes: (1) the United States was no longer a creditor; (2) wage inflation was increasing in the United States; and (3) there was a large quantity of assets which could be coverted into gold or dollars which lay outside the United States. In examining the dollar scarcity the author also examines the price and cost structure of the United States and England.

928 Hidy, Ralph W. "Anglo-American Merchant Bankers, 1815-1860." JOURNAL OF ECONOMIC HISTORY 1 (December 1941): 53-66.

Being largely a description of the financial, banking, and mercantile functions of the merchant bankers of England, the article shows how these bankers provided both long- and short-term credit to the United States.

929 Hinderliter, Roger H., and Rockoff, Hugh. "Banking under the Gold Standard: An Analysis of Liquidity Management in the Leading Financial Centers." JOURNAL OF ECONOMIC HISTORY 36 (June 1976): 379-98.

Using the period 1890-1907, the authors estimate a model to discover the behavior of commercial banks in response to the actions of central banks. A comparison is made among the three centers New York City, London, and Paris.

930 _____. "The Management of Reserves by Banks in Ante-Bellum Eastern Financial Centers." EXPLORATIONS IN ECONOMIC HISTORY 11 (Fall 1973): 37-54.

As a first step toward understanding pre-Civil War bank behavior, the authors develop a model of portfolio behavior and estimate it for eighty-two banks in Boston, New York, and Philadelphia. Reserve management is the focus of their attention.

931   Hogan, John V. "Bond Investments by National Banks." JOURNAL OF POLITICAL ECONOMY 21 (November 1913): 843-49.

        This is an examination of legislation concerning bank bond investment and the trends in the level and composition of security holdings.

932   Hollander, Jacob H. "The Probable Effects of the New Currency Act on Bank Investment." JOURNAL OF POLITICAL ECONOMY 22 (May 1914): 444-52.

        This is an examination of the effect of the new currency act upon present and future investment decision by banks.

933   Hoover, Ethel D. "Wholesale and Retail Prices in the Nineteenth Century." JOURNAL OF ECONOMIC HISTORY 18 (September 1958): 298-316.

        Hoover provides a summary of numerous attempts to compile wholesale and retail prices, including both techniques and sources of data used. Such summaries can be useful to economic historians.

934   Hoxie, Robert F. "The Silver Debate of 1890." JOURNAL OF POLITICAL ECONOMY 1 (September 1893): 535-87.

        A discussion of the political and economic environment of the 1890 silver debate, the bills in Congress are examined before the author examines the main economic postulates upon which the arguments are based.

935   Humphrey, Don D. "The Nature and Meaning of Rigid Prices, 1890-1933." JOURNAL OF POLITICAL ECONOMY 45 (October 1937): 651-61.

        An examination of the increasing rigidity of prices, the author attempts to analyze the effect of such rigidity on resource allocation.

936   James, John A. "Banking Market Structure, Risk, and the Pattern of Local Interest Rates in the United States, 1893-1911." REVIEW OF ECONOMICS AND STATISTICS 58 (November 1976): 453-62.

        This is an attempt to estimate a model of local interest rate determination using newly derived interest rate data for both country and reserve city banks in order to determine the relative influences of risk and local monopoly power on local interest rates.

937   _____. "Cost Functions of Post Bellum National Banks." EXPLORATIONS IN ECONOMIC HISTORY 15 (April 1978): 184-95.

This is an attempt to estimate the average cost functions of banks in order to determine the extent to which economies of scale existed. The effect of higher operating costs for southern banks is also considered as a possible explanation of the relative financial underdevelopment of the South. The cost levels for small banks were found to have declined significantly over the postbellum period.

938 _____. "The Development of the National Money Market, 1893-1911." JOURNAL OF ECONOMIC HISTORY 36 (December 1976): 878-916.

Using a model based on the capital-asset-pricing model, the author tests for interest rate convergence. The erosion of local monopoly power was found to have been of central importance for explaining convergence. The latter development was due more to the expansion of state banks than to that of national banks.

939 _____. MONEY AND CAPITAL MARKETS IN POSTBELLUM AMERICA. Princeton, N.J.: Princeton University Press, 1978. 293 p.

In an attempt to analyze the connection between the banking system and the short-term capital market, the author examines the causal factors for the convergence of interest rates. The institutional evolution is also examined, and appendixes of data and explanations of data are to be found at the back of the book.

940 Jones, Homer. "An Appraisal of the Rules and Procedures of Bank Supervision, 1929-1939." JOURNAL OF POLITICAL ECONOMY 48 (April 1940): 183-98.

He examines three periods: (1) panic and deposit contraction 1930-33; (2) reorganization and helping weaker banks 1933-34; and (3) recovery 1934 on. The latter period is one in which the supervisors were said to have impeded recovery and thus revised rules and procedures.

941 Kemmerer, Donald L. "The Marketing of Securities, 1930-1952." JOURNAL OF ECONOMIC HISTORY 12 (Fall 1952): 454-60.

Using three general periods--1776-1860, 1860-1929, and 1920-51--the author analyzes the evolution of the financial system. Most of the emphasis is on the third period and capital preservation, protection for the investors, and the elimination of costs in handling capital.

942 Kindahl, James K. "Economic Factors in Specie Resumption: The United States, 1865-79." JOURNAL OF POLITICAL ECONOMY 69 (February 1961): 30-48.

This article is an attempt to replace the inadequate explanations of how the premium on gold fell from its peak in 1865 to zero by the time of resumption in 1879. The author also tries to discover if resumption could have occurred earlier.

943 Kindleberger, Charles P. MANIAS, PANICS, AND CRASHES. New York: Basic Books, 1978. 271 p.

This is an attempt to examine the causes and problems of panics and crashes for a small group of countries for the period 1720 to the present.

944 Kohn, Ernest, and Speagle, Richard E. "Employment and Output in Banking, 1919-1955." REVIEW OF ECONOMICS AND STATISTICS 40 (February 1958): 22-35.

One of the first studies on the manpower needs of the service sectors, the author attempts to analyze the changes which have occurred in the manpower needs of the banking sector.

945 Krooss, Herman E., ed. DOCUMENTARY HISTORY OF BANKING AND CURRENCY IN THE UNITED STATES. 4 vols. New York: McGraw-Hill, 1969. 3,232 p.

This set contains over three hundred documents which record the history of currency and banking from 1637 to 1968. There is an introduction by Paul A. Samuelson and over thirty-one hundred pages of documents. It is the most comprehensive work published to date.

946 Kuh, Edwin. "Five Decades of United States Saving." JOURNAL OF ECONOMIC HISTORY 16 (June 1956): 211-18.

This is a highly favorable critique of Raymond Goldsmith's A STUDY OF SAVINGS IN THE U.S. (no. 918). The importance that this work will assume in future research is considered, especially the interaction between financial and real factors.

947 Kuznets, Simon. CAPITAL IN THE AMERICAN ECONOMY. Princeton, N.J.: Princeton University Press, 1961. 664 p.

Starting with 1870, the work is a mixture of estimation, classification, explanation, and speculation in order to explain long-term capital stock movements. Included is evidence on financing as well as formation of capital stock. Contains very extensive tables of data.

948 Lake, Wilfred S. "The End of the Suffolk System." JOURNAL OF ECONOMIC HISTORY 7 (November 1947): 183-207.

A system which served to guarantee convertibility of currencies, the Suffolk system broke down when the out-of-town banks refused to accept the Boston banks' notes in exchange for their own.

949 Laughlin, J. Laurence. "The Banking and Currency Act of 1913, Parts I & II." JOURNAL OF POLITICAL ECONOMY 22 (April 1914): 293-318; (May 1914): 405-35.

This article is a survey of recent reforms and proposals in order to understand the weaknesses of the U.S. banking and monetary system. The motives and results of these reforms are analyzed.

950 _____. "Elastic Currency and the Money Market." JOURNAL OF POLITICAL ECONOMY 15 (April 1907): 229-31.

Using the collapse of the New York Stock Exchange as a focal point, the author examines the importance of money stock elasticity. He discusses the inherent problems regarding the expansion of a bank's demand obligations as an expansion in its resources and assuming that all exchanges in the United States are facilitated by the use of bank notes.

951 _____. "Prices and the International Movement of Specie." JOURNAL OF POLITICAL ECONOMY 10 (September 1902): 514-36.

This is an examination of the rejection of the quantity theory of money and its relationship to the fundamental priciples of international trade. Price making and the international flow of gold are examined.

952 _____. "Withdrawls of the Treasury Notes of 1890." JOURNAL OF POLITICAL ECONOMY 6 (March 1898): 248-49.

How the treasury notes were retired and replaced by silver certificates is the focus of this work. Light is cast on the deficit of the treasury in 1890 and on future monetary reform.

953 Lerner, Eugene M. "Inflation in the Confederacy, 1861-1865." In STUDIES IN THE QUANTITY THEORY OF MONEY, edited by Milton Friedman, pp. 163-75. Chicago: University of Chicago Press, 1956.

Analyzing the causes of inflation--ever expanding stock of money, a sharp rise in velocity, and a drop in real income-- the author attempts to examine the behavior of these forces and their interrelation.

954 _____. "The Monetary and Fiscal Programs of the Confederate Government 1861-65." JOURNAL OF POLITICAL ECONOMY 62 (December 1954): 506-22.

This is an examination of wartime statistics on the Confederate government's monetary and fiscal policies.

955 McCusker, John J. "Sources of Investment Capital in the Colonial Philadelphia Shipping Industry." JOURNAL OF ECONOMIC HISTORY 32 (March 1972): 146-57.

This is a very general discussion of the sources of investment funds in the colonial period, using Philadelphia shipping as a point of analysis and measurement.

956 Macesich, George. "Sources of Monetary Disturbances in the United States, 1834-1845." JOURNAL OF ECONOMIC HISTORY 20 (September 1960): 407-34.

Arguing that internal disturbances may have been equally as important as external disturbances in this period, the author checks his arguments against what data was available. The hypothesis is not rigorously tested.

957 MacVeagh, Franklin. "Banking and Currency Reform." JOURNAL OF POLITICAL ECONOMY 19 (December 1911): 809-18.

This is a review of the needs for currency and banking reform based on a discussion of the panics, uncertainties, and rigidities of circulation. Recommendations for reform are proffered.

958 McVey, Frank L. "Reclassification of the Paper Currency." JOURNAL OF POLITICAL ECONOMY 10 (June 1902): 437-42.

Analyzing the composition of the currency in 1900 and 1902, the author reviews the progress of the reaffirmation of the gold stand, the systematization of the currency, and the provision for the circulation of silver certificates undertaken in 1900.

959 Magee, James D. "Food Prices and the Cost of Living." JOURNAL OF POLITICAL ECONOMY 18 (April 1910): 294-308.

Prices at the farm, wholesale, and retail level are examined, and the sources and methods of estimation are also included.

960 _____. "Money and Prices, I and II." JOURNAL OF POLITICAL ECONOMY 21 (October 1913): 681-711; (November 1913): 798-818.

This is a statistical analysis of the price-money relationship for prices in general and groups of prices in particular.

961 _____. "The World's Production of Gold and Silver from 1493 to 1905." JOURNAL OF POLITICAL ECONOMY 18 (January 1910): 50-58.

Tables of estimates of the world's production of gold and silver both by weight and value are provided along with a discussion of the sources and methods of estimation.

962 Martin, David A. "Bimetallism in the United States before 1850." JOURNAL OF POLITICAL ECONOMY 76 (May-June 1968): 428-42.

After examining the works of various "hard money" writers, Martin concludes that gold and silver prevailed in the United States except for 1822-33. The extension of legal tender to foreign coins also improved the performance of the bimetallic standard.

963 _____. "The Changing Role of Foreign Money in the United States." JOURNAL OF ECONOMIC HISTORY 37 (December 1977): 1009-1027.

This is an attempt at analyzing the early efforts to obtain a national currency and those which finally made it possible to terminate the lawful status of foreign money.

964 _____. "Metallism Small Notes, and Jackson's War with the B.U.S." EXPLORATIONS IN ECONOMIC HISTORY 11 (Spring 1974): 227-48.

Metallism and its underlying influence of Jacksonian policy is developed in this paper as a supplementary explanation of the confrontation between Jackson and the Second Bank of the United States. Jackson's plan was to replace all paper money of less than $20 with foreign and domestic specie.

965 _____. "1853: The End of Bimetallism in the United States." JOURNAL OF ECONOMIC HISTORY 33 (December 1973): 825-44.

The author argues that although bimetallism existed de jure, it was nonexistant on a de facto basis after the Coinage Act of 1853.

966 _____. "U.S. Gold Production Prior to the California Gold Rush." EXPLORATIONS IN ECONOMIC HISTORY 13 (October 1976): 437-49.

This is an attempt to assess the importance of gold production in the United States prior to the 1840s using new estimates of the percentages of total production deposited at the mints. One can conjecture that the United States was the world's major gold producer two decades before the California discoveries.

967 Mayer, Thomas. MONETARY POLICY IN THE UNITED STATES. New York: Random House, 1968. 238 p.

Although this book contains mostly post-World War II information, there is a section which treats the interwar period as well. It is an excellent treatment of monetary policy, tools, and theory.

968 _____. "Money and the Great Depression: A Critique of Professor Temin's Thesis." EXPLORATIONS IN ECONOMIC HISTORY 15 (April 1978): 127–45.

This is a discussion of at least seven issues raised by Temin in his book (see no. 1021). It is argued that although the book possesses some difficult problems in its analysis, Temin has raised some very interesting questions regarding the causes of the Great Depression.

969 Meade, Edward S. "The Deposit Reserve System of the National Bank Law." JOURNAL OF POLITICAL ECONOMY 6 (March 1898): 209–24.

Problems of rigidity in the banking system, of ascertaining the real value of reserves, and the adequacy of reserve levels are considered in this place.

970 _____. "The Fall in the Price of Silver since 1872." JOURNAL OF POLITICAL ECONOMY 5 (June 1897): 316–39.

This is an analysis of the demand for silver and the cost of producing it and the effects of the price of gold on the price of silver.

971 Meerman, Jacob P. "The Climax of the Bank War: Biddle's Contraction, 1833–34." JOURNAL OF POLITICAL ECONOMY 71 (August 1963): 378–88.

Although the data are not complete, the author argues that the situation is such a perfect laboratory experiment that it warrants study. It is an analysis of the monetary contraction which took place.

972 Million, John Wilson. "Debate on the National Bank Act of 1863." JOURNAL OF POLITICAL ECONOMY 2 (March 1894): 251–80.

Determining whence came the National Banking system is the objective of this article, along with an analysis of the goals of the original act.

973 Mitchell, Wesley C. "The Prices of American Stocks: 1890–1909." JOURNAL OF POLITICAL ECONOMY 18 (May 1910): 345–80.

An index of U.S. stock prices is presented in order to compare movements in these prices with changes in business prosperity. Comparisons are made on various groupings of the stocks vis-a-vis the economic condition.

974 _____. "The Prices of Preferred and Common Stocks: 1890-1909."
JOURNAL OF POLITICAL ECONOMY 18 (July 1910): 513-24.

> The causes of the fluctuations of stock prices during this peri-
> od and a large amount of statistical evidence are presented.

975 _____. "Rates of Interest and the Prices of Investment Securities: 1890-
1909." JOURNAL OF POLITICAL ECONOMY 19 (April 1911): 269-
308.

> Table of bond prices, interest yields on securities, commercial
> paper, and call loans are provided and a comparison is made
> between those for the United States and Europe during the
> period.

976 _____. "The Role of Money in Economic History." JOURNAL OF ECO-
NOMIC HISTORY 4 (December 1944): 61-67.

> An analysis of the development of a social organization when
> money is introduced and refined, the article considers the
> effects of different forms of money on men's thinking and habits.

977 _____. "Security Prices and Interest Rates in 1910-12." JOURNAL OF
POLITICAL ECONOMY 21 (June 1913): 500-522.

> This is an update of the previously published tables of security
> prices and interest rates for each month of the years 1890-
> 1909.

978 _____. "Suspension of Specie Payments, December 1861." JOURNAL
OF POLITICAL ECONOMY 7 (June 1899): 289-326.

> This is a comparison of the policies of S.P. Chase and H.
> Cobb, who were secretaries of the treasury under Lincoln,
> especially as related to borrowing, interest rates, and on the
> supervision of specie payments.

979 _____. "The Value of 'Greenbacks' during the Civil War." JOURNAL
OF POLITICAL ECONOMY 6 (March 1898): 139-67.

> An attempt is made to discern the reasons for fluctuations in
> the gold premium and to analyze the replacement of coin by
> paper in 1861.

980 Morton, Richard L. "The Virginia State Debt and Internal Improvements,
1820-38." JOURNAL OF POLITICAL ECONOMY 25 (April 1917): 339-
73.

> Starting with the debt position of Virginia when it entered the
> union, the author analyzes the sectional strife and political
> environment within which these internal improvements were
> made.

981   Moulton, Harold G. "Commercial Banking and Capital Formation, Part
       I, II, III and IV." JOURNAL OF POLITICAL ECONOMY 26 (May
       1917): 484-508; (June 1918): 638-63; (July 1918): 705-31; (November
       1918): 849-81.

       By studying the institutions which affect capital formation and
       the conventional theories of commercial banking, the author
       examines the effect of wars' reduction in the supply of capi-
       tal goods. Parts 2, 3, and 4 consider the commercial banks
       as they relate to commerce, not industry, and must therefore
       consider banking legislation. Various types of loans and
       liquidity problems are discussed.

982   _____. "The Surplus in Commercial Banking." JOURNAL OF POLITI-
       CAL ECONOMY 25 (December 1917): 1003-18.

       Examining the functions and the causes of the surplus in com-
       mercial banking, the author argues that they lessen the securi-
       ty of depositors rather than increase their security.

983   Newcomb, Simon. "Has the Standard Gold Dollar Appreciated?" JOUR-
       NAL OF POLITICAL ECONOMY 1 (September 1893): 503-12.

       Before attempting to determine whether the dollar has appreci-
       ated, the author discusses various abstract notions of value and
       its measurement.

984   North, Douglas C. "Life Insurance and Investments Banking at the Time
       of the Armstrong Investigation of 1905-1906." JOURNAL OF ECONOMIC
       HISTORY 14 (September 1954): 209-28.

       This is an attempt to fill a void in literature regarding invest-
       ment bankers and the organization of financial institutions as
       well as their reorientation toward the securities markets. North
       concentrates on the relationship between the large life insurance
       companies and investment banking.

985   Olmstead, Alan L. "David vs. Bigelow Revisited: Antebellum American
       Interest Rates." JOURNAL OF ECONOMIC HISTORY 34 (June 1974):
       483-91.

       The purpose of this work is to rescue Bigelow's estimates for
       the year 1848 and to offer an explanation for the differences
       between the two series. Some effort is also made to explain
       why rates were so high in 1848.

986   Patterson, E.M. "Certain Changes in New York's Position as a Financial
       Center." JOURNAL OF POLITICAL ECONOMY 21 (June 1913): 523-
       39.

       This is an analysis of the effects of cash withdrawls for crop

moving on the cash levels, reserves, and the declining positions of New York banks.

987   Patton, Eugene B.   "Secretary Shaw and Precedents as to Treasury Control over the Money Market."   JOURNAL OF POLITICAL ECONOMY
15 (February 1907):   65-87.

Whether or not the treasury should actively control the money
market is an issue, and the actual instances where Shaw did
so as well as the policy in the 1860s are all discussed.

988   Perkins, Edwin J.   "Foreign Interest Rates in American Financial Markets:
A Revised Series of Dollar-Sterling Exchange Rates 1835-1900."   JOUR-
NAL OF ECONOMIC HISTORY   38 (June 1978):   392-417.

This is a revision of the estimates produced by Lance Davis
and J.R.T. Hughes in "A Dollar-Sterling Exchange 1803-1894."
ECONOMIC HISTORY REVIEW   12 (March 1960):   52-78.   The
new estimates use the U.S. interest rates to discount the value
of time bills that were sold by the British to U.S. banks. This
alters the estimates of exchange rates considerably.

989   Powers, Fred Perry.   "No Silver Grievance Exists."   JOURNAL OF PO-
LITICAL ECONOMY   1 (September 1893):   596-600.

This is an argument against the demonetization of silver, which
cites the arguments used by congressmen as well.

990   Redlich, Fritz.   "American Banking and Growth in the Nineteenth Century: Epistemological Reflections."   EXPLORATIONS IN ECONOMIC
HISTORY   10 (Spring 1973):   305-14.

This is a reply to Sylla's work (see no. 1017) which brings
forth concepts from the German historical school as well as
some issues from current methodological discussions.

991   _____.   "Bank Administration, 1780-1914."   JOURNAL OF ECONOMIC
HISTORY   12 (Fall 1952):   438-53.

This is a test of Redlich's hypothesis regarding the role of
business administration in economic growth.   His data come
from American banking administrations for the years 1780-
1914.

992   Reed, Harold L.   "Federal Reserve Policy from the Spring of 1923 to the
Close of 1924."   JOURNAL OF POLITICAL ECONOMY   37 (August 1929):
400-429.

Starting with the trade recession of 1923, the absence of per-
plexities in the minds of monetary authorities during 1923, and
the gold inflow in 1923, the author examines the activities of

the reserve banks and the Federal Reserve, considering both foreign and domestic information.

993 _____. "Recent Federal Reserve Policy." JOURNAL OF POLITICAL ECONOMY 37 (June 1929): 249-84.

This is an evaluation of Federal Reserve policy within the context of the postwar crisis years, the credit situation at the beginning of 1922, the rate problem during that year, and industrial and credit developments in 1922.

994 Reynolds, George M. "The Effect of the European War on American Credits." JOURNAL OF POLITICAL ECONOMY 22 (December 1914): 925-36.

Have European hostilities affected U.S. financial condition, and if so, how? This is the focus of this paper as the author examines clearing house loan certificates and emergency notes authorized under the Aldrich-Vreeland Act of 1908. Historical references to periods of previous periods of interdependence are included.

995 Ritter, Lawrence S. "Official Central Banking Theory in the United States, 1939-61." JOURNAL OF POLITICAL ECONOMY 70 (February 1962): 14-29.

By examining the four editions of the Federal Reserve's publication PURPOSES AND FUNCTIONS, the author attempts to trace changes in the Federal Reserve's view regarding the objectives of monetary policy, methods employable, the channels of monetary policy, and the ideas of intellectuals.

996 Rix, M.S. "The Premium on U.S. Dollar Securities." ECONOMIC JOURNAL 60 (December 1950): 686-96.

This is an examination of the dollar premium which existed on the London stock exchange, how it came about, and the determination of its size.

997 Rockoff, Hugh. "Regional Interest Rates and Bank Failures, 1870-1914." EXPLORATIONS IN ECONOMIC HISTORY 14 (January 1977): 90-95.

Although nothing is proven in this article, it is argued and substantiated by some empirical evidences that the divergence among rates of return on bank stock was due to the premium investors' demand to place their funds in a particular bank's stock. The premium represented the risk of bank failure.

998 _____. "Varieties of Banking and Regional Economic Development in

the United States." JOURNAL OF ECONOMIC HISTORY 35 (March 1975): 160-81.

This is an assessment of the impact on financial development of three forms of regulation: (1) commercial banking laws; (2) usury laws; and (3) mutual savings bank laws.

999 Roll, Richard. "Interest Rates and Price Expectations during the Civil War." JOURNAL OF ECONOMIC HISTORY 32 (June 1972): 476-98.

It was found that the bond prices measured in gold did reflect the major battles, but gold's fluctuating greenback premium masked the movement of bond prices expressed in greenbacks. This illustrates the usefulness of capital asset price data in measuring the opinions of those who have long been dead. It also demonstrates that small efficient capital markets can exist in technologically less developed states.

1000 Roose, Kenneth D. "Federal Reserve Policy and the Recession of 1937-1938." REVIEW OF ECONOMICS AND STATISTICS 32 (May 1950): 177-83.

This is an examination of the policy role of the Federal Reserve just before and during the recession of 1937-38. References are made to other people's work dealing with the period of 1945-48 and with deflation.

1001 Rostow, W.W. "Some Aspects of Price Control and Rationing." AMERICAN ECONOMIC REVIEW 32 (June 1942): 486-500.

Why did the government freeze retail prices on May 18, 1942? What were the gaps in this freeze, the impact on replacement costs and production? These are questions addressed in this paper with respect to particular industries, such as sugar.

1002 Scheiber, Harry N. "The Pet Banks in Jacksonian Politics and Finance, 1833-1841." JOURNAL OF ECONOMIC HISTORY 23 (June 1963): 196-214.

This is an assessment of the economic impact of the financial policy of the Jackson and Van Buren administrations. Treasury operations during this period are reviewed to determine the relationship between the banks and the treasury.

1003 Schoffner, Robert C. "The Relation of the New Currency Act to the Work of Commercial Paper Houses." JOURNAL OF POLITICAL ECONOMY 22 (April 1914): 358-64.

The functions of commercial paper houses are examined and the effect of the new currency act on these houses is also discussed, with respect to method of operation, the extension of merchandise credits, the paper buying ability of the banks, the reserve levels, and the location of reserves.

1004 Schur, Leon M. "The Second Bank of the United States and the Inflation after the War of 1812." JOURNAL OF POLITICAL ECONOMY 68 (April 1960): 118-34.

As a central bank, the activities and policies of the Second Bank of the United States are analyzed in the framework of its responsibilities and problems. This is the first attempt at such an analysis.

1005 Schwartz, Anna J. "An Attempt at Synthesis in American Banking History." JOURNAL OF ECONOMIC HISTORY 7 (November 1947): 208-17.

This is a criticism of Fritz Redlich's THE MOLDING OF AMERICAN BANKING: MEN AND IDEAS: PART I. The author argues that it is an adequate history of banking but then proceeds to show why it is an inadequate treatment of bank practices and the contributions of leading theorists to the development of banking.

1006 _____. "The Beginning of Competitive Banking in Philadelphia, 1782-1809." JOURNAL OF POLITICAL ECONOMY 55 (October 1947): 417-31.

By tracing the evolution of banking in Philadelphia the author shows how banks responded to competition and that competition did not impede growth. The article tells how banks were able to adjust to competition and continue carrying on business.

1007 _____. "Monetary Trends in the United States and the United Kingdom, 1878-1970: Selected Findings." JOURNAL OF ECONOMIC HISTORY 35 (March 1975): 138-59.

Examining the development of both countries, the author finds financial unification but physical independence. Various financial variables are compared between the two countries.

1008 Scott, William A. "Rates on the New York Money Market, 1896-1906." JOURNAL OF POLITICAL ECONOMY 16 (May 1908): 273-98.

Illustrating the usual forces producing fluctuations in market rates, this study examines the factors contributing to these fluctuations during the period 1896-1906. The broader view of money market conditions and the general industrial situation are also examined.

1009 Selden, Richard T. "Monetary Velocity in the United States." In STUD-

IES IN THE QUANTITY THEORY OF MONEY, edited by Milton Friedman, pp. 179-257. Chicago: University of Chicago Press, 1956.

Covering velocity of money from 1839 to 1951, the author attempts to deal with the cause of change in velocity and both cyclical and secular trends in the series.

1010 Shushka, Marie Elizabeth. "The Antebellum Money Market and the Economic Impact of the Bank War." JOURNAL OF ECONOMIC HISTORY 36 (December 1976): 809-35.

The author constructs and tests a model of the antebellum money market. Due to its effect on the pattern of financial behavior the Bank War affected the economy. Wildcat banking was not characteristic of the post-Bank period, but the Panic of 1837 was the result of a severe monetary contraction.

1011 Simon, Matthew. "The Hot Money Movement and the Private Exchange Pool Proposal of 1896." JOURNAL OF ECONOMIC HISTORY 20 (March 1960): 31-50.

Arguing that the hot money movements and government intervention in the foreign exchange market during the great depression were not peculiar to the situation, the author examines the reaction in 1846 to the nomination of W.J. Bryan on his free silver platform.

1012 Smiley, Gene. "Interest Rate Movement in the United States, 1888-1913." JOURNAL OF ECONOMIC HISTORY 35 (September 1975): 591-620.

Using newly derived rate of return estimates for banks the convergence and/or divergence of short-term interest rates is examined. They are developed for both the state and city levels rather than the regional level alone, which allows for more accurate comparison across the United States.

1013 Sprague, O.M.W. "Commercial Paper and the Federal Reserve Banks." JOURNAL OF POLITICAL ECONOMY 22 (May 1914): 443-63.

An examination of the criteria the Federal Reserve should use in determining what constitutes eligible paper for discounting, the article also looks at safety and liquidity regulations as well as the implications for credit expansion.

1014 _____. "The Reserve Association and the Improvement of Methods of Making Payments between the Banks." JOURNAL OF POLITICAL ECONOMY 19 (December 1911): 831-40.

A review of the improvements in interbank transfers and the float are discussed with recommendations for further improvements being offered. The institutions involved with interbank check clearing are also considered.

1015 Stevens, Edward J. "Composition of the Money Stock Prior to the Civil War." JOURNAL OF MONEY CREDIT AND BANKING 3 (February 1971): 84-101.

> This is an analysis of the period 1847-57 in which gold is discovered in California, an independent treasury system is established, and coinage laws are revised. The author argues that the apparent impacts of gold were not those claimed by previous investigators, namely, that the three "proximate" determinants of the money stock were not independent. A comment on this article appears in the same journal, volume 5 (November 1973): 1000-1006, by Douglas Shetter.

1016 Swanson, William Walker. "The Crisis of 1860 and the First Issue of Clearing House Certificates, Parts I and II." JOURNAL OF POLITICAL ECONOMY 16 (February 1908): 65-75; (April 1908): 212-26.

> The industrial and agricultural climate of 1850-60 is examined, including the recovery from the panic of 1857 and the unsettled political condition of the United States and Europe in 1860. Part 2 examines the causes of the crisis of 1860, the drain on specie, and the discounting of southern paper. The role of the clearing house is evaluated.

1017 Sylla, Richard W. "American Banking and Growth in the Nineteenth Century: A Partial View of the Terrain." EXPLORATIONS IN ECONOMIC HISTORY 9 (Winter 1971-72): 197-228.

> This is an alternative framework for discussing the development of the U.S. banking system. It attempts to replace "quest for soundness" as a rationale for bank behavior.

1018 _____. "Federal Policy, Banking Market Structure, and Capital Mobilization in the United States, 1863-1913." JOURNAL OF ECONOMIC HISTORY 29 (December 1969): 657-86.

> Concentration is on the events beginning with the first National Banking Act and the subsequent developments in the banking industry and patterns of capital movements among the various industrial sectors.

1019 _____. "Forgotten Men of Money: Private Bankers in Early U.S. History." JOURNAL OF ECONOMIC HISTORY 36 (March 1976): 173-88.

> Using some relatively unknown quantitative evidence which provides rough measures of the private banker's numerical importance as compared with the incorporated banks, the author attempts to illustrate the importance of these types of banks in the financial system during the period. A comment by Lance E. Davis follows on pages 189-93 of the same journal number.

1020 _____. "The United States, 1863-1913." In BANKING AND ECO-
NOMIC DEVELOPMENT, edited by Rondo Cameron, pp. 232-62. New
York: Oxford University Press, 1972.

> This is an examination of the relationship between developments
> in the banking sector and the conditions for industrial finance.
> A cross-country comparison is also provided.

1021 Temin, Peter. DID MONETARY FORCES CAUSE THE GREAT DEPRESSION?
New York: W.W. Norton and Co., 1976. 201 p.

> This is an attempt to apply the tools of macroeconomic theory
> to the evidence that is available from the period 1929-31.
> Using this theoretical approach the author attempts to test
> various hypotheses regarding the causes of the Great Depres-
> sion.

1022 _____. "The Economic Consequences of the Bank War." JOURNAL OF
POLITICAL ECONOMY 76 (March-April 1968): 257-74.

> The author argues that Jackson's veto of the Second Bank of
> the United State's charter renewal was not responsible for the
> ensuing credit expansion and inflation. It was the result of
> a complex combination of events, most of which were uncon-
> nected with the political action of Jackson.

1023 _____. THE JACKSONIAN ECONOMY. New York: W.W. Norton
and Co., 1969. 208 p.

> This is an attempt to explain the occurrences which surrounded
> Jackson's vetoing of the charter renewal for the Second Bank
> of the United States up to and including the Panic of 1837.
> The author concludes that, contrary to traditional interpreta-
> tions, Jackson was not responsible for the economic difficulties
> which followed his veto. Appendixes on data are included for
> the reader.

1024 Timberlake, Richard H., Jr. "Ideological Factors in Specie Resumption
and Treasury Policy." JOURNAL OF ECONOMIC HISTORY 24 (March
1964): 29-52.

> In this examination of the period 1865-79, the conduct of
> Congress and the treasury are examined. The role of the
> treasury as a central bank is also discussed.

1025 _____. "Repeal of Silver Monetization in the Late Nineteenth Century."
JOURNAL OF MONEY CREDIT AND BANKING 10 (February 1978): 27-
45.

> Most have argued that the free silver movement died with the
> defeat of W.J. Bryan by McKinley in 1896, but the author

argues persuasively that silver had died in 1893 with repeal
of the silver purchase clause from the Treasury Note Act of
1890 by a Democratic Congress and president.

1026 _____. "The Specie Standard and Central Banking in the United States
before 1860." JOURNAL OF ECONOMIC HISTORY 21 (September 1961):
318-42.

Instead of judging central banking by today's criteria, the
author examines the emergence of central banking ideas and
institutions within the context of the specie standard.

1027 Trescott, Paul B. "Federal-State Financial Relations, 1790-1860." JOUR-
NAL OF ECONOMIC HISTORY 15 (September 1955): 227-45.

This is an analysis of federal-state interaction in the financing of particular programs. The trade-off between the stronger
revenue-raising ability of the federal government and the de-
sire for autonomy on the part of local and state governments
is the focal point of analysis.

1028 _____. FINANCING AMERICAN ENTERPRISE. New York: Harper &
Row, 1963. 304 p.

While not totally ignoring the monetary functions of banks,
the author concentrates his efforts on explaining the connection between bank credit control and capital formation in the
developing economy. Some considerable effort is spent on
the analysis of government regulations for banks.

1029 Veblen, Thorstein. "Credit and Prices." JOURNAL OF POLITICAL
ECONOMY 13 (June 1905): 460-72.

The relationship between uses of credit in business and the
price level are the focus of this study, with special emphasis
on the factors surrounding credit expansion and the resulting
movements in the price level. The functions of a bank are
also discussed.

1030 Venit, Abraham H. "Isaac Bronson: His Banking Theory and the Financial
Controversies of the Jacksonian Period." JOURNAL OF ECONOMIC HIS-
TORY 5 (November 1945): 201-14.

The thoughts, banking policies, and theories of Bronson are
used to illustrate the banking climate during the Jacksonian
era.

1031 Villard, Henry Hilgard. "The Federal Reserve System's Monetary Policy
in 1931 and 1932." JOURNAL OF POLITICAL ECONOMY 45 (December
1937): 721-39.

This is an examination of the impact of possible alternatives to the Federal Reserve's 1931-32 policy. An attempt is made to determine if such policies would have curved the rate of decline.

1032 Walker, Francis A. "The Free-Coinage of Silver." JOURNAL OF PO-LITICAL ECONOMY 1 (March 1893): 163-78.

The author divides the Silver party into three sections: (1) inflationist; (2) bimetallists; and (3) silver producers. Using these divisions, he is able to examine the reasons for the shared view of the party and the effects of the party on political decisions.

1033 Walters, Raymond, Jr. "The Origins of the Second Bank of the United States." JOURNAL OF POLITICAL ECONOMY 53 (June 1945): 115-32.

This is a revision of earlier writings introducing new concepts of economic theory which were not present at the turn of the century, and introducing newly exposed collections of pertinent manuscripts.

1034 Warburton, Clark. "Has Bank Supervision Been in Conflict with Monetary Policy?" REVIEW OF ECONOMICS AND STATISTICS 34 (February 1952): 69-74.

Using the period 1920-30, the author thoroughly examines the assumption that bank supervision during critical periods has run directly counter to monetary policy.

1035 _____. "Quantity and Frequency of Use of Money in the United States, 1919-1945." JOURNAL OF POLITICAL ECONOMY 54 (October 1946): 436-50.

This is a study of changes in the income velocity of money as well as the fluctuations that occur in the quantity of money itself. Special attention is given to periods of business fluctuation and wartime.

1036 _____. "Variations in Economic Growth and Banking Developments in the United States from 1835 to 1885." JOURNAL OF ECONOMIC HISTORY 18 (September 1958): 283-97.

This is a test of the hypothesis that banking and monetary developments should be regarded as the primary causal element in the variations in the rate of growth of the economy.

1037 Wattereau, James O. "The Branches of the First Bank of the United States." JOURNAL OF ECONOMIC HISTORY 2 (December 1942): 66-100.

This article focuses on the establishment of the eight branches, their operation, and the degree of liquidity that existed when the First Bank of the United States was discontinued.

1038 Weiss, Roger W. "The Issue of Paper Money in the American Colonies, 1720-1774." JOURNAL OF ECONOMIC HISTORY 30 (December 1970): 770-84.

This examination of the ability of the colonies to provide monetary elasticity through the issue of paper money also includes an estimate of the composition of the money stock.

1039 Wicker, Elmus R. "A Reconsideration of Federal Reserve Policy during the 1920-1921 Depression." JOURNAL OF ECONOMIC HISTORY 26 (June 1966): 223-38.

Arguing that others have underestimated the extent to which controlled deflation was a result of the Federal Reserve's view of the money supply mechanism, the author sets up a money supply model and examines the legal constraints on bank policy.

1040 _____. "Federal Reserve Monetary Policy, 1922-1933: A Reinterpretation." JOURNAL OF POLITICAL ECONOMY 73 (August 1965): 325-43.

This article provides an alternative interpretation of why Federal Reserve behavior appeared to be consistent and countercyclical in the period 1922-29, but inconsistent and procyclical between 1929 and 1933. The argument attempts to identify the concern for foreign currency convertibility as the crucial variable in the Federal Reserve's decision process.

1041 Willet, Thomas D. "International Specie Flows and American Monetary Stability, 1834-1860." JOURNAL OF ECONOMIC HISTORY 28 (March 1968): 28-50.

Examining earlier treatments of the interrelation of international and domestic monetary movements of funds, the author sets up his own model in which the money stock affects domestic stability. Analogies are also drawn to modern day problems.

1042 Wimmer, Larry T. "The Gold Crisis of 1869: Stabilizing or Destabilizing Speculation under Floating Exchange Rates?" EXPLORATIONS IN ECONOMIC HISTORY 12 (April 1975): 105-22.

This is an analysis of one man's attempt at manipulating gold markets during 1869. Jay Gould was successful for only a very short time and only then with the implicit sanction of the U.S. government. The author relates this to the current-day fears about floating exchange rates.

1043 Youngman, Anna. "The Growth in Financial Banking." JOURNAL OF POLITICAL ECONOMY 14 (July 1906): 435-43.

> Statistical data are presented regarding the relation of the level of bank investments in stock, bonds, and other securities to the level of individual deposits during the period 1889-1905. Reasons for growth and the decision-making process of the banks are examined.

7.2 GENERAL LISTINGS

1044 Abbott, Charles Cortez. THE NEW YORK BOND MARKET, 1920-1930. Cambridge, Mass.: Harvard University Press, 1937. 224 p.

1045 Bolles, A.S. THE FINANCIAL HISTORY OF THE UNITED STATES. 3 vols. New York: A. Appleton and Co., 1879-86. 371, 721, 585 p.

1046 Bullock, C.J. ESSAYS ON MONETARY HISTORY OF THE UNITED STATES. New York: Macmillan Co., 1900. 292 p.

1047 Burgess, George L. THE RESERVE BANKS AND THE MONEY MARKET. New York: Harper & Brothers, 1936. 342 p.

1048 Conant, Charles A. "The Gold Exchange Standard in the Light of Experience." ECONOMIC JOURNAL 19 (June 1909): 190-200.

1049 Davis, A.M. CURRENCY AND BANKING IN THE PROVINCE OF MASSACHUSETTS BAY. New York: Macmillan Co., 1901. 481 p.

1050 Dewey, Davis Rich. FINANCIAL HISTORY OF THE UNITED STATES. New York: Longmans, Green and Co., 1934. 600 p.

1051 Einzig, P. "Gold Points and Central Banks." ECONOMIC JOURNAL 39 (September 1939): 379-87.

1052 Eiteman, Wilford J. "The Economic Significance of Brokers' Loans." JOURNAL OF POLITICAL ECONOMY 40 (October 1932): 677-90.

1053 Gayer, A.D. "The Proposed Amendments of the U.S. Federal Reserve Act." ECONOMIC JOURNAL 45 (June 1935): 286-95.

1054 Goldenweisser, E.A.; Thurston, Elliot; and Hammond, Bray, eds. BANKING STUDIES. Washington, D.C.: Federal Reserve Board of Governors, 1941. 496 p.

1055 Gouge, William M. A SHORT HISTORY OF PAPER MONEY AND BANK-ING IN THE UNITED STATES. 2 vols. New York: A.M. Kelley, 1968. 140, 240 p.

1056 Greff, Albert O. THE COMMERCIAL PAPER HOUSE IN THE UNITED STATES. Cambridge, Mass.: Harvard University Press, 1938. 459 p.

1057 Hardy, Charles O. CREDIT POLICIES OF THE FEDERAL RESERVE SYSTEM. Washington, D.C.: Brookings Institution, 1932. 374 p.

1058 _____. IS THERE ENOUGH GOLD? Washington, D.C.: Brookings Institution, 1936. 212 p.

1059 Homan, Paul T., and Machlup, Fritz, eds. FINANCING AMERICAN PROSPERITY. New York: Twentieth Century Fund, 1945. 508 p.

1960 Jones, Homer. "Insurance of Bank Deposits in U.S.A." ECONOMIC JOURNAL 48 (December 1938): 695-706.

1061 Kemmerer, E.W. "Emergency Currency in the United States." ECO-NOMIC JOURNAL 24 (December 1914): 604-5.

1062 Keynes, J.M. "Member Bank Reserves in the United States." ECONOM-IC JOURNAL 42 (March 1932): 27-31.

1063 Kirk, J.H. "Silver: A Study in Monetary Instability." ECONOMIC JOURNAL 41 (September 1931): 385-94.

1064 Knox, John Jay. UNITED STATES NOTES. New York: Charles Scribner's Sons, 1885. 247 p.

1065 Krooss, Herman E., and Blyn, Martin. A HISTORY OF FINANCIAL IN-TERMEDIARIES. New York: Random House, 1971. 254 p.

1066 Lockhard, Oliver C. "The Development of Interbank Borrowing in The National System 1869-1914, Parts I and II." JOURNAL OF POLITICAL ECONOMY 29 (February 1921): 138-60; (March 1921): 222-40.

1066a McAvoy, Walter. "The Economic Importance of the Commercial Paper House." JOURNAL OF POLITICAL ECONOMY 30 (February 1922): 78-87.

1067 Mavor, James. "Recent Financial Movements in the United States." ECONOMIC JOURNAL 14 (June 1904): 169-87.

1068 Moulton, Harold G. THE FORMATION OF CAPITAL. Washington, D.C.: Brookings Institution, 1935. 207 p.

1069 Nugent, Rolf. CONSUMER CREDIT AND ECONOMIC STABILITY. New York: Russell Sage Foundation, 1939. 420 p.

1070 Pasvolsky, Leo. CURRENT MONETARY ISSUES. Washington, D.C.: Brookings Institution, 1933. 192 p.

1071 Riefler, Winfield W. MONEY RATES AND MONEY MARKETS IN THE UNITED STATES. New York: Harper & Brothers, 1930. 259 p.

1072 Ripley, W.Z. FINANCIAL HISTORY OF VIRGINIA, 1609-1776. New York: Columbia College, 1893. 170 p.

1073 Schlesinger, Arthur M. THE AGE OF JACKSON. Boston: Little, Brown and Co., 1945. 577 p.

1074 Slichter, Sumner H. TOWARDS STABILITY: THE PROBLEM OF ECONOMIC BALANCE. New York: Henry Holt and Co., 1934. 211 p.

1075 Starnes, George T. "Sixty Years of Branch Banking in Virginia." JOURNAL OF POLITICAL ECONOMY 36 (August 1928): 480-500.

1076 Stuart, Verrijn. "Metallic and Non-Metallic Standards of Money." ECONOMIC JOURNAL 33 (June 1923): 143-54.

1077 Studenski, Paul, and Krooss, Herman E. FINANCIAL HISTORY OF THE UNITED STATES. New York: McGraw-Hill, 1963. 605 p.

1078 Sumner, William G. THE FINANCIER AND THE FINANCES OF THE AMERICAN REVOLUTION. 2 vols. New York: Dodd, Mead, and Co., 1891. 309, 329 p.

1079 Tippetts, Charles S. "The Decline of Membership in the Federal Reserve System." JOURNAL OF POLITICAL ECONOMY 36 (April 1928): 185-211.

Chapter 8

INTERNATIONAL AND INTERREGIONAL
GROWTH AND DEVELOPMENT

This chapter is the most difficult of all the chapters to write, because of its wide range of interconnected topics. The wide range would usually have called for subdivision into two chapters, but the interconnectedness made such a division very unworkable. In addition to the large range of material encompassed within this topic heading, I have also chosen to reserve for this chapter most of the literature relating to both antebellum and postbellum southern development, that is, most of the economics of slavery literature.

Most of the references to works dealing with the economics of slavery are in this chapter. Although slavery affected the whole nation, it was a regional phenomena and had most of its impact on only one region--the South. Thus more of the regional studies cited concern the South than any other single region.

Needless to say, I have not included all of the works which each reader might feel are essential. I have included those that I felt were important and/or provided the reader with an excellent list of possible sources for further research. Many of the books possess very extensive bibliographies as do some of the articles, and users of this book should take advantage of such leads.

8.1 ANNOTATED LISTINGS

1080   Aldrich, Mark. "Flexible Exchange Rates, Northern Expansion, and the Market for Southern Cotton: 1866-1879." JOURNAL OF ECONOMIC HISTORY 33 (June 1973): 399-416.

   The article is an argument that the South's failure to rapidly recover the cotton markets lost during the war was in a major way due to certain aspects of nonsouthern economic development during the postwar decade and a half of flexible exchange rates. Exchange appreciation did not help the South.

1081   Andreano, Ralph, ed. ECONOMIC IMPACT OF THE AMERICAN CIVIL WAR. Cambridge, Mass.: Schenkman Publishing Co., 1967. 244 p.

This collection of thirteen essays considers four broad categories of the effect of the Civil War: (1) internal economic adjustment 1861-65; (2) monetary and physical costs of the War; (3) the tariff issue; and (4) the war and national economic growth. A fifth part contains various data series for the period 1850-80.

1082 _____. NEW VIEWS ON AMERICAN ECONOMIC DEVELOPMENT. Cambridge, Mass.: Schenkman Publishing Co., 1965. 434 p.

A major portion of this book is given over to the discussion of regional growth performance, with contributions from various authors.

1083 Aufhauser, R. Keith. "Slavery and Scientific Management." JOURNAL OF ECONOMIC HISTORY 33 (December 1973): 811-24.

This is an attempt to discover how closely the slaveholders' behavior matches that of F.W. Taylor's school of scientific management. The author argues that the slaveholders carefully studied worker productivity behavior.

1084 _____. "Slavery and Technological Change." JOURNAL OF ECONOMIC HISTORY 34 (March 1974): 36-50.

This is an attempt to illustrate that slavery did not hinder the application or adoption of new techniques and/or activities.

1085 Baack, Bennet D., and Ray, Edward J. "Tariff Policy and Income Distribution: The Case of the U.S. 1830-1860." EXPLORATIONS IN ECONOMIC HISTORY 11 (Winter 1973-74): 103-22.

This is an attempt to illustrate the role of the Metzler effect in any determination of the income effect of tariffs and to test for the importance of this effect in the study of antebellum textile tariffs. The principal finding is that the evidence does not support the contention that the tariffs may have benefitted the antebellum South.

1086 _____. "Tariff Policy and Comparative Advantage in the Iron and Steel Industry: 1870-1929." EXPLORATIONS IN ECONOMIC HISTORY 11 (Fall 1973): 3-24.

This paper is an argument that tariffs were significant in the promotion of domestic industry and that substitution effects tended to mask the extent to which tariffs were prohibitive to foreign competition prior to 1900.

1087 Bailyn, Bernard. "Communication and Trade: The Atlantic in the Seventeenth Century." JOURNAL OF ECONOMIC HISTORY 13 (Fall 1953): 378-87.

This is an examination of the social consequences of early commercial growth and the network of communication that resulted from explorations and settlement.

1088   Baldwin, Robert E.   "The Commodity Composition of Trade: Selected Industrial Countries, 1900-1954." REVIEW OF ECONOMICS AND STATISTICS 40 (February 1958): 50-71.

An attempt to classify imports of leading industrial nations in a way similar to that already used for exports, allows for the calculation of net trade balances by commodity group. Changes in the composition of trade by groups and country, the effects of structural changes on the distribution of trade, and trends in trade among industrial countries are all discussed.

1089   Ball, R.J., and Marwak, K. "The U.S. Demand for Imports, 1948-1958." REVIEW OF ECONOMICS AND STATISTICS 4 (November 1962): 395-401.

Using quarterly postwar data, the authors attempt to estimate the elasticities of imports with respect to income and the relative prices of import. They were unable to reject the hypothesis that both elasticities were greater than one, that is, elastic.

1090   Bamford, Paul Walden. "France and the American Market in Naval Timber and Masts, 1776-1786." JOURNAL OF ECONOMIC HISTORY 12 (Winter 1952): 21-34.

An analysis of the competition between Britain and France for the timber and masts, this paper also discusses some of the barriers and problems between the French and the Americans, namely, language, conservation, and ignorance.

1091   Bateman, Fred, and Weiss, Thomas. "Comparative Regional Development in Antebellum Manufacturing." JOURNAL OF ECONOMIC HISTORY 35 (March 1975): 182-208.

This is a comparative study of the manufacturing development in the South, West, and East during the antebellum period. Little difference was found in the level of industrialization for the South and West. Size and structure of markets appear not to have greatly affected industrial levels. Two discussions follow by Edward P. Duggan and George D. Green on pages 209-11 and 212-15 respectively.

1092   Bateman, Fred; Foust, James; and Weiss, Thomas. "Profitability in Southern Manufacturing: Estimates for 1860." EXPLORATIONS IN ECONOMIC HISTORY 12 (July 1975): 211-32.

The authors do not attempt to answer whether the South had

too little investment in manufacturing. This article is an attempt only to examine the evidence on rates of return in antebellum southern manufacturing. The results indicate such returns were quite high.

1093 Bernstein, Edward M. "American Productivity and the Dollar Payments Problem." REVIEW OF ECONOMICS AND STATISTICS 32 (May 1955): 101-9.

Concerned with payments difficulties, scarce currencies, productivity, and exports and imports, this study concludes that although not perfect there is a relationship between increasing productivity and business prosperity.

1094 Berry, Brian J.L. "City Size Distribution and Economic Development." ECONOMIC DEVELOPMENT AND CULTURAL CHANGE 9 (July 1961): 573-88.

This is an international consideration of city size distribution. The degree of urbanization in counting is also considered. It is a very thorough and extensive article.

1095 Bjork, G.C. "Regional Adjustment to Economic Growth: The U.S. 1880-1950." OXFORD ECONOMIC PAPERS 20 (March 1968): 81-97.

A model is developed to explain the movements of labor from surplus areas to deficit areas. Evidence is considered regarding interstate wage differences, industrial structure, per capita income, migration, and long-term disequilibrium in labor markets. The model is empirically tested.

1096 Bogue, Donald J. "The Spread of Cities." AMERICAN ECONOMIC REVIEW 46 (May 1956): 284-92.

This article deals primarily with the location of U.S. cities after the early 1900s. It discusses how efficiently these cities were set up regarding the allocation of resources.

1097 Bonomo, Vittorio. "International Capital Movements and Economic Activity: The United States Experience, 1870-1968." EXPLORATIONS IN ECONOMIC HISTORY 8 (Spring 1971): 321-42.

Using both regression and spectral techniques to analyze the time series, the relationship between capital movements and economic activity for the United States is examined and compared to findings by earlier writers. The effect of differences in timing and amplitude are discussed and compared with those of the United Kingdom.

1098 Borts, George H. "Growth and Capital Movements among U.S. Regions in the Postwar Period." AMERICAN ECONOMIC REVIEW 58 (May 1968): 155-61.

The author uses an open neoclassical growth model to analyze the flow of capital among the regions. He argues that the construction and testing of such models is useful for the analysis of the past as well as the present.

1099 Borts, George H., and Stein, Jerome L. ECONOMIC GROWTH IN A FREE MARKET. New York: Columbia University Press, 1964. 235 p.

A very thorough treatment of various aspects of the disaggregated analysis of economic growth. Much of it is theoretical, but empirical evidence is introduced whenever possible. Discussion is directed to both the state and industry level.

1100 Bourque, Philip J. "The Domestic Importance of Foreign Trade of the United States, by Producing Regions, Manufacturing Sector, 1947." REVIEW OF ECONOMICS AND STATISTICS 36 (November 1954): 401-8.

Using the data from the 1947 U.S. CENSUS OF MANUFACTURING, the author classifies commodities as either exports, import competing, or nontraded. The evidence suggests that foreign trade is highly uneven (absolutely and relatively) in its importance to particular regions.

1101 _____. "Geographic Earnings Differentials and Foreign Trade." REVIEW OF ECONOMICS AND STATISTICS 40 (May 1958): 177-79.

The conclusion is that, contrary to the findings of others, the geographic wage differentials in the export- and import-competing industries are not largely the result of differences in the durability of the products.

1102 Bowman, John D., and Keehn, Richard H. "Agricultural Terms of Trade in Four Midwestern States, 1870-1900." JOURNAL OF ECONOMIC HISTORY 34 (September 1974): 592-609.

Using price data on goods purchased and goods sold for Iowa, Illinois, Indiana, and Wisconsin, the authors construct alternative measures of agricultural sector terms of trade, vis-a-vis the rest of the economy. These data are used to study short-run variations in farm purchasing power.

1103 Broude, Henry W. "The Significance of Regional Studies for the Elaboration of National Economic History." JOURNAL OF ECONOMIC HISTORY 20 (December 1960): 588-96.

This paper discusses the idea of analyzing rational differences and growth and generalizing from these to a national view of growth. Some review is provided for the conventional views on regionalism.

1104   Bruce, Philip A. ECONOMIC HISTORY OF VIRGINIA IN THE SEVEN-
TEENTH CENTURY. 2 vols. New York: P. Smith, 1935. 634, 647 p.

Economic conditions as well as social, religious, and political
aspects of the area are discussed and many periods of analysis
are set out: 1607-24; 1624-50; 1650-85; and 1685-1700. The
roles of both foreign and domestic supplies of manufactured
goods are discussed.

1105   _____. THE RISE OF THE NEW SOUTH. Philadelphia: G. Barrie
and Sons, 1905. 491 p.

This book contains a thorough treatment of demographic, economic, and political changes which took place in the South
between 1876 and 1905. Not only domestic trade and industrial growth but foreign trade as well are discussed.

1106   Bullock, C., et al. "The Balance of Trade of the United States." RE-
VIEW OF ECONOMICS AND STATISTICS 7 (July 1919): 215-66.

Covering the period 1789 to 1914, the author seeks to explain the trade position existing in 1919 and also to learn
what must be done to prepare for the reversal.

1107   Caves, Richard E. "Export-Led Growth and the New Economic History."
In TRADE, BALANCE OF PAYMENTS AND GROWTH, edited by Jagdish
N. Bhagwati et al., pp. 403-42. Amsterdam: North-Holland, 1971.

This is a very thorough review of the various applications of
the export-led theory of growth in explaining past economic
growth. The benefits and hazards are examined in some detail. The work includes a large bibliography on this topic.

1108   Checkland, S.G. "American versus West Indian Traders in Liverpool,
1793-1815." JOURNAL OF ECONOMIC HISTORY 18 (June 1958):
141-60.

This is an examination of the changing structure of trade at
Liverpool as a result of the war between Britain and France,
namely, the decline of West Indian trade and the growth of
American trade.

1109   Christy, David. COTTON IS KING, OR SLAVERY IN THE LIGHT OF
POLITICAL ECONOMY. New York: Derby and Jackson, 1856. 298 p.

The conditions of slavery along with the economic relations
of slavery and the impact on foreign trade restrictions generated by the South as a result of its economic structure are
all discussed, along with other less economic topics.

1110 Church, R.A. "The British Leather Industry and Foreign Competition 1870-1914." ECONOMIC HISTORY REVIEW 24 (November 1971): 543-70.

The key factor in the examination of the effect of competition is the relationship between science and technology in the leather industry.

1111 _____. "The Effect of the American Export Invasion on the British Boot and Shoe Industry, 1885-1914." JOURNAL OF ECONOMIC HISTORY 28 (June 1968): 223-54.

Besides a short historical perspective of the American export invasion, the circumstances and factors preceding the industrial response of the British boot and shoe industry are examined.

1112 Clark, John G. "The Antebellum Grain Trade of New Orleans: Changing Patterns in the Relation of New Orleans with the Old Northwest." AGRICULTURAL HISTORY 38 (July 1964): 131-42.

The hazards of trade and the nature of the trade formed the pattern of relations between the two areas. It is pointed out that as alternate transportation means became available, the importance of the Mississippi River and New Orleans diminished.

1113 Coelho, Philip, and Shepherd, James. "Differences in Regional Prices: The United States, 1851-1880." JOURNAL OF ECONOMIC HISTORY 34 (September 1974): 551-91.

A series of regional price indexes for the West, South, and East are developed in this article. The findings are that the cost of living for the West was much lower than for the East, which would have tended to equalize income differentials when considered in real terms.

1114 Conrad, Alfred H., and Meyer, John R. THE ECONOMICS OF SLAVERY. Chicago: Aldine Publishing Co., 1964. 241 p.

These essays are exceptionally good both for methological purposes as well as for analytic empirical work testing various hypotheses regarding the economics of slavery. National income growth in the nineteenth century and an input-output evaluation of British industrial production during the late nineteenth century are also included as separate chapters.

1115 _____. "The Economics of Slavery in the Antebellum South." JOURNAL OF POLITICAL ECONOMY 66 (April 1958): 95-130.

This was the earliest attempt to measure the economic profitability of slavery. Capital theory is employed to organize the historical data. Slave functions and the concept of efficiency are defined. The hypothesis that slavery was an efficient maintainable economic institution is tested. A comment by Douglas Dowd and a reply by the authors appear in this journal, volume 66 (October 1958): 448-53. ". . . Another Comment." by John E. Moes and a reply by the authors appears in volume 68 (April 1960): 183-89.

1116   Crowther, Simeon J. "Urban Growth in the Mid-Atlantic States, 1785-1850." JOURNAL OF ECONOMIC HISTORY 36 (September 1976): 624-44.

This is a study of urban growth in two systems of cities--New York and Philadelphia. Successive cross-sections of urban population data are analyzed, and it was found that each city center had various satellite cities for increasing commerce.

1117   Danhof, Clarence H. "Economic Validity of the Safety-Value Doctrine." JOURNAL OF ECONOMIC HISTORY 1 (December 1941): 96-106.

This is a thorough examination of Frederick Jackson Turner's theory, including the conditions needed to make the theory fit the situation, namely, free land, superior labor force, and a pool of unemployed.

1118   David, Paul A. "Learning by Doing and Tariff Protection: A Reconsideration of the Case of the Ante-Bellum United States Cotton Textile Industry." JOURNAL OF ECONOMIC HISTORY 30 (September 1970): 521-601.

Using the New England cotton textile industry as a case study, the author examines the relationship between tariff policy and technical characteristics of production. The argument for protection rests upon a learning-by-doing thesis, and the author examines the implications for government policy.

1119   David, Paul A., and Temin, Peter. "Slavery: The Progressive Institution?" JOURNAL OF ECONOMIC HISTORY 34 (September 1974): 739-83.

This is an extensive critical review of Fogel and Engerman's TIME ON THE CROSS (see no. 1141).

1120   David, Paul A., et al. RECKONING WITH SLAVERY. New York: Oxford University Press, 1976. 398 p.

This collection of eight essays, with an introduction by Kenneth Stamp, all form a formidable critique of Fogel and Engerman's TIME ON THE CROSS (see no. 1141). Six authors contributed to this work and each article is a substantive work addressing such issues as the noneconomic treatment of the slaves, the care and feeding of slaves, and the sexual mores and conduct of slaves as well as the profitability of using slaves.

1121　Davis, E.G., and Swanson, J.A.　"On the Distribution of City Growth Rates in a Theory of Regional Economic Growth."　ECONOMIC DEVELOPMENT AND CULTURAL CHANGE　20 (April 1972):　495-503.

Characterizing city growth rates as a stochastic process, the growth rates of population centers are explained.　The distribution of efficiency progress and the growth of the labor force are combined to get at this problem of explaining the growth pattern of city sizes.

1122　Davis, Lance E., and Hughes, J.R.T.　"A Sterling Dollar Exchange, 1803-1895."　ECONOMIC HISTORY REVIEW　13 (August 1960):　52-78.

Utilizing a totally new series of quarterly data on exchange rates, the authors explain the exchange rate behavior of the nineteenth century.　Using trade and finance bills for 1831 to 1895, they also derive a pure rate of exchange series. These data are all used to discuss gold points and the great monetary crises that occurred between 1803 and 1895.

1123　DeBow, J.D.B.　THE INDUSTRIAL RESOURCES OF THE SOUTHERN AND WESTERN STATES.　3 vols.　New Orleans:　Office of DeBow's Review, 1852-53.

This is one of the better contemporary discussions of the economic situation in the South in the antebellum period, dealing with population, agriculture, commerce, and manufacture.

1124　DeCanio, Stephen.　"Productivity and Income Distribution in the Post-Bellum South."　JOURNAL OF ECONOMIC HISTORY　34 (June 1974):　422-46.

The author develops a model to test the two hypotheses that blacks were low-productivity farmers relative to whites, and that the South lost potential income by specializing in cotton. The suggestion is that wealth distribution and geographical location are more important in explaining southern income and productivity differences than were discrimination and alleged institutional rigidities.

1125　Degler, Carl N.　"The Locofocos:　Urban 'Agrarians'."　JOURNAL OF ECONOMIC HISTORY　16 (September 1956):　322-33.

This is an analysis of the monetary policy of the Locofocos political party--New York City Democrats.　This policy was not expansionary, and was in direct opposition to the Jacksonians.

1126   Dillard, Dudley. ECONOMIC DEVELOPMENT OF THE NORTH ATLAN-
TIC COMMUNITY. Englewood Cliffs, N.J.: Prentice-Hall, 1967. 747 p.

This study is built around the concept of an interrelated European
and U.S. economy both progressing along the same evolutionary
process. The author also explores the relationship between
capital accumulation and the characteristic instability of capitalism.

1127   Doane, David P. "Regional Cost Differentials and Textile Location: A
Statistical Analysis." EXPLORATIONS IN ECONOMIC HISTORY 9
(Fall 1971): 3-34.

The author examines new empirical evidence on the rise of
southern cotton cloth production and compares it to New England's new monopoly and the respective decline of New England industry by 1920. Analysis is also made of the North-
South wage differential using point-in-time data.

1128   Dowd, Douglas F. "A Comparative Analysis of Economic Development
in the American West and South." JOURNAL OF ECONOMIC HIS-
TORY 16 (December 1953): 558-74.

This is a comparison of the development process with respect
to available resources, utilized resources, and the social con-
texts of industrialization. The problems of underdevelopment
are discussed for each region along with the inhibiting factors
characteristic of southern organization and industrialization.

1129   Edwards, Richard C. "Economic Sophistication in Nineteenth Century
Congressional Tariff Debates." JOURNAL OF ECONOMIC HISTORY 30
(December 1970): 802-38.

The impact of protective tariffs on economic growth, employment, and the dispersion of new technology are examined by
the author along with the theory used by congressmen in the
debates over protective tariffs between 1824 and 1894.

1130   Ellsworth, P.T. "The Structure of American Foreign Trade: A New View
Examined." REVIEW OF ECONOMICS AND STATISTICS 36 (August 1954):
279-85.

In agreement with the earlier findings by Leontief, the author
argues that his reasons are much different. It is argued that
due to the relatively higher labor cost for import competing
industries, the United States uses more capital in these industries. This is where Leontief's evidence that the U.S. imported capital-intensive goods and exported labor-intensive goods
originated, that is, it is true only in the sense of U.S. factor
proportions.

1131 Engerman, Stanley. "The Economic Impact of the Civil War." EX-PLORATIONS IN ECONOMIC HISTORY 3 (Spring 1966): 176-99.

This article reviews the original works in the area and then some of the more recent attacks upon the defenses of these earlier views. He concludes that aside from commercial banking, the Civil War appears not to have started or created any new patterns of economic institutional change. Most of the author's reservations regarding the original works seem justified. Topics considered include income distribution, wages and profits and inflation, and "war industries."

1132 _____. "The Effects of Slavery upon the Southern Economy: A Review of the Recent Debate." EXPLORATIONS IN ECONOMIC HISTORY 4 (Spring 1967): 71-97.

This is a review of earlier work and the attacks leveled against it with regard to these three issues: profitability of slavery to the individual slave owner; the viability of slavery as an economic system; and the effects of the slave system on the economic development of the South.

1133 Farbman, Michael. "Income Concentration in the Southern United States." REVIEW OF ECONOMICS AND STATISTICS 55 (August 1973): 333-40.

A six-variable model is used to identify the factors most influential in producing a concentration of income. These factors were found to vary in importance from state to state.

1134 Fisher, Franklin M., and Temin, Peter. "Regional Specialization and the Supply of Wheat in the United States, 1867-1914." REVIEW OF ECONOMICS AND STATISTICS 52 (May 1970): 134-49.

This attempt at applying a rather rigorous economic model to the wheat market introduces the effect of supply elasticity for the first time. Differences in labor productivity are examined in some detail. A comment by Robert Higgs and a reply appear in this journal, volume 53 (February 1971): 101-2 and 102-3.

1135 Fishlow, Albert. "Ante-Bellum Interregional Trade Reconsidered." AMERICAN ECONOMIC REVIEW 54 (May 1964): 352-64.

The author argues that the trade between the South and the West was never of significance except for possibly New Orleans. The South was not in need of imported foodstuffs. Trade and consumption both grew over the period. Robert W. Fogel has a discussion in AMERICAN ECONOMIC REVIEW 24 (December 1964): 561-66, where he criticizes Fishlow's statistical work. Both of these are reprinted in Andreano (see no. 1082).

1136   Fleisig, Heywood. "Slavery, the Supply of Agricultural Labor, the Industrialization of the South." JOURNAL OF ECONOMIC HISTORY 36 (September 1976): 572-97.

It is argued that slavery relieved the labor constraint on agriculture and permitted larger farms, larger absolute profits in farming and thereby shifted entrepreneurs into agriculture at the expense of industry. It is also shown that the relaxation of this restraint also reduced the size of the market and the incentive to invent and innovate farm machinery.

1137   Fletcher, Max E. "The Suez Canal and World Shipping, 1869-1914." JOURNAL OF ECONOMIC HISTORY 18 (December 1958): 556-73.

The opening of the Suez Canal altered shipbuilding techniques and practices and contributed to the decline of sailing ships. This article discusses the above transition and the changing trade routes and patterns between eastern and Australian trade routes.

1138   Floyd, John E., and Hynes, Allan. "The Economic Growth, Price Trends and the U.S. Balance of Trade: 1925-1962." JOURNAL OF POLITICAL ECONOMY 76 (November-December 1968): 1209-23.

Examining the effects of secular price trends at home and abroad and differing rates of income growth on the trade balance of the United States, the authors use an aggregated general-equilibrium model of two countries and their goods. Theoretical issues regarding income and price trends are considered.

1139   Fogel, Robert W., and Engerman, Stanley L. "The Economics of Slavery." In their THE REINTERPRETATION OF AMERICAN ECONOMIC HISTORY, pp. 311-41. New York: Harper & Row, 1971.

This work reviews the works of others, presents an index of the sanquinity of slaveholders, estimates the price of slaves in 1890 if slavery had persisted, and presents new data on the rate of growth of southern per capita income between 1840 and 1860.

1140   _____. "Explaining the Relative Efficiency of Slave Agriculture in the Antebellum South." AMERICAN ECONOMIC REVIEW 67 (June 1977): 275-96.

This is a progress report or interior report on the work that has been done regarding the criticism of such authors as David and Temin (see no. 1119) about the measurement of efficiency. The authors are quick to caution that slavery's relative efficiency is not necessarily good due to the loss of freedom. A series of comments appears in this journal, volume 69 (March 1970): 206-21.

1141 _____. TIME ON THE CROSS: THE ECONOMICS OF AMERICAN NEGRO SLAVERY. 2 vols. New York: Little, Brown and Co., 1974. 286, 267 p.

> The first volume is an analysis of the plight of the American Negro slave from an economic point of view. Volume 2 contains the data to support the discussions of volume 1. Nearly four hundred sources are listed at the conclusion of volume 2.

1142 Genovese, Eugene D. THE POLITICAL ECONOMY OF SLAVERY. New York: Vintage Books, 1967. 304 p.

> This is a collection of essays by the author on various aspects of the economic and social condition of antebellum South. Most of the evidence relates to the plight of the slave and/or the resulting conditions of slavery.

1143 Gilbert, Geoffrey. "The Role of Breadstuffs in American Trade, 1770-1790." EXPLORATIONS IN ECONOMIC HISTORY 14 (October 1977): 378-87.

> This examination of the role of breadstuffs finds that the annual volume of breadstuff exports increased by over 50 percent this period, their terms of trade improved, growth in demand was not evenly distributed among major markets, and the percentage of output exported remained nearly the same.

1144 Gilchrist, David T., and Lewis, W. David, eds. ECONOMIC CHANGE IN THE CIVIL WAR ERA. Greenville, Del.: Eleutherian Mills-Hagley Foundation, 1965. 180 p.

> This collection of essays by some of the leading people in the field treats all aspects of the antebellum and postbellum development of the economy. International markets and finance, science and technology, the structure of manufacturing, and the relationship between business and government are all considered.

1145 Ginsberg, Alan L. "The Determination of the Factors Afflicting American and British Exports in the Interwar and Postwar Periods." OXFORD ECONOMIC PAPERS 17 (July 1965): 263-78.

> Improving upon earlier works, this is an investigation of the influence of relative prices, commodity characteristics, time, and region of destination as determinants of the quantities of U.S. and British exports.

1146 Goldin, Claudia G., and Lewis, Frank D. "The Economic Cost of the American Civil War: Estimates and Implications." JOURNAL OF ECONOMIC HISTORY 35 (June 1975): 299-326.

This is an attempt to improve on various attempts to assess the costs of the Civil War. The authors use a direct measure and two forms of an indirect measure. The former contains the fiscal costs of equipment men and human capital. The indirect cost is calculated on the basis of foregone consumption during the period 1861-65. The conclusion is that the Civil War did not help the United States or any of its regions in terms of growth.

1147   Goldsmith, Raymond W. "The Quantitative International Comparison of Financial Structure and Development." JOURNAL OF ECONOMIC HISTORY 35 (March 1975): 216-37.

This is an attempt to shed light on the role of financial systems in the growth process. The author compares various countries to discover the various relationships. Much of the work discusses what must be done to answer questions regarding the relationship between the financial superstructure and the real infrastructure.

1148   Goodrich, Carter. "Internal Improvements Reconsidered." JOURNAL OF ECONOMIC HISTORY 30 (June 1970): 289-311.

In an attempt to ascertain the extent of public action, the role of government in the development of internal improvement is surveyed for the antebellum period. Some evidence is provided for capital flows after the Civil War.

1149   Graff, Henry F. "The Early Impact of Japan on American Agriculture." AGRICULTURAL HISTORY 23 (April 1949): 110-15.

The topics are the impact that the 1854 opening of trade with Japan had on U.S. agriculture and the information transmission mechanism.

1150   Gregg, Josiah. COMMERCE OF THE PRAIRIES: THE JOURNAL OF A SANTA FE TRADER. Dallas: Southwest Press, 1933. 438 p.

The nature and organization of the trading parties along with an account of the natural resources of New Mexico are included along with a large amount of social history about the people and their lives.

1151   Gunderson, Gerald. "The Origin of the American Civil War." JOURNAL OF ECONOMIC HISTORY 34 (December 1974): 915-50.

The author concludes that slavery was the cause of the Civil War. Without slavery as the initiating issue the other factors would not have been sufficient to cause the war.

1152 _____. "Southern Ante-Bellum Income Reconsidered." EXPLORATIONS IN ECONOMIC HISTORY 10 (Winter 1973): 151-76.

This is a criticism of regional income estimates by Richard A. Easterlin (see no. 141), for the South in particular. By re-computing the data, the author argues that the 1840 data for the west south central region as reported by Easterlin was overstated. A comment by Robert E. Gallman and a reply by the author appear in this journal, volume 12 (January 1975): 89-102.

1153 Hanna, Frank A. "A Contribution of Manufacturing Wages to Regional Differences in Per Capita Income." REVIEW OF ECONOMICS AND STATISTICS 33 (February 1951): 18-28.

This compares wages paid to production workers in the same industry but according to state of employment. These differences are compared with differences in per capita income for each state and geographic division.

1154 Hanna, Frank A., ed. REGIONAL INCOME. National Bureau of Economic Research Studies in Income and Wealth, vol. 21. Princeton, N.J.: Princeton University Press, 1957. 408 p.

This is a collection of studies by various authors on many aspects of regional income: economic progress assessment; the value of the regional approach in economic analysis; conceptual issues of regional income estimation; the geographical area in regional research; analysis of interstate income differentials; city size and income; measurement of agricultural income for countries; and alternative ways of estimating local area incomes.

1155 Harley, C. Knick. "Western Settlement and the Price of Wheat, 1872-1913." JOURNAL OF ECONOMIC HISTORY 38 (December 1978): 865-78.

This is an attempt to explain western expansion by examining the changes in wheat prices or more exactly the reasons why they did not change significantly. It is argued very forcefully that the railroad and reduced transport costs maintained the price of wheat and fostered expansion.

1156 Harper, Lawrence A. "The Effect of the Navigation Acts of the Thirteen Colonies." In THE ERA OF THE AMERICAN REVOLUTION, edited by Richard B. Morris, pp. 3-39. New York: Columbia University Press, 1959.

This is an attempt to analyze the effect of the navigation acts by looking at the alternative cost or benefit of not levying them. A comparison is made between the situation under the acts and the post-Revolution period when they did not exist. Estimates of the price paid by the colonists are derived.

1157   Harris, Seymore E.   "Interregional Competition with Particular Reference to North South Competition." AMERICAN ECONOMIC REVIEW 44 (May 1954): 367-80.

The theoretically predicted adjustment did not take place due to rigidities and imperfections in the capital and labor markets. Trade unions played a large role in maintaining the rigidity of wages in the North. Public policy had much to do with the speed of adjustment in the South.

1158   Hawill, Richard A. "The Economy of the South." JOURNAL OF PO-LITICAL ECONOMY 48 (February 1940): 33-61.

Focusing on the changed role of the South, from one of leader-ship to that of decline, the author investigates southern politi-cal, educational, and manufacturing areas. Declining leader-ship in income, population, agriculture, and manufacturing are all discussed.

1159   Hawke, G.R. "The United States Tariff and Industrial Protection in the Late Nineteenth Century." ECONOMIC HISTORY REVIEW 28 (Febru-ary 1975): 84-99.

The author surveys much of the previous work on tariffs and U.S. industry and applies the relatively new concept of "effec-tive protection" to the analysis of the late nineteenth century U.S. tariffs. This analysis shows that tariffs were not as pro-tective as earlier works have argued for the period 1879-1904.

1160   Hazami, Yujiro, and Puttan, V.W. "The United States and Japan, 1880-1960." JOURNAL OF POLITICAL ECONOMY 78 (September-October 1970): 1115-41.

This is the test of a hypothesis on the progress of technological change and the choice of inputs for the United States and Japan in terms of a dynamic adjustment process. Trends in factor prices, and in several factor-product or factor-factor ratios in both countries are discussed. Concern is primarily with agri-cultural output production.

1161   Henderson, John P. "An Intercity Comparison of Differential in Earnings and the City Worker's Cost of Living." REVIEW OF ECONOMICS AND STATISTICS 37 (November 1955): 407-11.

Some evidence is found for the inverse relationship between earnings and cost of living, and there is no apparent relation-ship between income and expenditure upon any one classification of goods or service. The cost of living was observed to have remained constant while consumption habits were influenced by diverse local and institutional factors. Edwin Mansfield has a comment in the same journal, 39 (February 1957): 90, in which he refutes some of Henderson's conclusions.

1162 Hicks, John D. THE POPULIST REVOLT. Lincoln: University of Nebraska Press, 1961. 473 p.

This is a very lengthy study of the postbellum economic relationships which fed into the discontent that prompted the Populist movement. The political issues and debates are also discussed. A twenty-page bibliography is included.

1163 Hidy, Ralph. THE HOUSE OF BARING IN AMERICAN TRADE AND FINANCE. Cambridge, Mass.: Harvard University Press, 1949. 421 p.

This is an examination of the broad policy, general organization, and techniques of operation used by the Barings. It is a clarification of the role of the Anglo-American banking group and the effect of London policies on U.S. economic development.

1164 Higgs, Robert. "Patterns of Farm Rental in the Georgia Cotton Belt, 1880-1900." JOURNAL OF ECONOMIC HISTORY 34 (June 1974): 468-82.

Although the tenancy arrangements were always in a state of adjustment, many questions remain unanswered: (1) what determined the proportion of farms which were rented?; (2) what determined the proportion of share-rent versus fixed-rent tenancy?; and (3) did the farmer's race affect the form of rental contract he obtained? This article is an attempt to answer these questions for one region.

1165 _____. "Race, Tenure, and Resource Allocation in Southern Agriculture, 1910." JOURNAL OF ECONOMIC HISTORY 33 (March 1973): 149-69.

This is an attempt to determine the role of race in determining the distribution of farm rental contract between fixed-rent and share-rent forms and the effect of race upon the form of land tenure and the size distribution of farms. A discussion by Gavin Wright appears on pages 170-76 of this issue of the journal.

1166 Hoxie, Robert F. "Colonial Policy and the Tariff." JOURNAL OF POLITICAL ECONOMY 11 (March 1903): 198-219.

This is an examination of the Republican party's apparently
incongruous policy of imperialism and protectionism during the
colonial period.

1167   Hutchinson, William K., and Williamson, Samuel H. "The Self-Sufficiency of the Antebellum South: Estimates of the Food Supply." JOUR-
NAL OF ECONOMIC HISTORY 31 (September 1971): 591-612.

This is an attempt to ascertain whether the seven southern
states were possibly self-sufficient during the period 1840-60
in the area of food production. Feeding techniques used by
southern agricultural producers are examined in the process of
deriving estimates of swine weights.

1168   Hyde, Francis Edwin. "British Capital and American Enterprise in the
North-West." ECONOMIC HISTORY REVIEW 6 (April 1936): 201-8.

This is an account of how British bondholders through bond-
holder committees helped to free the promoters of the North-
ern-Pacific from the hold of conservative German financial
interests.

1169   Imlay, Gilbert. A TOPOGRAPHICAL DESCRIPTION OF THE WESTERN
TERRITORY OF NORTH AMERICA. New York: A.M. Kelley, 1969.
598 p.

This is an account of the land, climate, agriculture, and other
features of the part of the United States that lies east of the
Mississippi River, particularly Kentucky, Tennessee, Louisiana,
and west Florida. Various original colonies are included in
the topographical discussions.

1170   James, John A. "The Welfare Effects of the Antebellum Tariff: A
General Equilibrium Analysis." EXPLORATIONS IN ECONOMIC HIS-
TORY 15 (July 1978): 231-56.

Using rather sophisticated general equilibrium techniques, the
author attempts to ascertain the effect of the tariff on U.S.
economic growth. This is accomplished by posing a counterfactual case with no tariff, and comparing the results against
the actual growth data.

1171   Jenks, L. THE MIGRATION OF BRITISH CAPITAL. New York: Nelson,
1963. 289 p.

The cycles of Anglo-American finance, postwar foreign investment, railroad investment, and government activity are all
examined in an attempt to discover how the invisible empire
of British enterprise was created.

1172 Keene, Charles A. "American Shipping and Trade, 1798-1820: The Evidence from Leghorn." JOURNAL OF ECONOMIC HISTORY 38 (September 1978): 681-700.

Using data from reports submitted to the Department of State by the American consuls, the author argues that productivity was rising. The characteristics of the U.S. reexport trade to southern Europe are also examined.

1173 Keynes, Lord J.M. "The Balance of Payments of the United States." ECONOMIC JOURNAL 56 (June 1946): 172-87.

A warning against attempts to project prewar statistics into the postwar period, this article indicates the data that are required for an informed judgment. Keynes argues that more of an examination of the details is required especially as the future gradually unfolds.

1174 Klingaman, David C., and Vedder, Richard K., eds. ESSAYS IN NINETEENTH CENTURY ECONOMIC HISTORY: THE OLD NORTH-WEST. Athens: Ohio University Press, 1975. 356 p.

This collection of eleven essays contains some works that are based on more than the old Northwest. Topics covered are population; migration; wealth; sectoral growth; financial institutions; and transportation.

1175 Koo, Anthony Y.C. "British and American Productivity and Regional Patterns of Exports--A Further Addendum." OXFORD ECONOMIC PAPERS 17 (March 1965): 158-61.

The author sets the relative share of British and U.S. exports to various regions of the world as functions of their net cost ratio. The sample is limited to twenty-two industries.

1176 Kotlikoff, Lawrence J., and Pinera, Sebastian E. "The Old South's Stake in the Inter-Regional Movement of Slaves, 1850-1860." JOURNAL OF ECONOMIC HISTORY 37 (June 1977): 434-50.

This article is an argument that interregional slave sales may not have been as beneficial to the selling region as many have argued. In fact, the authors state that it may have reduced the wealth of the eastern south.

1177 Kravis, Iwing B. "The Role of Exports in Nineteenth-Century United States Growth." ECONOMIC DEVELOPMENT AND CULTURAL CHANGE 20 (April 1972): 387-405.

This examination of the export-led theory of growth considers price, relative importance of exports, the timing of changes in exports and in domestic production, and the role of exports in key sectors.

1178   Kreinin, Mordechai. "United States Imports and Income in the Postwar Period." REVIEW OF ECONOMICS AND STATISTICS 42 (May 1960): 223-25.

This is an examination of various balance of payments items and GNP. Imports are also broken out in their five major components and compared with GNP.

1179   Kuznets, Simon. "Quantitative Aspects of the Economic Growth of Nations: Level and Structure of Foreign Trade, Long-Term Trends." ECONOMIC DEVELOPMENT AND CULTURAL CHANGE 15 (January 1967): 1-140.

Long-term movements in foreign trades proportions relative to product, the structure of exports and imports by economic categories, terms of trade, and the problems involved with financing imports are all discussed in this lengthy work. The findings of cross-sectional data are examined for their information value in explaining long-term changes and trends.

1180   _____. "Quantitative Aspects of the Economic Growth of Nations, Level and Structure of Foreign Trade: Comparisons for Recent Years." ECONOMIC DEVELOPMENT AND CULTURAL CHANGE 13 (October 1964): 1-106.

This large study examines the structure of trade, especially in commodities, along with the extent of geographic concentration in exports. The extent of the imbalance and the related problem of financing are also discussed.

1181   Kuznets, Simon, et al. POPULATION REDISTRIBUTION AND ECONOMIC GROWTH, UNITED STATES, 1870-1950. 3 vols. Philadelphia: American Philosophical Society, 1957. 759, 289, 368 p.

These three volumes contain an unbelievable amount of information on population, income, wealth, employment, manufacturing, and so forth, on a state-by-state basis. They are an invaluable source of information and data.

1182   Land, Aubrey C. "Economic Base and Social Structure: The Northern Chesapeake in the Eighteenth Century." JOURNAL OF ECONOMIC HISTORY 25 (December 1965): 639-59.

An examination of the inventories of the estates of all free men in Maryland is carried out in order that one may ascertain the economic base and social structure. The standard of living, possible social status, and income distribution are also considered.

1183   Laursen, Svend. "Productivity, Wages, and the Balance of Payments."

REVIEW OF ECONOMICS AND STATISTICS 37 (May 1955): 180–88.

This examination of the hypothesis that differential national productivity growth rates lead to persistent imbalance in the world finds little evidence to support it. Special effort is given to discussing the possible effects of the postwar intent of many industrialized nations to maintain full employment.

1184 Lederer, Walther. "Major Developments Affecting the United States Balance of International Payments." REVIEW OF ECONOMICS AND STATISTICS 38 (May 1956): 177–92.

This is a study of characteristics of balance of payments data, structural factors which affect the relationships of international transactions to the level of business activity, the effect of structural developments on credit-debt relations, and cyclical effects.

1185 Lipsey, Robert E. "Foreign Trade." In AMERICAN ECONOMIC GROWTH, edited by Lance E. Davis et al., pp. 548–81. New York: Harper & Row, 1972.

This chapter of the larger, more comprehensive work dealing with economic growth is concerned with the relationship between international trade and economic growth.

1186 _____. PRICE AND QUANTITY TRENDS IN THE FOREIGN TRADE OF THE UNITED STATES. National Bureau of Economic Research Studies in International Economic Relations, no. 2. Princeton, N.J.: Princeton University Press, 1963. 487 p.

This is a very extensive and disaggreated study of exports and imports for the United States between 1870 and 1960. Of the six chapters, the first two are summaries of the analysis and the last four are more technically oriented toward descriptions of the data and how it was used to construct the various indexes.

1187 Lord, Daniel. THE EFFECT OF SECESSION ON THE COMMERCIAL RELATIONS BETWEEN THE NORTH AND SOUTH. London: H. Stevens, 1861. 341 p.

The effects of secession on trade with the North and upon direct trade with Europe are examined. Growth in population prior to the Civil War is traced and the proportion of the population that was slave is kept for each state.

1188 McCalla, Alex F. "Protectionism in International Agricultural Trade, 1850–1968." AGRICULTURAL HISTORY 43 (July 1969): 329–44.

This is a study of national policies toward trade in temperate-

zone agricultural products. An attempt is made to learn the
reasons for the continuance of national restrictions to the inflow of agricultural commodities.

1189   McClelland, Peter D. "The Cost to America of British Imperial Policy."
AMERICAN ECONOMIC REVIEW 59 (May 1969): 370-85.

The author argues that the conceptual framework used by previous authors has been seriously lacking, and offers an alternative for estimating the cost of British policy, based on an opportunity cost measure.

1190   McCormick, William W., and Franks, Charles M. "A Self-Generating
Model of Long-Swings for the American Economy, 1860-1940." JOUR-
NAL OF ECONOMIC HISTORY 31 (June 1971): 295-343.

It is argued that a stable socioeconomic structure of long-term
economic change exists and this is what shapes the long swings
in economic activity. There is a concurrence of relationships
between certain economic and demographic variables which in
combination determine the dynamic pattern of economic growth.

1191   MacDougall, G.D.A. "British and American Exports: A Study Suggested
by the Theory of Comparative Costs, Parts I and II." ECONOMIC JOUR-
NAL 61 (December 1951): 697-724; 62 (September 1952): 487-521.

Analyzing British and U.S. data, the author attempts to test
the theory of comparative cost. Part 1 is concerned with explaining the deviations from the prediction of this theory.
Part 2 examines elasticities and substitution, exports and factors other than price, for example, imperfect markets.

1192   Macesich, George. "Sources of Monetary Disturbance in the United
States, 1834-1845." JOURNAL OF ECONOMIC HISTORY 20 (September 1960): 407-26.

Another examination of the effects of dissolution of the Second
Bank of the United States, this article proffers the hypothesis
that the major source of instability due to monetary disturbances
was external. A comment by Jeffrey G. Williamson and a reply by Macesich appear in this journal, volume 21 (September
1961): 372-85.

1193   Machlup, Fritz. "Three Concepts of the Balance of Payments and the
So-called Dollar Shortage." ECONOMIC JOURNAL 60 (March 1950):
46-68.

Discussing three variations in the concept of balance of payments and their usefulness, the author attempts to illustrate
the implications of running persistent deficits in terms of these

definitions. The effects of such policy upon development are also considered.

1194 McVey, Frank L. "Trusts and the Tariff." JOURNAL OF POLITICAL ECONOMY 7 (June 1899): 382-84.

This article contains an examination of a list of millionaires in the United States in an attempt to determine the effects of protective tariffs on the creation of trusts.

1195 Mak, James. "Intraregional Trade in the Antebellum West: Ohio, A Case Study." AGRICULTURAL HISTORY 46 (October 1972): 489-97.

This article questions whether the Midwest was a homogeneous region. Was there subregional specialization to the extent that trade occurred among areas of specialization within the region in wheat, corn, pork, and beef? Estimates are made for Ohio in 1846, 1850, and 1860.

1196 Mandle, Jay R. "The Plantation States as a Sub-Region of the Post-Bellum South." JOURNAL OF ECONOMIC HISTORY 34 (September 1974): 732-38.

This author argues that the traditional Census Bureau definitions of regions are covering up much more economically meaningful regions. By using Census Bureau data the concentrations of poverty and growth are not observed in their fullest extent. He observes differences between the economic performance in states where plantation agriculture was concentrated as compared to other southern states.

1197 Mansfield, Edwin. "Community Size, Region, Labor Force, and Income, 1950." REVIEW OF ECONOMICS AND STATISTICS 37 (November 1955): 418-23.

Arguing from the viewpoint that substantial differences in income levels per consumer unit exist among community size categories, the author tries to determine if the number of income earners per consumer unit explains the income differences among communities.

1198 Melman, Seymore. "An Industrial Revolution in the Cotton South." ECONOMIC HISTORY REVIEW 2 (April 1950): 59-72.

Examining the process by which the economic and technological arrangements of sharecropping replaced slavery with the wage labor, the author analyzes the effects on output, labor force, the agricultural system, organization, and markets.

1199 Mendershausen, Horst. "Foreign Aid with and without Dollar Shortage."

REVIEW OF ECONOMICS AND STATISTICS 33 (February 1951): 38-48.

This is a comparison of two views on the dollar shortage: (1) the outside world is persistently short of dollars; and (2) the outside need not be persistently short of dollars and was not, prior to the 1940s. The identification of the dollar shortage is discussed.

1200   Meyer, Hugo R. "Railway Rates as Protective Tariffs." JOURNAL OF POLITICAL ECONOMY 14 (January 1906): 1-13.

Using various test cases, the author illustrates how the Interstate Commerce Commission carried out practices that reestablished the doctrine that "each locality is entitled to the enjoyment of the advantages occurring to it by virtue of its location."

1201   Miller, Ronald E. "Impact of the Aluminum Industry on the Pacific Northwest: A Regional Input-Output Analysis." REVIEW OF ECONOMICS AND STATISTICS 39 (May 1957): 200-209.

This is an analysis of the locational problems incurred by the aluminum industry in the United States, with particular emphasis on the application of modified Weberian analysis. A brief discussion of the Pacific Northwest is also included.

1202   Miller, William L. "A Note on the Importance of the Interstate Slave Trade of the Antebellum South." JOURNAL OF POLITICAL ECONOMY 73 (February 1965): 181-87.

This author concludes that interstate slave trade was not necessary for the preservation of slavery as an institution. Although it may have served to more efficiently reallocate labor and to generate profits for the sellers, it was not necessary.

1203   Mintz, Ilse. CYCLICAL FLUCTUATIONS IN THE EXPORTS OF THE UNITED STATES SINCE 1879. National Bureau of Economic Research Studies in Business Cycles, no. 15. New York: Columbia University Press, 1967. 332 p.

This work uses much of the same data as did Lipsey (see no. 1186), but this author directs all of the analysis to the relationship between exports and the business cycle. Price and quantity trends and trends in world imports are examined along with the trends of U.S. exports during U.S. business cycles.

1204   Morgan, Theodore. "The Long-Run Terms of Trade between Agriculture and Manufacturing." ECONOMIC DEVELOPMENT AND CULTURAL CHANGE 8 (October 1959): 1-23.

Using data for seven countries, criticisms are offered for sev-

eral existing doctrines which imply adverse or worsening terms
of trade for producers of primary products.

1205   Morriss, Margaret Shove. COLONIAL TRADE OF MARYLAND, 1689-
1715. Baltimore: Johns Hopkins Press, 1914. 157 p.

This work discusses the role of Maryland (1) as a source of
raw materials, (2) as a market for British manufacturers and
goods passed through England as an entrepôt, and (3) as the
terminus of a line of trade employing British ships and sea-
men. Trade routes, chief commodities exported and imported,
and illicit trade are also discussed.

1206   National Bureau of Economic Research, ed. TRENDS IN THE AMERICAN
ECONOMY IN THE NINETEENTH CENTURY. Studies in Income and
Wealth, no. 24. Princeton, N.J.: Princeton University Press, 1960.
682 p.

This collection of papers includes such topics as trends in output, income, factor payments, and international payments.
The origin of income by sector, factor payments, and railroad
and capital investment are also discussed.

1207   Neisser, Hans P. "The United States Demand for Imports." AMERICAN
ECONOMIC REVIEW 43 (May 1953): 134-47.

This is a discussion of the author's work on attempting to derive import functions for the United States using data from 1919
to 1937 from various sources. A discussion follows by John H.
Adler, pages 160-63.

1208   Nettels, Curtis P. "British Mercantilism and the Economic Development
of the Thirteen Colonies." JOURNAL OF ECONOMIC HISTORY 12
(Spring 1952): 105-14.

Starting with a discussion of mercantilism and the conditions
for its perpetuation, the author discusses how these characteristics might have affected the development of the thirteen
colonies.

1209   Nicholls, William H. "Industrial Urban Development and Agricultural
Adjustments, Tennessee Valley and Piedmont, 1939-1954." JOURNAL
OF POLITICAL ECONOMY 68 (April 1960): 135-49.

This is comparative analysis of these two regions, and the
process of worker income equalization in both areas is compared. The impediments to the equilibrating factors are examined and this rate of redirection is compared between the
regions.

1210 _____. "Relative Economic Development of the Upper East Tennessee Valley, 1850-1950." ECONOMIC DEVELOPMENT AND CULTURAL CHANGE 5 (April 1957): 308-24.

Comparing the performance of this region with that of the national economy of the basis of a set of socioeconomic characteristics, the author found that the Upper East Tennessee Valley study area remained in a relatively disadvantaged state.

1211 _____. "Some Foundations of Economic Development in the Upper East Tennessee Valley, 1850-1900, Parts I and II." JOURNAL OF POLITICAL ECONOMY 64 (August 1956): 277-302; (October 1956): 400-415.

Why certain southern areas experienced substantial industrial urban development and others did not is the central theme of part 1. Particular industries are considered individually and counties contiguous to the developing ones are examined to discover why they were not also developing. Part 2 examines trends in population and population characteristics of this area.

1212 Niemi, Albert W., Jr. "Inequality in the Distribution of Slave Wealth: The Cotton South and Other Southern Agricultural Regions." JOURNAL OF ECONOMIC HISTORY 37 (September 1977): 747-54.

This analysis of the distribution of wealth finds that it is not only unequally distributed in the cotton South but also in the other agricultural areas as well.

1213 North, Douglas C. GROWTH AND DEVELOPMENT IN THE AMERICAN PAST. Englewood Cliffs, N.J.: Prentice-Hall, 1966. 304 p.

Developing an export-led model of regional growth, the author attempts to use existing data to produce an explanation of regional as well as aggregate growth. This is one of the earliest works that reopens this area of research.

1214 _____. "International Capital Flows and the Development of the American West." JOURNAL OF ECONOMIC HISTORY 16 (December 1956): 493-505.

Summarizing the institutional framework and characteristics of the Atlantic economy, North discusses the development of the western resources and land where the primary obstacles were accessibility not quality. It is argued that western development was spurred by favorable long-run movements of the prices of key staple goods, which resulted from flows of long-term foreign investment used for internal and plantation development.

1215 _____. "Location Theory and Regional Economic Growth." JOURNAL OF POLITICAL ECONOMY 63 (June 1955): 243-58.

The author lays out an export base model for the development of regions within a country, and attempts to describe the location choice of particular types of industry, that is, why does it develop where and when it does. A comment by Charles M. Tiebout, a reply by North, and a rejoinder by Tiebout appear in this journal, volume 64 (April 1956): 160-69.

1216 _____. "Ocean Freight Rates and Economic Development, 1750-1913." JOURNAL OF ECONOMIC HISTORY 18 (December 1958): 537-55.

Contained in this article are discussions of the effects of reductions in ocean freight rates on agricultural stimulation and economic interdependence.

1217 _____. "The United States in the International Economy, 1790-1950." In AMERICAN ECONOMIC HISTORY, edited by Seymore Harris, pp. 181-206. New York: McGraw-Hill Book Co., 1961.

This looks at the evolving structure of world trade with the United States as integral parts, so that the patterns of trade and factor movements become intelligible. In this way the author examines the frictions and barriers that developed. The analysis is broken down into time periods.

1218 Notz, William. "Export Trade Problems and an American Foreign Trade Policy." JOURNAL OF POLITICAL ECONOMY 26 (February 1918): 105-24.

The author is considering the need for a foreign trade policy for the United States as a result of the changes generated by the war. The effect of U.S. trade on the foreign trade of other countries and anticipated foreign trade problems are considered.

1219 Novack, David, and Simon, Matthew. "Commercial Response to the American Export Invasion, 1871-1914: A Essay in Attitudinal History." EXPLORATIONS IN ECONOMIC HISTORY 3 (Winter 1966): 121-47.

After reviewing the various ways in which expectations are formed, the authors attempt to assess the attitudes of U.S. businessmen toward the export invasion. Because it does not separate cause and effect, the work is primarily a description of patterns in attitudinal behavior of the export community.

1220 Nugent, Jeffrey B. "Exchange-Rate Movements and Economic Development in the Late Nineteenth Century." JOURNAL OF POLITICAL ECONOMY 81 (September-October 1973): 1110-35.

Using the period 1873-94, the author tests the hypothesis that devaluation will stimulate exports and income growth. Silver standard countries are compared with gold standard countries, since those on silver depreciated nearly 50 percent faster.

1221   Olmsted, F.L. THE COTTON KINGDOM. 2 vols. New York: Mason Brothers, 1861. 276, 283 p.

These are a traveler's observations on cotton production and slavery, as he passes from Washington, D.C., to Virginia, South Carolina, Georgia, southwest Alabama, Mississippi, Louisiana, and Texas. The railroad economy of Virginia is also discussed.

1222   Ostrander, Gilman M. "The Colonial Molasses Trade." AGRICULTURAL HISTORY 30 (April 1956): 77-84.

This is an examination of the importance of the molasses trade and the effect on the distribution of molasses of the prohibitive duty of the Molasses Act.

1223   Page, Thomas Walker. "Earlier Commercial Policy of the United States." JOURNAL OF POLITICAL ECONOMY 10 (March 1902): 161-92.

This is a review of early U.S. commercial policy within the perspective of free trade.

1224   Parker, William N., ed. THE STRUCTURE OF THE COTTON ECONOMY OF THE ANTEBELLUM SOUTH. Washington, D.C.: Agricultural History Society, 1970. 169 p.

This is a reprint of the January 1970 issue of AGRICULTURAL HISTORY, and includes articles by William N. Parket, Robert E. Gallman, Raymond C. Battalio and John Kagel, James D. Foust and Dale E. Swan, Gavin Wright, Diane L. Lindstrom, Stanley L. Engerman, Eugene D. Genovese, and Morton Rothstein. These articles treat nearly every aspect of the antebellum southern economy.

1225   Passell, Peter. "The Impact of Cotton Land Distribution on the Antebellum Economy." JOURNAL OF ECONOMIC HISTORY 31 (December 1971): 917-37.

In this analysis of the effect of cotton land sales, the issues considered are the effect on factor proportions from the shaping of the pool of available farm land; the effect on aggregate national output as a result of changing the quantity of land in productive use, the effect on federal spending as a result of the revenues; and the effect of the added export earnings.

1226   Perkins, Edwin J. "Foreign Interest Rates in American Financial Markets: A Revised Series of Dollar-Sterling Exchange Rates, 1835-1890." JOURNAL OF ECONOMIC HISTORY 38 (June 1978): 392-417.

The author presents a new series of nineteenth-century Anglo-American foreign exchange rates. It was found that domestic interest rates serve as better reflections for English than U.S. money markets.

1227 Perloff, Harvey S. HOW A REGION GROWS. New York: Committee for Economic Development, 1963. 147 p.

This book is devoted to analyzing the patterns of regional growth between 1870 and 1960. Factors behind various aspects of growth are examined as well as long-term changes in the regional distribution of economic activity. Particular industries are examined for their regional characteristics.

1228 Perren, Richard. "The North American Beef and Cattle Trade with Great Britain, 1870-1914." ECONOMICS HISTORY REVIEW 24 (August 1971): 430-44.

Development of refrigeration methods, methods of transport to England, regulation of the livestock trade, costs involved, and competition are all considered in this examination of the demand for chilled North American beef.

1229 Pfister, Richard L. "External Trade and Regional Growth: A Case Study of the Pacific Northwest." ECONOMIC DEVELOPMENT AND CULTURAL CHANGE 11 (January 1963): 134-51.

The author tests three hypotheses regarding trade and growth using data for the Pacific Northwest: (1) foreign trade (external trade) declines as a proportion of total output as growth occurs; (2) specialization in primary products means slower growth relative to the more industrialized areas; and (3) if an economy's exports are a large proportion of output and they are mainly primary products, the economy will be subject to relatively greater instability.

1230 Phinney, J.T. "The Growth of Trade to 1913." JOURNAL OF POLITICAL ECONOMY 42 (August 1934): 492-507.

Using data derived from indexes of the physical volume of production, deflated clearing and, the true indexes of the volume of trade, the author concludes that the rate of growth of trade had been primarily negative before World War I.

1231 Pope, Clayne. "The Impact of the Ante-Bellum Tariff on Income Distribution." EXPLORATIONS IN ECONOMIC HISTORY 9 (Summer 1972): 375-422.

A review of the literature on tariffs and income distribution is presented along with analysis of the effects of the antebellum tariffs. A model of the antebellum economy is presented and used to examine the data on tariffs and income by sectors (sectors which approximate regions).

1232   Price, Jacob M. "The Economic Growth of the Chesapeake and the European Market, 1697-1775." JOURNAL OF ECONOMIC HISTORY 24 (December 1964): 496-516.

Examining trade data for both Virginia and Maryland, the author ascertains the pattern of the tobacco trade. The article also focuses on the nature of the tobacco markets and the regulation of the markets to account for economic growth as well as the movement of trade centers and credit expansion.

1233   _____. "A Note on the Value of Colonial Exports in Shipping." JOURNAL OF ECONOMIC HISTORY 36 (September 1976): 704-24.

This is an examination of the ship-building industry in the colonial United States--the average number of ships per year and their tonnage.

1234   Reid, Joseph D., Jr. "Antebellum Southern Rental Contracts." EXPLORATION IN ECONOMIC HISTORY 13 (January 1976): 69-84.

The evidence presented in this study shows that tenancy was not new to the postbellum South, but had been practiced for at least forty years before the Civil War. The evidence also allows one to learn more about why one tenure was chosen over another.

1235   _____. "Sharecropping as an Understandable Market Response--The Post-Bellum South." JOURNAL OF ECONOMIC HISTORY 33 (March 1973): 106-30.

The author shows that sharecropping should have increased productivity during the postbellum period, which leaves the reduction in the availability of capital and labor as the main explanatory variables for the relative reduction in southern per capita income between 1860 and 1880. A discussion by Gavin Wright follows on pages 170-76 of the same issue of this journal.

1236   Reimer, Richard. "The United States Demand for Imports of Materials, 1923-1960." REVIEW OF ECONOMICS AND STATISTICS 46 (February 1964): 65-75.

This article is an attempt at measuring the influence that changes in the volume of U.S. imports had on the countries that exported these goods to the United States. The level of imports is also compared to the level of economic activity and prices within the U.S. economy. The evidence for the postwar period is very similar to that for the interwar period.

1237 Robertson, M.L. "Scottish Commerce and the American War of Independence." ECONOMIC HISTORY REVIEW 9 (August 1957): 123-31.

This is an examination of the effect of the war on Scottish trade with the United States, and the pivotal role played by the Navigation Acts.

1238 Rogers, J.M. THE DEVELOPMENT OF THE NORTH SINCE THE CIVIL WAR. Philadelphia: G. Barrie and Sons, 1906. 482 p.

The panic of 1873 and the completion of the Transcontinental Railroad are a couple of the many economic as well as noneconomic topics discussed.

1239 Ronsom, Roger, and Sutch, Richard. "The Impact of the Civil War and of Emancipation on Southern Agriculture." EXPLORATIONS IN ECONOMIC HISTORY 12 (January 1975): 1-28.

The authors find that the devastation of the South cannot be blamed for its slow rate of recovery in per capita income, because the devastation was not that serious. They cite emancipation, instead, as the cause of slow rate of recovery, due to the voluntary decline in the per capita supply of labor.

1240 _____. ONE KIND OF FREEDOM: THE ECONOMIC CONSEQUENCES OF EMANCIPATION. Cambridge, Engl.: Cambridge University Press, 1977. 409 p.

This is a slightly technical historical narrative of the economic changes that occurred in the postbellum South. The authors have used sampling techniques when possible to reduce the difficulties at hand in attempting to study the cotton South. The effects of noneconomic forces are discussed whenever they were felt to have been influential. It is a perfect follow-up to TIME ON THE CROSS (see no. 1141), although the authors do not necessarily agree with one another on issues in either period.

1241 Rostow, Walter W. "The Past Quarter-Century as Economic History and the Tasks of International Economic Organization." JOURNAL OF ECONOMIC HISTORY 30 (March 1970): 150-87.

Defining five clusters of sectors crucial to the growth process, the author attempts to explain the interwar years and the evaluation of the world economy since 1945. Aggregate concepts such as productivity and investment are compared between sectors.

1242 Rothstein, Morton. "The Antebellum South as a Dual Economy: A Tentative Hypothesis." AGRICULTURAL HISTORY 41 (October 1967): 373-82.

This is a test of the profitability of the plantation system and the southern economy as a whole. It does not consider individual slaveholders.

1243 _____. "Antebellum Wheat and Cotton Exports: Contrast in Marketing Organization and Economic Development." AGRICULTURAL HISTORY 40 (April 1966): 91-100.

This is a comparison of the development and marketing organization of the cotton South and the wheat-growing north central region before the Civil War. An attempt is made to explain these differences.

1244 Salant, Walter S. "International Transactions in National Income Accounts." REVIEW OF ECONOMICS AND STATISTICS 33 (November 1951): 304-15.

This study of the international accounts contains suggestions for improving the accounting concepts and illustrates how various accounting measures have been applied to analysis.

1245 Schafer, Joseph. HISTORY OF THE PACIFIC NORTHWEST. New York: Macmillan Co., 1918. 323 p.

Dealing frequently with the Oregon territory, the author discusses migration, railways, agriculture, industry, and general commerce.

1246 Schmidt, Louis B. "Internal Commerce and the Development of National Economy before 1860." JOURNAL OF POLITICAL ECONOMY 47 (December 1939): 798-822.

This is an assessment of the effect of internal commerce on specialization and the development of a national economy. The streams of commerce among the East, West, and South are outlined.

1247 Schmitz, Mark D., and Schaefer, Donald F. "Slavery, Freedom, and The Elasticity of Substitution." EXPLORATIONS IN ECONOMIC HISTORY 15 (July 1978): 327-37.

This is an attempt to determine the degree to which input substitutability existed for farms using slave labor and for farms using only free labor. The finding was that the elasticity was less than one for slave farms and greater than or equal to one for free labor farms.

1248 Scrivenor, H.A. A COMPREHENSIVE HISTORY OF THE IRON TRADE. London: Cass, 1967. 327 p.

The book is an attempt to place in a clear and correct per-spective the development and growth of the trade in all coun-tries where iron may be considered to be a staple manufacture. The production of the British colonies in America up to the War of Independence is covered quite thoroughly.

1249 Shepherd, James F., and Walton, Gary M. "Economic Change after the American Revolution: Pre- and Post-War Comparisons of Maritime Shipping and Trade." EXPLORATIONS IN ECONOMIC HISTORY 13 (October 1976): 397-422.

These authors present new data on trade and shipping for the period between the colonial years and the adoption of the Constitution. A considerable amount of space is devoted to comments on the works of other writers.

1250 _____. SHIPPING, MARITIME TRADE AND THE ECONOMIC DEVELOP-MENT OF COLONIAL NORTH AMERICA. New York: Cambridge Uni-versity Press, 1972. 255 p.

Applying economic theory to the empirical evidence from the period 1650 to 1776, the author provides a detailed quantita-tive study of the role of trade in colonial development. Pro-ductivity change in shipping and distribution are also discussed.

1251 Shepherd, James F., and Williamson, Samuel H. "The Coastal Trade of the British North American Colonies, 1768-1772." JOURNAL OF ECONOMIC HISTORY 32 (December 1972): 783-810.

This attempt at discovering the importance of trade to colonial development examines the patterns of coastal trade by commod-ity. The values of most of the traded goods are estimated along with the central tendencies of direction and the distance trav-eled by each commodity.

1252 Shepherd, W. Geoffrey. "Development Loans to Private Borrowers, 1945-1961." ECONOMIC DEVELOPMENT AND CULTURAL CHANGE 12 (April 1964): 305-11.

Covering six major agencies for international lending, data are presented for analysis of the lenders and borrowers.

1253 Sheridan, Richard B. "The Molasses Act and the Market Strategy of the British Sugar Planters." JOURNAL OF ECONOMIC HISTORY 17 (March 1957): 62-83.

This is an examination of tensions between British sugar plant-ers and North American and Irish merchants. The changing

nature of the British market for sugar and rum, and the planters' attempts to adjust the Navigation Acts to these changes
are examined.

1254 Simon, Matthew, and Novack, David E. "Some Dimensions of the American Commercial Invasion of Europe, 1871-1914: An Introductory Essay."
JOURNAL OF ECONOMIC HISTORY 24 (December 1964): 591-608.

It was commonly believed that the United States commercially
invaded Europe during this period. The authors evaluate data
on U.S. exports to Europe to determine the validity of this
belief.

1255 Smolensky, Eugene. "Industrial Location and Urban Growth." In
AMERICAN ECONOMIC GROWTH, edited by Lance E. Davis et al.,
pp. 582-610. New York: Harper & Row, 1972.

This chapter develops a theoretical view of city growth and
then examines the hypotheses produced, to see if they are
verified.

1256 Smolensky, Eugene, and Ratajezak, Donald. "The Conception of Cities."
EXPLORATIONS IN ECONOMIC HISTORY 3 (Spring 1965): 90-131.

This is an analysis of why cities grow and why they locate
where they do as well as their impact on economic growth.
The requisite investment in social overhead capital is also examined.

1257 Sorrell, Lewis C. "Dislocations in the Foreign Trade of the United States
Resulting from the European War." JOURNAL OF POLITICAL ECONOMY
24 (January 1916): 25-75.

World War I altered many things, some of which are examined
here: levels of exports and imports, levels of trade with bel-
ligerent nations, changes in commodities involved, changes in
international gold movements, and changes in shipping facilities. No attempt is made to assess the benefits of these changes.

1258 Southard, F.A., Jr. "American Industry Abroad since 1929." JOUR-
NAL OF POLITICAL ECONOMY 41 (August 1933): 530-47.

In light of the 1930s, the growth of U.S. investment abroad
is discussed with regard to motive and rate of growth. The
effects of falling profits, exchange restrictions, and the oc-
currence of such disorders as strikes and political unrest are
all considered.

1259 Spicer, A.D. THE PAPER TRADE. London: Methuen and Co., 1907.
282 p.

This discussion of the mechanical developments and the introduction of steam power which took place in the paper industry also considers foreign sources of inputs and the regional
localization of production.

1260   Stampp, Kenneth M. PECULIAR INSTITUTION: SLAVERY IN THE
ANTE-BELLUM SOUTH. New York: Vintage Books, 1956.

This is one of the earlier attempts at a new approach to this
topic and one often cited by more recent authors. Many aspects of the slaves' condition are considered, including profitability of the arrangement. A fairly long list of manuscripts
which were consulted is provided.

1261   _____, ed. CAUSES OF THE CIVIL WAR. Englewood Cliffs, N.J.:
Prentice-Hall, 1965. 186 p.

This is a collection of ninety-two works by various writers,
which the editor has divided into seven groups. The one on
economic sectionalism deals more strictly with economic issues,
but the others provide considerable background reading.

1262   Stanwood, Edward. AMERICAN TARIFF CONTROVERSIES IN THE NINE-
TEENTH CENTURY. New York: Houghton Mifflin and Co., 1903.

This work traces the recurring reliance upon protection and
tariff revenues for various purposes during the period, from
pre-Civil War to 1902.

1263   Stern, Robert M. "British and American Productivity and Comparative
Costs in International Trade." OXFORD ECONOMIC PAPERS 14 (October 1962): 275-96.

Using a new sample of data, tests are made of the comparative
cost doctrine. These tests were previously not possible due to
the lack of data. A brief discussion of export elasticities is
also given.

1264   Sterns, Worthy P. "The Foreign Trade of the United States from 1821-
1930." JOURNAL OF POLITICAL ECONOMY 8 (September 1900):
452-90.

This article explores the importance of exports and the U.S.
consumption of imports. Special attention is given to the
most important export, cotton.

1265   Sutch, Richard. "The Treatment Received by American Slaves: A Critical Review of the Evidence Presented in TIME ON THE CROSS." EX-
PLORATIONS IN ECONOMIC HISTORY 12 (October 1975): 335-438.

This article is an extensive in-depth critical analysis of Fogel

and Engerman's book (see no. 1141), which attempts to re-
fute many of the calculations generated by the two authors
in their treatment of American slavery.

1266   Sutch, Richard, and Ransom, Roger. "The Ex-Slave in the Post-Bellum
        South: A Study of the Economic Impact of Racism in a Market Environ-
        ment." JOURNAL OF ECONOMIC HISTORY 33 (March 1973): 131-
        48.

        This discussion of the size distribution of farms attempts to dis-
        cern why incomes are so diverse, and uses information costs as
        one of the major variables to explain income differences. A
        discussion by Gavin Wright appears on pages 170-76 in this
        issue of the journal.

1267   Taeuber, Conrad. "Rural-Urban Migration." AGRICULTURAL HISTORY
        15 (July 1941): 151-60.

        Covering the whole nineteenth century, this article examines
        the reasons for and the magnitude of urban-rural migration in
        the United States.

1268   Taussig, Frank W. "New United States Tariff." ECONOMIC JOURNAL
        4 (December 1894): 573-94.

        The effect of the tariff on minerals and raw materials is con-
        sidered and found to be completely different from the effects
        on manufactured articles. The conclusion is that the act makes
        no new change in the character of U.S. tariff legislation.

1269   _____. SOME ASPECTS OF THE TARIFF QUESTION. Cambridge,
        Mass.: Harvard University Press, 1931. Reprint. Clifton, N.J.:
        Augustus M. Kelley Publishers, 1972. 497 p.

        The purpose of this work was to "consider and illustrate some
        questions of principle in the controversy on free trade and pro-
        tection." The sugar, iron and steel, and textile industries are
        all considered in great detail.

1270   _____. STATE PAPERS AND SPEECHES ON THE TARIFF. Cambridge,
        Mass.: Harvard University Press, 1893. 385 p.

        This collection includes a paper by Alexander Hamilton and
        speeches by Clay and Webster on the Tariff Act of 1824, as
        well as various other papers of the pre-1860 period.

1271   _____. TARIFF HISTORY OF THE UNITED STATES. New York: G.P.
        Putnam's Sons, 1931. Reprint. New York: Augustus M. Kelley Publishers,
        1967. 536 p.

        Starting with the beginning of the country, the author traces
        out the development of tariff policies up to 1930. Particular

industries are examined at some length in the discussions of particular tariffs. Each tariff act is considered in some detail.

1272 Taylor, G.W. Langworthy. "The Relative Importance of Our Foreign Trade." JOURNAL OF POLITICAL ECONOMY 12 (December 1903): 18-33.

Analyzing statistics on world trade, the author attempts to determine the importance of the United States in this world market.

1273 Temin, Peter. "The Post-Bellum Recovery of the South and the Cost of the Civil War." JOURNAL OF ECONOMIC HISTORY 36 (December 1976): 898-907.

This article is an attempt to reconcile the works of Ransom and Sutch (no. 1266), Wright (no. 1301), and Goldin and Lewis (no. 1146) and to provide a unified interpretation. By accounting for the demand factors noted by Wright and the supply factors cited by Ransom and Sutch, the author argues that the Goldin and Lewis estimates of the cost of the Civil War are overstated by a factor of four. An alternative calculation is offered.

1274 Thistlethwaite, Frank. "Atlantic Partnership." ECONOMIC HISTORY REVIEW 7 (August 1954): 1-17.

This is an examination of the effects of the British partnership with the Atlantic communities on western expansion, economic development, innovation, credit expansion, social organizations, political radicalism, finance, and capital formation.

1275 Thomas, Brinley. "Long Swings and the Atlantic Economy: A Reappraisal." In NATIONS AND HOUSEHOLDS IN ECONOMIC GROWTH, edited by Paul A. David and Melvin Reder, pp. 383-406. New York: Academic Press, 1974.

This article examines America's weight in the pre-1913 international economy. A model of the Atlantic economy is developed and used to analyze long swings in productivity and real income.

1276 Thomas, Robert Paul. "A Quantitative Approach to the Study of the Effects of British Imperial Policy upon Colonial Welfare: Some Preliminary Findings." JOURNAL OF ECONOMIC HISTORY 25 (December 1965): 615-38.

The hypothesis, that the British Navigation Acts severely burdened

the thirteen colonies, is tested by examining the costs and benefits of these regulations. A comment by Roger L. Ransom and
a reply appear in this journal, volume 28 (September 1968):
427-40.

1277   Thomas, Robert Paul, and Anderson, Terry L.   "White Population, Labor
Force and Extensive Growth of the New England Economy in the Seventeenth Century."   JOURNAL OF ECONOMIC HISTORY   33 (September
1973):   634-67.

This is an attempt to integrate the population parameters and
aggregate growth for the region.   Labor force data are generated as well as the note of employment of this force that
were employed.

1278   Thomas, Robert Paul, and Bean, Richard Nelson.   "The Fishers of Men:
The Profits of the Slave Trade."   JOURNAL OF ECONOMIC HISTORY
34 (December 1974):   885-914.

This is an attempt to discern who received the profits from the
slave trade.   The market structure is examined at each stage
of the slave trade and from that inferences are made regarding
the existence of profits.   They found that the only true gainers
from the existence of the slave trade were possibly the European
consumers.

1279   Thornblade, James B.   "Textile Imports from the Less Developed Countries: A Challenge to the American Market."   ECONOMIC DEVELOP-
MENT AND CULTURAL CHANGE   19 (January 1971):   277-86.

Labor costs, productivity, quality of machinery, and the changes
for a reversal of comparative advantage are all discussed with
respect to the presence and increased role of textile imports
from less well developed countries.

1280   Upgren, Arthur P.   "Triangular Trade."   JOURNAL OF POLITICAL
ECONOMY   43 (October 1935):   653-73.

Investigating the trade policies of the United States and other
countries, the source of later contrary trade policies is dis-
covered.   Triangular trade is defined and various methods of
measurement are discussed.

1281   Vanek, Jaroslav.   "The Natural Resource Content of Foreign Trade, 1870-
1955, And the Relative Abundance of Natural Resources in the United
States."   REVIEW OF ECONOMICS AND STATISTICS   41 (February
1959):   146-53.

This is an attempt to provide statistical evidence on the natural resource requirements in an economic aggregate such as exports or imports.   The relative abundance of factors of pro-

duction in the U.S. economy are also discussed.

1282 _____. NATURAL RESOURCE CONTENT OF U.S. FOREIGN TRADE, 1870-1955. Cambridge: MIT Press, 1963. 142 p.

Economic theory implies we should export those commodities that use our relatively more abundant factors most intensively. To test this hypothesis the resource content of exports and imports is necessary, for we should also import those commodities that use our relatively more scarce resources most intensively. The patterns have changed over time and explanations are offered for why and the subsequent impacts.

1283 Vatter, Harold G. "An Estimate of Input Substitution for Manufactured Products in the U.S. Economy, 1859 and 1899." ECONOMIC DEVELOPMENT AND CULTURAL CHANGE 18 (October 1969): 40-43.

The ratio of net imported manufacturers to total domestic absorption is used to obtain a gross import substitution figure, which is further modified for analysis.

1284 Vedder, Richard K. "The Slave Exploitation (Expropriation) Rate." EXPLORATIONS IN ECONOMIC HISTORY 12 (October 1975): 453-57.

This is an examination of the concept of exploitation and a calculation of the extent of the exploitation as determined by one conventional method of measurement. These losses must be compared with the exploitation of free workers in order to judge the relative degree of exploitation of slaves.

1285 Viner, Jacob. "The Most-Favored-Nation-Clause in American Commercial Treaties." JOURNAL OF POLITICAL ECONOMY 32 (February 1924): 101-29.

Explaining the conditional and unconditional forms of this policy, the author compares the results of the two policies and discusses the consequences of abandoning the conditional form.

1286 Walton, Gary M. "The New Economic History and the Burdens of the Navigation Acts." ECONOMIC HISTORY REVIEW 24 (November 1971): 533-42.

This is a reexamination of such earlier works as Harper (no. 1156) and Thomas (no. 1276), where the author attempts to sort out the errors of each. The work by Thomas was found to be the more adequate in its treatment of the subject matter from the point of view of the author and his analysis. None were found to be totally adequate. Comments by Frank J.A. Broeze and Peter D. McClelland appear in this journal, volume 26 (November 1973): 668-86.

1287   Wardwell, A.R.   REGIONAL TRENDS IN THE U.S. ECONOMY.   Washington, D.C.:   Government Printing Office, 1951.   121 p.

This regional analysis of the United States considers changes in industrial structure, production technology, and the growth of new products.   This is printed as a supplement to the SURVEY OF CURRENT BUSINESS.

1288   Weeden, William B.   ECONOMIC AND SOCIAL HISTORY OF NEW ENGLAND.   New York: Houghton Mifflin and Co., 1891.   195 p.

This is an account of the commercial development of New England from about 1630 to 1745.   The economic use of wampum is part of the discussion of the early development.

1289   Williams, Eric.   CAPITALISM & SLAVERY.   Chapel Hill: University of North Carolina Press, 1944.   285 p.

This work is described as a study of the contribution of slavery to the development of British capitalism, and not a study of the institution of slavery.   Slavery in non-United States places is discussed at some length in terms of its role in the development of these regions.

1290   Williamson, Jeffrey G.   "Antebellum Urbanization in the American Northeast."   JOURNAL OF ECONOMIC HISTORY   25 (December 1965): 592-614.

This preliminary discussion of research which was then under way includes explanations of the rate and character of economic growth, regional timing of development, and comparisons of regional differences of urbanization with the spread of growth outward from the development poles.

1291   _____.   LATE NINETEENTH-CENTURY AMERICAN DEVELOPMENT: A GENERAL EQUILIBRIUM HISTORY.   New York: Cambridge University Press, 1974.   350 p.

An attempt at applying general equilibrium techniques to regional growth, this book is a very thorough and quantitative study of the northeast and north central regions of the United States.   In his analysis the author uses a large simulation model from which he can make judgments about various regional and aggregate occurrences.

1292   _____.   "Late Nineteenth-Century American Retardation: A Neoclassical Analysis."   JOURNAL OF ECONOMIC HISTORY   33 (September 1973): 581-607.

By using a full employment neoclassical model to simulate the behavior of the economy with two regions defined, the author

is able to ask and sometimes answer a great many questions.
Money is neutral in this model and does not affect the growth
of income.

1293 _____. "The Long Swing: Comparisons and Interactions between British
and American Balance of Payments, 1820-1913." JOURNAL OF ECO-
NOMIC HISTORY 22 (March 1962): 21-46.

The response to similar long-swings in economic activity are
compared for Britain and the United States in terms of flows
of international capital, goods, and specie. The possibility
of an inverse Kuznets cycle is also explored.

1294 _____. "Regional Inequality and the Process of National Development."
ECONOMIC DEVELOPMENT AND CULTURAL CHANGE 13 (July 1965):
1-84.

This is a description of the aggregate patterns of labor migration, capital migration, interregional linkages, and central
government policies in an international cross-section analysis.
It is an attempt to fill a void in the so-called North-South
problem.

1295 Williamson, Jeffrey G., and Swanson, Joseph A. "Growth of Cities
in the American Northeast, 1820-1870." EXPLORATIONS IN ECO-
NOMIC HISTORY 4, no. 1 (1966): supplement, 1-101.

This is a test of scale hypotheses regarding city growth, and
the results are less than conclusive for or against the existence
of economies, external for firms in growing cities, but internal
to the cities. It is a first attempt to account for the effect of
city age and the impact of the "hinterland" upon city growth.
A comment by Robert Higgs and a reply by Swanson and Williamson
appear in this journal, volume 8 (Winter 1970-71): 203-22.

1296 Willis, H. Parker. "The Tariff of 1909." JOURNAL OF POLITICAL
ECONOMY 17 (November 1909): 589-619.

This examination of the Tariff Act considers the political environment surrounding its passage and its implications for U.S.
commercial dealings.

1297 _____. "The Tariff of 1913, Parts I, II, and III." JOURNAL OF PO-
LITICAL ECONOMY 22 (January 1914): 1-42; (February 1914): 105-
31; (March 1914): 218-38.

This is a study of the effect of the 1913 Tariff Act on industrial development over the next few years. The effects of
this act are compared with those for the 1909 act.

1298   Winther, Oscar O. "Promoting the American West in England, 1865–1890." JOURNAL OF ECONOMIC HISTORY 16 (December 1956): 506–13.

        This article examines the people and the methods they used to attract immigrants from England to the American West. Aspects that were stressed included climate, land, opportunities, and the social freedom of the West.

1299   Wolfson, Robert J. "An Econometric Investigation of Regional Differentials in American Agricultural Wages." ECONOMETRICA 26 (April 1958): 225–57.

        This is an examination of the relation between productivity of labor and wages, and the relation between labor mobility and wages. The stability, persistence, and existence of the differentials are estimated and explained by use of the specific model.

1300   Wright, Chester W. WOOL GROWING AND THE TARIFF. New York: Russell and Russell, 1910. 362 p.

        Although this work traces the growth and development of the wool industry in the United States, many of the influences that the industry had on the economy, and conversely, are discussed at some length.

1301   Wright, Gavin. "Cotton Competition and the Post-Bellum Recovery of the American South." JOURNAL OF ECONOMIC HISTORY 34 (September 1974): 610–35.

        The author analyzes the arguments for unfavorable exchange rate changes and new sources of cotton supply as reasons for the initial retardation of the South. He ranks these reasons well below lagging world demand for cotton as causes. Deeper causes are felt to be in southern institutions, investment patterns, and concentration on staple crops.

1302   _____. "An Economic Study of Cotton Production and Trade, 1830–1860." NEW ECONOMIC HISTORY, edited by Peter Temin, pp. 63–80. Baltimore: Penguin Books, 1973. Reprinted from REVIEW OF ECONOMICS AND STATISTICS 53 (May 1971): 111–20.

        A model is developed which provides estimates of supply and demand elasticities for cotton. The author attempts to analyze the effects of these elasticities and the expansion of the market for cotton.

1303   _____. THE POLITICAL ECONOMY OF THE COTTON SOUTH. New York: W.W. Norton and Co., 1978. 205 p.

This is a summary and reinterpretation of the works which had been done during the previous decade or so. It includes both antebellum as well as postbellum times in the discussion. The purpose is to understand the historical background, the origins of the economic structure, and institutions of the cotton South as well as their evolution over the nineteenth century. A rather complete bibliography is provided at the conclusion of this book.

1304 _____. "Slavery and the Cotton Boom." EXPLORATION IN ECONOMIC HISTORY 12 (October 1975): 439-52.

This paper argues that the economic success of slavery would not have persisted much after 1860 due to the collapse of the demand for cotton and its subsequent stagnation. It also is a critique of the evidence offered by Fogel and Engerman (see no. 1141).

1305 Zassernhaus, Herbert K. "Net Material on United States Imports." REVIEW OF ECONOMICS AND STATISTICS 35 (February 1953): 92-97.

In reviewing evidence from various works, the author analyzes a large number of time series of imports from major countries and areas. He examines the relation between changes in imports from the various areas and U.S. GNP, production volume, and of prices of imports from one area to another. Some of the evidence found by the author calls into question the significance of earlier findings by others.

1306 Zepp, Thomas M. "On Returns to Scale and Input Substitutability in Slave Agriculture." EXPLORATIONS IN ECONOMIC HISTORY 13 (April 1976): 165-78.

This is an attempt to estimate the elasticity of substitution for slave labor where the author finds that inputs may well have been elastic substitutes. As a result, the inference of economies of scale in slave agriculture need not rest upon the assumption of unitary elasticity of substitution.

8.2 GENERAL LISTINGS

1307 Ankli, Robert E. "Canadian-American Reciprocity: A Comment." JOURNAL OF ECONOMIC HISTORY 30 (June 1970): 427-31.

1308 Berglund, Abraham. "Our Trade Balance and Our Foreign Loans." JOURNAL OF POLITICAL ECONOMY 26 (September 1918): 732-43.

1309 Fisk, George M. "German-American 'Most-Favored-Nation' Relations." JOURNAL OF POLITICAL ECONOMY 11 (May 1903): 220-36.

1310   Goldin, Claudia. "'N' Kinds of Freedom: An Introduction to the Issues." EXPLORATIONS IN ECONOMIC HISTORY 16 (January 1979): 8-30.

1311   Heaton, Herbert. "Non-Importation, 1806-1812." JOURNAL OF ECONOMIC HISTORY 1 (November 1941): 178-98.

1312   Hill, William. "Protective Purpose of the Tariff Act of 1789." JOURNAL OF POLITICAL ECONOMY 2 (December 1893): 54-76.

1313   Kiaer, Anders Nicolai. "The Shipping Trade between the United States and the United Kingdom." JOURNAL OF POLITICAL ECONOMY 5 (December 1896): 1-22.

1314   Krause, Lawrence B. "United States Imports, 1947-1958." ECONOMETRICA 30 (April 1962): 221-38.

1315   McClellan, William S. SMUGGLING IN THE AMERICAN COLONIES. New York: Moffat, Yard, and Co., 1912. 105 p.

1316   Morton, W.L. "The Significance of Site in the Settlement of the American and Canadian Wests." AGRICULTURAL HISTORY 25 (July 1951): 97-103.

1317   Officer, Lawrence H., and Smith, Lawrence B. "Canadian-American Reciprocity: A Reply." JOURNAL OF ECONOMIC HISTORY 30 (June 1970): 432-34.

1318   _____. "The Canadian-American Reciprocity Treaty of 1855 to 1866." JOURNAL OF ECONOMIC HISTORY 28 (December 1968): 598-623.

1319   Ransom, Roger, and Sutch, Richard. "Credit Merchandising in the Post-Emancipation South: Structure, Conduct, and Performance." EXPLORATIONS IN ECONOMIC HISTORY 16 (January 1979): 64-89.

1320   Reid, Joseph D., Jr. "White Land, Black Labor, and Agricultural Stagnation. The Causes and Effects of Sharecropping in the Postbellum South." EXPLORATIONS IN ECONOMIC HISTORY 16 (January 1979): 31-55.

1321   Salley, Alexander S. NARRATIVES OF EARLY CAROLINA, 1650-1708. New York: C. Scribner's Sons, 1911. 388 p.

1322   Shepherd, James F. "Commodity Exports from the British North American Colonies to Overseas Areas, 1768-1772: Magnitudes and Patterns of Trade." EXPLORATIONS IN ECONOMIC HISTORY 8 (Fall 1970): 5-76.

1323 Shepherd, James F., and Walton, Gary M. "Estimates of 'Invisible' Earnings in the Balance of Payments of the British North American Colonies, 1768-1772." JOURNAL OF ECONOMIC HISTORY 29 (June 1969): 230-63.

1324 Shideier, James H. "Flappers and Philosophers, and Farmers: Rural-Urban Tensions of the Twenties." AGRICULTURAL HISTORY 47 (October 1973): 283-99.

1325 Skelton, O.D. "Wood Pulp and the Tariff." JOURNAL OF POLITICAL ECONOMY 14 (December 1906): 632-36.

1326 Sterns, Worthy P. "The International Indebtedness of the United States in 1789." JOURNAL OF POLITICAL ECONOMY 6 (December 1897): 27-53.

1327 Swerling, B.C. "United States Commodity Imports in the Longer Run." ECONOMIC JOURNAL 62 (March 1952): 35-41.

1328 Taylor, Rosser H. "Post-Bellum Southern Rental Contracts." AGRICULTURAL HISTORY 17 (April 1943): 121-28.

1329 Temin, Peter. "Freedom and Coercion: Notes on the Analysis of Debt Peonage in ONE KIND OF FREEDOM." EXPLORATIONS IN ECONOMIC HISTORY 16 (January 1979): 56-63.

1330 Walton, Gary M. "New Evidence on Colonial Commerce." JOURNAL OF ECONOMIC HISTORY 28 (September 1968): 363-89.

1331 Willis, H. Parker. "The Tariff of 1909, II and III." JOURNAL OF POLITICAL ECONOMY 18 (January 1910): 1-33; (March 1910): 173-96.

1332 Wright, Gavin. "Freedom and the Southern Economy." EXPLORATIONS IN ECONOMIC HISTORY 16 (January 1979): 90-108.

Chapter 9

THE ROLE OF GOVERNMENT

This is a peculiar chapter in that it overlaps with many other chapters. Here we have sources that examine the government's role in every aspect of economic growth and development. Topics include land development, shipping, and trade agreements.

Government has played a large and very significant role in the development process of the United States. We have always been a legalistic society which could not always find what was needed for a particular situation within the common law doctrines.

These few sources by no means account for a majority of the works available on governmental effects upon matters economic. In fact the entire area of the effect of fiscal policy has been left to a work devoted to twentieth-century macroeconomics. Another area only touched on in this chapter is the role of government in antitrust operations.

Be that as it may, the beginning researcher should find some material with which to begin his/her work as well as leads to further sources.

9.1 ANNOTATED LISTINGS

1333   Adams, T.S. "Separation of the Sources of State and Local Revenues." JOURNAL OF POLITICAL ECONOMY 16 (January 1908): 1-12.

> The author argues that separation moves are counter-productive because we lose efficiency when we decentralize, for example, home rule cannot materially increase the positive fiscal free-dom of the local government.

1334   _____. "Valuation of Railway Property for Purposes of Taxation." JOURNAL OF POLITICAL ECONOMY 23 (January 1915): 1-16.

> For purposes of taxation it may be better to base valuation on the earnings and this may be more advantageously done by the

federal government or through some central bureau of states.

1335   Allen, R.G.D. "Post-War Economic Policy in the U.S." ECONOMIC JOURNAL 55 (April 1945): 28-46.

This discussion of the function of government, especially in the postwar period, argues for low interest rates, control of the flow of short-term government securities, and discusses the possibility of integrating social security schemes with general postwar economic policies.

1336   Andrews, Charles M. COLONIAL SELF-GOVERNMENT. New York: Harper and Brothers, 1904. 369 p.

This is an examination of the political, social, and economic development of each of the groups of colonies as well as the individual colonies. The period of analysis is about 1689.

1337   Arrington, Leonard J. "Science, Government, and Enterprise in Economic Development: The Western Beet Sugar Industry." AGRICULTURAL HISTORY 41 (January 1967): 1-18.

Dealing with the rise of the beet sugar industry (1888-1913), the major contention is that the effect of protection has been greatly exaggerated. A variety of factors led to the development and expansion of the industry: science, engineering, government, entrepreneurship, and labor.

1338   Backstrom, Philip N. "The Mississippi Valley Trading Company: A Venture in International Cooperation, 1875-1877." AGRICULTURAL HISTORY 46 (July 1972): 425-37.

This is an account of the exchange of products between American Grangers and British cooperators, which was facilitated by the Mississippi Valley Trading Company.

1339   Bassett, John S. THE FEDERALIST SYSTEM. New York: Harper and Brothers, 1906. 327 p.

The time period examined is from 1789 to 1801 and the issues center around the formation of a financial system and all the other machinery of government.

1340   Batchelder, Charles C. "The Character and Powers of Governmental Regulation." JOURNAL OF POLITICAL ECONOMY 20 (April 1912): 373-405.

The author argues that we must construct a framework for governing and/or restricting the combination of capital. He goes so far as to argue for compulsory federal incorporation of large organizations.

1341 Bauer, John, and Brown, Harry Gunnison. "Rate Base for Effective and Non-Speculative Railroad and Utility Regulation." JOURNAL OF POLITICAL ECONOMY 34 (August 1926): 479-513.

> After examining the conclusions of other writers, the author concludes that the easy way is usually the best and that one should not take into account general economic conditions when setting a rate base.

1342 Beard, C.A., ed. AN ECONOMIC INTERPRETATION OF THE CONSTITUTION OF THE UNITED STATES. 2d ed., rev. New York: Free Press, 1965. 330 p.

> Surveying the various economic interests of 1787, the author relates these economic data to the constitutional convention voting and the ratification process. This is a second edition (first edition was in 1913) and the major changes are Benjamin Franklin's writing concerning public debt and Hamilton's funding system based on the authority of the Constitution.

1343 Beer, George L. THE COMMERCIAL POLICY OF ENGLAND TOWARD THE AMERICAN COLONIES. New York: P. Smith, 1948. 167 p.

> This is a discussion of England's colonial shipping policy before the Restoration Acts of Charles V and the basis for the colonial system. The author discusses the history of enumerated commodities (1660-1763), restrictions on manufactures, bounties, and other inducements offered to colonial industry and commerce before 1763. The Molasses Act and its administration is also discussed.

1344 _____. THE OLD COLONIAL SYSTEM, 1660-1754, I and II. New York: Macmillan Co., 1912. 763 p.

> This book is concerned with colonial policy, the laws of trade and navigation and imperial defense, the English fiscal system and imperial finances, and the slave trade for plantation colonies.

1345 _____. THE ORIGINS OF THE BRITISH COLONIAL SYSTEM, 1578-1660. New York: Macmillan Co., 1908. 438 p.

> This is a study of the underlying principles of the English fiscal system and colonial legislation regarding slavery, customs duties, currency, and bankruptcy. Export restrictions are also examined.

1346 Bemis, Edward W. "The Homestead Strike." JOURNAL OF POLITICAL ECONOMY 2 (June 1894): 369-96.

> This is based upon the U.S. Congress's investigation regarding

the causes of the strike, and the result of the recognition on the part of workers of a new property right--the right of the employee to employment. The tariff issue in the presidential election at that time is also discussed.

1347 Benedict, M.K. "Attempts to Restrict Competition in Agriculture: The Government Programs." AMERICAN ECONOMIC REVIEW 44 (May 1954): 93-106.

This analysis points out that government has interfered to an increasing extent with agriculture as it has become progressively more commercial. One issue dealt with is the lack of countercyclical behavior on the part of the government.

1348 Berry, Thomas S. "The Effect of Business Conditions on Early Judicial Decisions Concerning Restraint of Trade." JOURNAL OF ECONOMIC HISTORY 10 (May 1950): 30-44.

Prior to 1880 it was found that the courts tended to consider current prices and market conditions when deciding cases dealing with restraint of trade.

1349 Bing, Alexander M. "The Work of the Wage-Adjustment Boards." JOURNAL OF POLITICAL ECONOMY 27 (June 1919): 421-56.

This is a very thorough examination of the various agencies and boards that governed the labor relations for various industries.

1350 Bloomburg, Laurence N. "The Role of the Federal Government in Urban Housing." AMERICAN ECONOMIC REVIEW 41 (May 1951): 586-98.

Starting with the Home Loan Bank Board in 1932, the federal government has had an increasing impact on the housing market. This article attempts to explain why the board entered this field and what its effect has been.

1351 Blum, Jay W. "The Federal Securities Act, 1933-36." JOURNAL OF POLITICAL ECONOMY 46 (February 1938): 52-96.

This paper is an examination of the required reporting procedures for companies who sell stock, and a statistical summary of refusal, suspensions, and effective issues. Investigations of alleged violations and civil liabilities are also presented.

1352 Bronfenbrenner, Martin. "The Incidence of Collective Bargaining." AMERICAN ECONOMIC REVIEW 44 (May 1954): 293-307.

This study of the effects of collective bargaining shows that there has been little change in either the functional or per-

sonal distribution of income and relative gains have been
made only in times of slow economic growth. These relative gains have come at the expense of the remainder of the
work force and the consuming public, not the employer or
"capitalist".

1353   Brown, Harry Gunnison. "The Shifting of Taxes and the Sales of Land
        and Capital Goods and on Loans." JOURNAL OF POLITICAL ECON-
        OMY 29 (October 1921): 643-53.

        Studying the incidence of taxes on land capital goods, or
        loans, the author examines the income level and type of in-
        come that ultimately pays these taxes. Taxes on the sales
        of corporate securities are discussed.

1354   Buchanan, Norman S. "The Capital Account and the Rate of Return in
        Public Utility Operating Companies." JOURNAL OF POLITICAL ECON-
        OMY 43 (February 1935): 50-68.

        This is a discussion of the debate over how to best establish
        the book value of assets and thus the rate base for purposes
        of setting rates and determining the rate of return or invest-
        ment.

1355   Butler, Pierce. "Valuation of Railway Property for Purposes of Rate
        Regulation." JOURNAL OF POLITICAL ECONOMY 23 (January 1915):
        17-33.

        As a practical matter rates cannot be based solely on value
        of merchandise. Confiscatory rates may not be wrong in some
        cases, and other criteria must be considered.

1356   Cam, Gibert A. "United States Government Activity in Low-Cost Hous-
        ing, 1932-38." JOURNAL OF POLITICAL ECONOMY 47 (June 1939):
        357-78.

        This is a discussion of various projects: limited dividend pro-
        jects under Reconstruction Finance Corporation; Public Works
        Administration; alley dwelling authority of the District of
        Columbia; the Suburban Resettlement Division; and the U.S.
        Housing Act of 1937.

1357   Channing, Edward. THE JEFFERSONIAN SYSTEM. New York: Harper
        and Brothers, 1906. 299 p.

        This book discusses the expansionary policy of Jeffersonians
        as well as the prohibition of slave trade, and the exploration
        of the West.

1358   Christensen, Alice M. "Agricultural Pressure and Governmental Response in the United States, 1919-1929." AGRICULTURAL HISTORY 11 (January 1937): 33-42.

This is an explanation of the government's role in assisting farmers through the formation of farm bureaus from 1919 to 1929.

1359 Commons, John R. "Taxation in Chicago and Philadelphia." JOURNAL OF POLITICAL ECONOMY 3 (September 1895): 434-60.

This is a detailed examination of both the state and city tax systems for Philadelphia and Chicago.

1360 Compton, Wilson. "Recent Tendencies in the Reform of Forest Taxation." JOURNAL OF POLITICAL ECONOMY 23 (December 1915): 971-79.

Through new means of scientifically estimating the value of a forest, states are more easily able to tax all types of wealth more equally.

1361 Conklin, W.D. "Building Cost in the Business Cycle: With Particular Reference to Building Sponsored by Governments in the United States." JOURNAL OF POLITICAL ECONOMY 43 (June 1935): 365-92.

This is an examination of wholesale prices of individual building materials, labor costs, and building costs in the business cycle.

1362 Davis, Joseph S. "Experience under Intergovernmental Commodity Agreements, 1902-45." JOURNAL OF POLITICAL ECONOMY 54 (June 1946): 193-220.

Intergovernmental Commodity Agreements (ICA) usually relate to a single commodity or well-defined group of commodities, and this article is a study of these agreements which involve study of the international aspects of the commodity and the regulations on its trade and price.

1362a Davis, Lance E., and Legler, John. "The Government in the American Economy, 1815-1902: A Quantitative Study." JOURNAL OF ECONOMIC HISTORY 26 (December 1966): 514-52.

This study deals mostly with regional differences, because data at the state level are most readily available. Many regional differences existed with respect to the level of activity, and this activity may have produced different rates of regional growth. Federal finance may be analyzed only on a qualitative basis because of the lack of quantitative data.

1363 Denison, Edward F. "The Influence of the Walsh-Healey Public Con-

tracts Act upon Labor Conditions." JOURNAL OF POLITICAL ECON-
OMY 49 (April 1941): 225-46.

This act was to control labor market conditions via government purchasing, and this article is a discussion of its direct
economic influence.

1364 Dewey, D.R. NATIONAL PROBLEMS. New York: Harper and Brothers,
1907. 360 p.

Although many problems are dealt with in this book, three
economic problems are considered: the tariffs; silver; and
railroads.

1365 Donaldson, Thomas. THE PUBLIC DOMAIN. Washington, D.C.: Government Printing Office, 1884. 1343 p.

This is an extensive examination of government actions relating to the regulation of use of the national domain. The
time period is primarily from 1784 to 1880 and also 1882 and
1883.

1366 Dorfman, Joseph. "The Principles of Freedom and Government Intervention in American Economic Expansion." JOURNAL OF ECONOMIC
HISTORY 19 (December 1959): 570-83.

This discussion of the role of the state in a developing nation
argues that the state should enter only to get things started
and should subsequently fade out of these projects.

1367 Duncan, Bingham. "Diplomatic Support of the American Rice Trade,
1835-1845." AGRICULTURAL HISTORY 23 (April 1949): 92-95.

This is an examination of two examples where diligent officers
abroad sought to maintain a policy to protect domestic rice
planters and traders in foreign markets.

1368 Duncan, C.S. "The Chicago Milk Inquiry." JOURNAL OF POLITICAL
ECONOMY 26 (April 1918): 321-46.

An example of the classic problem of defining monopoly, this
article focuses on the cost of production, cost of distribution,
and what constitutes a reasonable profit. The author argues
the outcome was unsatisfactory.

1369 Egerton, H.E. A SHORT HISTORY OF BRITISH COLONIAL POLICY.
London: Methuen and Co., 1950. 516 p.

This deals with the period of systematic colonization and the
granting of responsible government, which is the period of
trade ascendency as well.

1370   Falkus, M.E.   "United States Economic Policy and the 'Dollar Gap' of the 1920's."   ECONOMIC HISTORY REVIEW   24 (November 1971): 599-623.

This is an assessment of U.S. trade policy in the setting of tariffs.   A comment by Sean Glynn and Alan L. Lougheed appears in this journal, volume 26 (November 1973):   692-94.

1371   Fitch, Lyle C.   "Trends in Federal, State, Local Government Expenditures since 1890."   AMERICAN ECONOMIC REVIEW   43 (May 1953): 216-33.

Analyzing per capita spending by functional categories of government spending, the author concludes that state and local government have continuously accounted for most of the spending on internal issues, while the federal government has spent most of its efforts on external affairs.

1372   Freund, Ernst.   "Limitations of Hours of Labor and the Supreme Court."   JOURNAL OF POLITICAL ECONOMY   13 (September-December 1905): 597-99.

This is a discussion of the importance of the case of Lochner v. New York where the Supreme Court declared unconstitutional the states' ten-hour law for bakeries.

1373   Gates, R.C.   "The Weight of Taxation in Five Countries, 1938 to 1950."   ECONOMIC RECORD   28 (November 1952): 222-36.

This cross-country comparison covers thirteen years and attempts to calculate the weight of taxation for each of the five countries: Australia, Canada, New Zealand, the United Kingdom, and the United States.

1374   Goodrich, Carter.   GOVERNMENT PROMOTION OF AMERICAN CANALS AND RAILROADS.   New York: Columbia University Press, 1960. 283 p.

Focusing the issue of competition versus cooperation between government and business, the author examines in some detail the importance of state, local, and federal government assistance in the development of the transportation infrastructure.

1375   Graham, Gerald S.   "The Gypsum Trade of the Maritime Provinces: Its Relation to American Diplomacy and Agriculture in the Early Nineteenth Century."   AGRICULTURAL HISTORY   12 (July 1938):   209-23.

This is an account of the effect the U.S. gypsum trade had on foreign policy and diplomacy.

1376   Hamilton, W.B. "Early Cotton Regulation in the Lower Mississippi
        Valley." AGRICULTURAL HISTORY 15 (January 1941): 20-25.

        Starting from the late 1700s up to the early 1800s, cotton
        exports were inspected. The methods of inspection and the
        enforcement are the topics of this article.

1377   Hamilton, Walton H. "The Requisites of a National Food Policy." JOUR-
        NAL OF POLITICAL ECONOMY 26 (June 1918): 612-37.

        This is a discussion of the food problem in Europe after World
        War I, and how the burden of solving this problem fell upon
        the United States.

1378   Haney, Lewis H. "Magazine Advertising and the Postal Deficit." JOUR-
        NAL OF POLITICAL ECONOMY 19 (April 1911): 338-43.

        The author states the hierarchy that he feels should exist, and
        then argues that the postal service sets rates in illogical fash-
        ion. He discusses a proposal by government to change these
        rates.

1379   Harris, Seymore E. "The Economic Legislation of the United States,
        1933." ECONOMIC JOURNAL 43 (December 1933): 619-51.

        In this contemporary analysis of the major pieces of emergency
        economic legislation of 1933, the author points out that higher
        prices were an objective of the Roosevelt administration. Cre-
        ation of additional purchasing power for farmers and laborers
        was another objective.

1380   Heilman, Ralph E. "The Control of Interstate Utility Capitalization by
        State Commissions." JOURNAL OF POLITICAL ECONOMY 24 (May
        1916): 474-88.

        States may exercise considerable control over corporations that
        issue securities secured by liens on property in other states.
        This is an examination of such regulation for utilities.

1381   House, Albert V., Jr. "Proposals of Government Aid to Agricultural
        Settlement during the Depression of 1873-1879." AGRICULTURAL HIS-
        TORY 12 (January 1938): 46-66.

        This is a discussion of land policy that was used to attract
        unemployed industrial workers from the East.

1382   Howenstine, E. Jay, Jr. "Public Works Programs after World War I."
        JOURNAL OF POLITICAL ECONOMY 51 (December 1943): 523-37.

        An examination of the federal government's construction policy
        and its effects on given buying, this article considers such

agencies as federal public works; railroad administration; shipping board; and the land-settlement agency.

1383   Hoyt, Homer. "The Economic Function of the Common Law." JOUR-
        NAL OF POLITICAL ECONOMY 26 (February 1918): 167-99.

        When economies develop rapidly, as the United States did,
        the common law does not evolve as rapidly. This article
        focuses on the attacks against and the defenses of the com-
        mon law.

1384   Hultgren, Thor. "Divisions of Freight Rates and the Interterritorial Rate Prob-
        lem." JOURNAL OF POLITICAL ECONOMY 50 (February 1942): 99-116.

        This paper is a discussion of the problems of equalizing freight
        rates among the five major regions both from an economic and
        a nationalistic point of view.

1385   Jenks, Jeremiah W. "Economic Aspects of the Recent Decisions of the
        United States Supreme Court on Trusts." JOURNAL OF POLITICAL
        ECONOMY 20 (April 1912): 346-57.

        Discussing sources of the more recent cases and the economic
        arguments used to establish monopolization, the author argues
        that insufficient concern is given to the benefits, such as
        energy saving, that may result from industrial combination.

1386   Johnson, E.A.J. "Federalism, Pluralism, and Public Policy." JOUR-
        NAL OF ECONOMIC HISTORY 22 (December 1962): 427-44.

        This is a debate of these issues during the early era--founding
        period--in the United States.

1387   Kelley, Arthur C. "Federal Taxation of Income from the Production of
        Minerals." JOURNAL OF POLITICAL ECONOMY 29 (April 1921):
        265-92.

        This is a full discussion of ways in which the law must be
        amended to provide large revenues with a minimum of in-
        justice, inequality, and unnecessary administrative labor.

1388   Kendrick, M. Slade. "The Collection of Taxes by the State Government
        and the Division of These Revenues with Units of Local Government, with
        Emphasis on New York." JOURNAL OF POLITICAL ECONOMY 39
        (February 1931): 25-41.

        This discussion entails the decisions as to what taxes should
        be divided, how they should be divided, what local units
        should participate, and should the state exercise any power
        over the expenditure of funds.

1389   Kessler, W.C. "A Statistical Study of the New York General Incorpora-
       tion Act of 1811." JOURNAL OF POLITICAL ECONOMY 48 (Decem-
       ber 1940): 877-82.

       A review of the importance of this act shows that it was far
       more important than many had previously supposed.

1390   Lambert, C. Roger. "Want and Plenty: The Federal Surplus Relief
       Corporation and the AAA." AGRICULTURAL HISTORY 46 (July 1972):
       390-400.

       This is a discussion of the operation undertaken through the
       Agricultural Adjustment Act of 1933 and later through the
       FSRC after 1934. Both worked to solve the problems of un-
       employment and poverty and the author discusses how this
       occurred.

1391   Lester, Richard A. "The Economic Significance of Unemployment Com-
       pensation, 1948-1959." REVIEW OF ECONOMICS AND STATISTICS
       42 (November 1960): 349-72.

       The analysis includes a measure of the earnings loss from un-
       employment and estimates the extent to which unemployment
       insurance compensated for this loss from 1948 to 1959. Dur-
       ing this period various federal-state programs were introduced.

1392   Levinson, Harold M. "Collective Bargaining and Income Distribution."
       AMERICAN ECONOMIC REVIEW 44 (May 1954): 308-16.

       Examining the empirical evidence regarding collective bargain-
       ing and income distribution, the author discusses the theoreti-
       cal implications of his findings.

1393   Lewis, Ben W. "Public Policy and the Growth of the Power Industry."
       JOURNAL OF ECONOMIC HISTORY 7 (1947): supplement, 47-55.

       This is an analysis of the ways in which regulation has affected
       the growth of regulated industries. The author discusses whether
       the effect has been positive, negative, or neutral.

1394   Libecap, Gary D. "Economic Variables and the Development of the
       Law: The Case of Western Mineral Rights." JOURNAL OF ECONOMIC
       HISTORY 38 (June 1978): 338-62.

       The author attempts to describe and quantify the progression
       of property law from general rules to highly specified statutes
       and court verdicts. The author also attempts to relate these
       legal developments to economic conditions.

1395   Lytton, Henry D. "Recent Productivity Trends in the Federal Government:

An Exploratory Study." REVIEW OF ECONOMICS AND STATISTICS 41 (November 1959): 341-59.

Stating the general problems encountered, the author explains why such a study should be useful. The size and scope of each agency studied, the measurement problems, and the year-by-year productivity trends are provided.

1396 MacAvoy, Paul. THE ECONOMIC EFFECTS OF REGULATION. Cambridge: MIT Press, 1965. 376 p.

This book examines the effect of control by cartels of the railroads, and the setting of trunk-line rates prior to 1879 and the Interstate Commerce Commission. The performance of the industry and the I.C.C. from 1877 to 1899 are also analyzed.

1397 MacDonald, William. JACKSONIAN DEMOCRACY. New York: Harper and Brothers, 1906. 345 p.

Many issues are considered which arose in the time of Jackson's presidency: disposal of excess revenues; public lands policy; bank controversies.

1398 McLaughlin, Andrew C. THE CONFEDERATION AND THE CONSTITUTION. New York: Harper and Brothers, 1905. 348 p.

The financial, commercial, and diplomatic sectors, paper money circulation, and the culmination of the Confederation in Shay's Rebellion are all discussed in this book. A great deal of effort is also given to considering the Constitutional Convention and the process of producing a ratifiable Constitution.

1399 McLean, S.J. "State Regulation of Railways in the United States, Parts I & II." ECONOMIC JOURNAL 10 (June 1900): 151-71; (September 1900): 349-69.

From 1832 until 1862 the federal government allowed states to govern the railroads. The conditions in the West and the South made it impossible for these states to adopt the advisory type commissions used in the eastern states.

1400 McVey, Frank L. "Subsidizing Merchant Marines." JOURNAL OF POLITICAL ECONOMY 14 (June 1906): 370-91.

The author defines two types of subsidy which fit the three phases of the subsidy question. Besides the distinction between natural and artifical influences on commerce, the author also discusses the government attitude toward these commercial restrictions.

1401   May, Irvin M., Jr. "Cotton and Cattle: The FSRC and Emergency Work Relief." AGRICULTURAL HISTORY 46 (July 1972): 401-13.

> In the second year of the New Deal the Federal Surplus Relief Corporation was created to procure and distribute agricultural surpluses to the needy. This is a discussion of their various activities.

1402   Merritt, Albert N. "Shall the Scope of Government Functions be Enlarged so as to Include the Express Business?" JOURNAL OF POLITICAL ECONOMY 16 (July 1908): 417-35.

> Merritt argues that the government should not attempt to provide parcel post service to particular industry types using the already available cheaper but slower means of freight movement.

1403   Meyers, R.J. "The Effect of the Social Security Act on the Life Insurance Needs of Labor." JOURNAL OF POLITICAL ECONOMY 45 (October 1937): 681-86.

> Dealing with the direct tax and benefit results rather than any indirect effects, the article concludes that the Social Security Act plus group insurance will adequately take care of the life insurance needs of labor in the future.

1404   Mezer, Balthasar H. "Government Regulation of Railway Rates." JOURNAL OF POLITICAL ECONOMY 14 (February 1906): 86-106.

> This is a discussion of certain opinions upon the railway rate question. References to regulatory practices in other countries are also provided.

1405   Miller, John Perry. "Military Procurement Policies: World War II and Today." AMERICAN ECONOMIC REVIEW 42 (May 1952): 453-75.

> Given the size of total procurements, one must be aware of their effect on economic activity. In this study they are judged according to their ability to: (1) fulfill requirements; (2) function productively; (3) satisfy budgetary economy; (4) maintain economic stabilization and (5) affect sociopolitical objectives.

1406   Moore, John B. HISTORY AND DIGEST OF THE INTERNATIONAL ARBITRATIONS TO WHICH THE UNITED STATES HAS BEEN A PARTY. Washington, D.C.: Government Printing Office, 1898. 5,239 p.

> This is a detailed discussion of various agreements between the United States and her contiguous neighbors regarding the use of lands or waterways that lie on the border.

1407   Musgrave, Richard A., and Thin, Tun. "Income Tax Progression, 1929–1948." JOURNAL OF POLITICAL ECONOMY 56 (December 1948): 498–514.

The authors examine the rates for various types of progressiveness: average rate progression; marginal rate progression; liability progression; and residual income progression. Policy implications of the various measures are considered.

1408   Mushkin, Selma J. "Distribution of Federal Expenditures among the States." REVIEW OF ECONOMICS AND STATISTICS 39 (November 1957): 435–47.

Much of the discussion is about the difficulties involved with getting data, but the data obtained were sufficient to provide an approximate basis for the relative distribution of federal expenditures among the states. Two basic ways of approaching the problem are discussed: the program purpose of benefits approach and the dollar-flow approach.

1409   Nichols, Jeanette P. "The United States Congress and Imperialism, 1861–1897." JOURNAL OF ECONOMIC HISTORY 21 (December 1961): 526–38.

This is a study of action of the U.S. Congress regarding imperialism between 1865 and 1897. The actions are classified under three headings: (1) negative reference groups centered around domestic politics; (2) negative reference groups centered around attitudes toward costs and wealth; and (3) negative reference groups centered around hostile attitudes toward foreigners.

1410   Page, Thomas Walker. "The Movement for Tax Reform in Virginia." JOURNAL OF POLITICAL ECONOMY 24 (October 1916): 737–54.

Starting with the 1912 state constitution, this article traces the development of tax legislation through to 1915. The breakdown of "segregation" as a self-enforcing system is also discussed.

1411   Patterson, Robert T. "Government Finance on the Eve of the Civil War." JOURNAL OF ECONOMIC HISTORY 12 (Winter 1952): 35–44.

This assessment of the financial position of the U.S. government indicates that it was ill prepared for such a demand for rapid expenditure. Its current credit condition had developed as a result of financial policies in the preceding period, and this made short-term borrowing and the printing of paper money very costly.

1412   Peterson, Arthur G. "Governmental Policy Relating to Farm Machinery in World War I." AGRICULTURAL HISTORY 17 (January 1943): 31-40.

> Although various conservation measures were enacted during 1917 and early 1918, most were lifted by the end of 1918. This article discusses the effects of these measures.

1413   Phelps, Orme W. "Public Policy in Labor Disputes: The Crisis of 1946." JOURNAL OF POLITICAL ECONOMY 55 (June 1947): 189-211.

> An attempt to establish the proper limits to government intervention in labor disputes for the purpose of protecting the general welfare, the article also contains suggested criteria for limiting this intervention.

1414   Plehn, Carl C. "The Nature and Causes of the Tax Reform Movement in the United States." ECONOMIC JOURNAL 20 (March 1910): 1-12.

> This is a study of the sources of the tax reform movement in the United States vis-a-vis that in Europe. Two sets of causes of unrest are singled out: ethical or intellectual convictions and great untaxed or undertaxed resources outside the existing tax system.

1415   Pyle, J. Freeman. "The Taxation of Incomes in Oklahoma." JOURNAL OF POLITICAL ECONOMY 30 (October 1922): 709-16.

> The evolution of Oklahoma income tax laws from 1908 to 1915 is the topic of this article. The discussion illustrates how the new version is a more efficient revenue producer.

1416   Rimlinger, Gaston V. "Welfare Policy and Economic Development: A Comparative Historical Perspective." JOURNAL OF ECONOMIC HISTORY 26 (December 1966): 556-71.

> An examination of the shift from "poor relief" programs to modern "welfare" programs, this author hypothesizes that the shift is in part due to increased worker productivity and scarcity of labor. The labor-economics aspects of welfare programs are also discussed.

1417   Rosenberg, Laurence C. "Natural-Gas-Pipeline Rate Regulation: Marginal Cost Pricing and The Zone-Allocation Problem." JOURNAL OF POLITICAL ECONOMY 75 (March-April 1967): 159-68.

> An extension of the theory of peak-responsibility pricing to include zone allocations, the author evaluates the performance of the Federal Power Commission for consistency with the theoretical results.

1418 Ruggles, C.O. "Discrimination in Public-Utility Rates." JOURNAL OF POLITICAL ECONOMY 32 (April 1924): 191-206.

The varying rate schedules and criteria for determining who is charged which rate are the topics of this article.

1419 _____. "Problems of Public Utility Rate Regulation and Fair Return." JOURNAL OF POLITICAL ECONOMY 32 (October 1924): 543-66.

This is an examination of all of the factors besides cost of capital that affect the cost of operating a public utility. Finally, the appropriate base upon which one should calculate a rate of return is proffered.

1420 Schaller, Howard G. "Social Security Transfer Payments and Differences in State Per Capita Incomes, 1929, 1930, and 1949." REVIEW OF ECONOMICS AND STATISTICS 37 (February 1955): 83-89.

There was no perceptible difference in per capita incomes that could be traced to Social Security payments. Lower income states had a higher proportion of their population receiving transfer payments, but the payments were lower in these states.

1421 _____. "Veterans' Transfer Payments and State Per Capita Incomes, 1929, 1939, and 1949." REVIEW OF ECONOMICS AND STATISTICS 35 (November 1953): 325-32.

The analysis showed that the differences in 1929 and 1939 were nearly all due to veterans benefits, but that in 1949 the difference was due primarily to G.I. Bill payments and pensions.

1422 Schaub, Edward L. "The Regulation of Rentals during the War Period." JOURNAL OF POLITICAL ECONOMY 28 (January 1920): 1-36.

This is an account of the difficulties encountered in obtaining housing for military personnel during World War I, both in this country and abroad. Emphasis is placed upon domestic problems.

1423 Scheiber, Harry N. "Property Law, Expropriation, and Resource Allocation by Government: The United States, 1789-1910." JOURNAL OF ECONOMIC HISTORY 33 (March 1973): 232-51.

This is an explanation of how the government aids in the land development process.

1424 _____. "State Policy and the Public Domain: The Ohio Canal Lands." JOURNAL OF ECONOMIC HISTORY 25 (March 1965): 86-113.

This is an examination of the three land grants made to fund canals in Ohio; one in 1827 and two in 1828. The author discusses the policy of the state in supporting the building of this canal network.

1425 Seligman, Edwin Robert Anderson. "The American Income Tax." ECONOMIC JOURNAL 4 (December 1894): 639-67.

Examining the first national income tax in the United States, the author discusses the origin of the tax and the reason for its present form. An explanation of why it was enacted along with a forecast of its consequences and probable future are also presented.

1426 _____. "The United States Federal Income Tax." ECONOMIC JOURNAL 24 (March 1914): 57-77.

A critique of the 1913 income tax law, this article argues that there are a number of respects in which the laws was not well drawn and numerous issues remain for the courts to settle.

1427 Smullyan, Emile Benoit. "Public Works in the Depression." AMERICAN ECONOMIC REVIEW 38 (March 1948): 134-39.

This examination of the growth of public works argues that although the federally funded public works were replacing local and state funded public works, public works in general were not growing during the depression.

1428 Spencer, William H. "Recent Cases on Price Maintenance." JOURNAL OF POLITICAL ECONOMY 30 (April 1922): 189-200.

This is an assessment of the current position of the Supreme Court with respect to price maintenance.

1429 Spengler, Joseph J. "The Role of the State in Shaping Things Economic." JOURNAL OF ECONOMIC HISTORY 7 (1947): supplement, 123-43.

This is a study of (1) the state and how it is related to the other components of the social system; (2) how economists view the state as an economic determinant; (3) what the state can theoretically do to shape economic affairs; and (4) whether the future role of the state is predictable.

1430 Stein, Bruno. "Labor's Role in Government Agencies during World War II." JOURNAL OF ECONOMIC HISTORY 17 (September 1957): 389-408.

The agencies discussed included the National Defense Advisory Commission, the Office of Production Management, the War

Production Board, the War Manpower Commission, and the
Office of Price Administration.

1431   Stoke, Harold W. "Economic Influences upon the Corporation Laws of
New Jersey." JOURNAL OF POLITICAL ECONOMY 38 (October
1930): 551-79.

An analysis of early development in New Jersey corporation
laws, this article also contains a discussion of the development of incorporation laws in New Jersey. The time period
is from 1846 to 1919.

1432   Tanzer, Michael D. "State and Local Government Debt in the Post
War Period." REVIEW OF ECONOMICS AND STATISTICS 46 (August
1964): 237-44.

State debt flows were shown to be positively related to new
capital expenditures and negatively related to the movement
of interest rates. The debt of state governments was found
to have a stronger relationship to interest rates than did the
debt of local governments.

1433   Tatter, Henry. "State and Federal Land Policy during the Confederation
Period." AGRICULTURAL HISTORY 9 (October 1935): 176-86.

A comparison of the state and federal land policies with the
new British policy, the study examines state and federal policies
during the period 1776-89.

1434   Teele, Ray P. "Water Rights in the Arid West." JOURNAL OF PO-
LITICAL ECONOMY 8 (September 1900): 524-34.

A discussion of the potential benefits to be had from irrigation,
this article cites the lack of certainty in titles to water and
the inability to coordinate labor and capital for the slow progress in the irrigation of arid western lands.

1435   Trescott, Paul B. "Federal Government Receipts and Expenditures, 1861-
1875." JOURNAL OF ECONOMIC HISTORY 26 (June 1966): 206-22.

Three sets of data were used in this study of the governmental
operations: (1) annual expenditures classified by major function; (2) annual estimates of federal revenue and expenditures
on a moneyflow basis (compatible with national income accounts); and (3) quarterly estimates of the transactions of the
treasury, both in total and by major component elements.

1436   Turvey, Ralph. "Inflation as a Tax in World War II." JOURNAL OF
POLITICAL ECONOMY 69 (February 1961): 70-73.

An examination of the effects of a 10 percent price increase on consumer's buying, this article also examines the indirect effect of the reduction in real wealth. The yield is computed and compared with ordinary taxes.

1437　Virtue, George O. "Public Ownership of Mineral Lands in the United States." JOURNAL OF POLITICAL ECONOMY 3 (March 1895): 185-202.

This is a study primarily of salt and lead ownership in the United States.

1438　Whittlesey, Charles R. "Political Aspects of the Gold Problem." JOURNAL OF ECONOMIC HISTORY 9 (1949): supplement, 50-60.

This paper discusses the "gold problem" in terms of the silver situation, arguing that one is merely the adverse of the other.

9.2 GENERAL LISTINGS

1439　Allen, Edward D. "Treasury Tax Policies in 1943." AMERICAN ECONOMIC REVIEW 34 (December 1944): 707-33.

1440　Bernard, Sir Francis. SELECT LETTERS ON THE TRADE AND GOVERNMENT OF AMERICA. London: T. Payne, 1774. 130 p.

1441　Cain, Louis. "The Sanitary District of Chicago: A Case Study in Water Use and Conservation." JOURNAL OF ECONOMIC HISTORY 30 (March 1970): 256-61.

1442　Cooke, Gilbert W. "The North Dakota State Mill and Elevator." JOURNAL OF POLITICAL ECONOMY 46 (February 1938): 23-51.

1443　Duncan, Julian S. "The Effect of the N.R.A. Lumber Code on Forest Policy." JOURNAL OF POLITICAL ECONOMY 49 (February 1941): 91-102.

1444　Havens, R.M. "Laissez-Faire Theory in Presidential Messages." JOURNAL OF ECONOMIC HISTORY 1 (December 1941): 86-95.

1445　Henrich, F.K.; Handlin, O.; Hartz, L.; and Health, M.S. "The Development of American Laissez-Faire." JOURNAL OF ECONOMIC HISTORY 3 (December 1943): 51-100.

1446　Hoffmann, I. Newton. "The Cotton Futures Act." JOURNAL OF POLITICAL ECONOMY 23 (May 1915): 465-89.

1447   Howenstine, E. Jay, Jr.   "The Industrial Board, Precursor of the N.R.A.:
        The Price-Reduction Movement after World War I."   JOURNAL OF PO-
        LITICAL ECONOMY 51 (June 1943): 235-50.

1448   Hoxie, George L.   "City Taxation and Skyscraper Control."   JOURNAL
        OF POLITICAL ECONOMY 23 (February 1915): 166-76.

1449   Killingsworth, Charles C.   "Public Relations of Labor Relations--The
        Wisconsin Experiment."   AMERICAN ECONOMIC REVIEW 33 (June
        1943): 247-63.

1450   Sidlo, T.L.   "Consolidation of Public Utilities in Ohio."   JOURNAL
        OF POLITICAL ECONOMY 18 (May 1910): 388-92.

1451   Sikes, George C.   "Public Policy Concerning Franchise Values."   JOUR-
        NAL OF POLITICAL ECONOMY 9 (September 1901): 527-39.

1452   Slichter, Sumner H.   "The Impact of Social Security Legislation upon
        Mobility and Enterprise."   AMERICAN ECONOMIC REVIEW 30 (March
        1940): 44-60.

1453   Twentieth Century Fund.   ELECTRIC POWER AND GOVERNMENT POLI-
        CY. New York: 1948. 261 p.

1454   U.S. Senate. Temporary National Economic Committee. A STUDY OF
        THE CONSTRUCTION AND ENFORCEMENT OF THE FEDERAL ANTI-
        TRUST LAWS. Monograph no. 38. Washington, D.C.: Government
        Printing Office, 1941. 106 p.

1455   Vanderblue, Homer B.   "Federal Valuation of Railroads."   JOURNAL
        OF POLITICAL ECONOMY 30 (December 1922): 841-49.

1456   White, Gerald T.   "Financing Industrial Expansion for War: The Origin
        of the Defense Plant Corporation Leases."   JOURNAL OF ECONOMIC
        HISTORY 9 (November 1949): 156-83.

1457   Wright, Almon R.   "World War Food Controls and Archival Sources for
        Their Study."   AGRICULTURAL HISTORY 15 (April 1941): 72-83.

Chapter 10

ASSESSING THE PERFORMANCE OF GROWTH

The works cited in this chapter are primarily those which analyze or examine various topics and/or issues in the growth of the United States. Some of these articles and books are of a more general nature treating growth in general, that is, not for a specific country. Many of the sources compare and contrast the growth of the United States to the performance of other nations.

The works of other chapters will undoubtedly overlap into this area and the works of this chapter overlap into the areas of previous chapters. The user is thus cautioned to search other chapters, particularly the ones dealing with technological change, regional growth, industrial structure and growth, and population.

10.1 ANNOTATED LISTINGS

1458   Abramovitz, Moses. "Economic Growth in the U.S.: 'A Review'." AMERICAN ECONOMIC REVIEW 52 (September-December 1962): 762-82.

> This review of two or three major works on growth in the United States is very thorough and compares measurement techniques, definitions of variables, and conclusions reached by the various writers.

1459   _____. "The Nature and Significance of Kuznets Cycles." ECONOMIC DEVELOPMENT AND CULTURAL CHANGE 9 (April 1961): 225-48.

> The author argues that long swings are the outcome of interactions among the pace at which resources are developed, the generation of effective demand, and the intensity of resource use.

1460   _____. "Resource and Output Trends in the U.S. since 1870." AMERICAN ECONOMIC REVIEW 46 (May 1956): 5-23.

It is not clear that trends in the rates of growth exist, because growth has occurred very erratically. Growth was said to have followed approximately a twenty-year cycle since 1870 and cannot be attributed to growth in labor or growth in capital productivity.

1461 Adler, John H. "World Economic Growth--Retrospect and Prospects." REVIEW OF ECONOMICS AND STATISTICS 38 (August 1956): 273-85.

Covering the previous ten years, the author examines the most important factors for long-run economic growth, for example, the volume of savings and investing, the role of international trade and capital movements, and the effect of price changes. Future prospects are also discussed.

1462 Balogh, T. "Some Theoretical Implications of International Aspects of the United States Recession 1953/54." ECONOMIC JOURNAL 64 (December 1955): 641-53.

This is an examination of the European response to our recession and how this recession affected the balance of payments.

1463 Bilkey, Warren J. "Equality of Income Distribution and Consumption Expenditures." REVIEW OF ECONOMICS AND STATISTICS 38 (February 1956): 81-87.

Using the periods 1921-41 and 1951-52, the author attempts to examine the relationship between income equality and consumer expenditure in order to evaluate the comparative propensity to consume theory and the emulation theory. He also examines shifts in conspicuous versus nonconspicuous consumption and income inequality.

1464 Bjork, Gordon C. "The Weaning of the American Economy: Independence, Market Changes and Economic Development." JOURNAL OF ECONOMIC HISTORY 24 (December 1964): 541-66.

This is an examination of the trade position of the United States immediately after the Revolution, and its short-term prospects.

1465 Blyth, C.A. "The 1948-49 American Recession." ECONOMIC JOURNAL 64 (September 1954): 486-510.

The author argues that the recession was due to a reduction in private investment along with a downswing in inventory investment for nondurable goods, retailers, and farmers.

1466 Brady, Dorothy S., ed. OUTPUT, EMPLOYMENT AND PRODUCTIVITY

IN THE UNITED STATES AFTER 1800. In Studies in Income and Wealth, no. 30. New York: National Bureau of Economic Research, 1967. 660 p.

This collection of papers and commentary upon the papers covers (1) consumption, investment and employment; (2) output of final products; (3) minerals and fuels; (4) power and machines; and (5) sources of productivity change.

1467 Budd, Edward C. "Postwar Changes in the Size Distribution of Income in the U.S." AMERICAN ECONOMIC REVIEW 60 (May 1970): 247-60.

Using a method of examining changes in the income distribution among component recipient groups, rather than changes in overall inequality, the author compares single groups over time as well as various groups against each other.

1468 Burton, Theodore E. FINANCIAL CRISES AND PERIODS OF INDUSTRIAL DEPRESSION. New York: D. Appleton and Co., 1908. 392 p.

The nature and causes of disturbances and some practical suggestions for anticipating and offsetting these disturbances are the crux of this book. The author attempts to identify various indicators.

1469 Cochran, Thomas C. "Cultural Factors in Economic Growth." JOURNAL OF ECONOMIC HISTORY 20 (December 1960): 515-30.

Using the United States and Latin America, the author examines the differences between the two that would explain different rates of growth.

1470 Cooper, Richard. "Growth and Trade: Some Hypotheses about Long-Term Trends." JOURNAL OF ECONOMIC HISTORY 24 (December 1964): 609-28.

The growth in U.S. and world trade as well as evidence on interregional growth are the focus of this paper.

1471 David, Paul A. "The Growth of Real Product in the United States before 1840: New Evidence Controlled Conjectures." JOURNAL OF ECONOMIC HISTORY 27 (June 1967): 151-97.

After setting out his assumptions, the author examines farm labor productivity, intrasectoral productivity growth, foreign trade, and the causes of economic growth.

1472 David, Paul A., and Reder, Melvin W., eds. NATIONS AND HOUSEHOLDS IN ECONOMIC GROWTH. New York: Academic Press, 1974. 411 p.

This collection of essays is not totally devoted to economic history, but a major portion of the work deals with growth in a historical manner. The writers are leading scholars in the field of economics as well as economic history.

1473 Davis, Lance E., and North, Douglas C. INSTITUTIONAL CHANGE AND AMERICAN ECONOMIC GROWTH. New York: Cambridge University Press, 1971. 283 p.

This work discusses the various legal and institutional changes that have occurred along with the growth of the U.S. economy. Some changes preceded growth, others followed. A whole foundation of the relationship between the two topics is presented by the authors.

1474 Denison, Edward F. "Income Types and the Size Distribution." AMERICAN ECONOMIC REVIEW 44 (May 1954): 254-69.

Examining the distribution of income by proportion among industries, the author argues that shares have remained relatively constant if one adjusts for structural change. Before, tax shares had remained stable.

1475 _____. THE SOURCES OF ECONOMIC GROWTH IN THE U.S. New York: Committee for Economic Development, 1962. 297 p.

The author attempts to assign proportions of growth to the particular crafts, that is, to determine which factors contributed to growth the most and the least. Changes in particular factors affect the productivity of other factors.

1476 Diamond, Sigmund. "Values on an Obstacle to Economic Growth: The American Colonies." JOURNAL OF ECONOMIC HISTORY 27 (December 1967): 561-75.

This is an examination of the effects of relaxation of the rules and bases of the original settlements in North America.

1477 Domar, Evsey D., et al. "Economic Growth and Productivity in the United States, Canada, United Kingdom, Germany, and Japan in the Post-War Period." REVIEW OF ECONOMICS AND STATISTICS 46 (February 1964): 33-40.

Total factor productivity as well as labor and capital productivity are calculated and compared over time as well as among countries.

1478 Dunning, William A. RECONSTRUCTION, POLITICAL AND ECONOMIC. New York: Harper and Brothers, 1907. 378 p.

This is an examination of the period 1865–77, when much
was occurring both domestically and internationally. Most
of the emphasis is on the domestic economic and political
problems.

1479   Dunsing, Marilyn, and Reid, Margaret B. "Effect of Variability of Incomes on Level of Income Expenditure Curves of Farm Families." RE-
VIEW OF ECONOMICS AND STATISTICS 38 (February 1956): 90–95.

Families are differentiated by income change for all families
and for subgroups of families. The subgroups were determined
according to those who had common income classes in the
prior year. Transitory income was found to be more important
for farm families than for nonfarm families.

1480   Easterbrook, W.T. "Long-Period Comparative Study: Some Historical
Cases." JOURNAL OF ECONOMIC HISTORY 17 (December 1957):
571–95.

Focusing on entrepreneurial decision makers, the author studies
a vast number of factors which contribute to growth, using
Canada and the United States as examples.

1481   Fels, Rendigs. "The American Business Cycle of 1879–1885." JOUR-
NAL OF POLITICAL ECONOMY 60 (February 1952): 60–75.

Using current business cycle theory, the author concludes that
investment opportunities remained the same or improved in many
important areas. He does, however, argue that it was a major recession because of the cycle in long-term investment opportunities in railroads, the comparative severity of the depression, and precedent.

1482   Fisher, Franklin M.; Griliches, Zvi; and Kaysen, Carl. "The Costs
of Automobile Model Changes since 1949." JOURNAL OF POLITICAL
ECONOMY 70 (October 1962): 433–51.

The authors estimate the direct costs of model change as well
as the effects on advertising expenditures, retooling expenditures, and gasoline expenditures.

1483   Fishlow, Albert. "Trends in the American Economy in the Nineteenth
Century." JOURNAL OF ECONOMIC HISTORY 22 (March 1962):
71–80.

Reviewing new historical statistics, the author discusses real
output growth, sector income measurement, and capital formation in transportation before 1860.

1484   Fite, E.D. SOCIAL AND INDUSTRIAL CONDITIONS IN THE NORTH

DURING THE CIVIL WAR. New York: P. Smith, 1930. 318 p.

Examining the occupations and pursuits in various industries in the North, the author finds the North was more active and prosperous during the Civil War than ever before.

1485   Goldsmith, Selma, et al. "Size Distribution of Income since the Mid-Thirties." REVIEW OF ECONOMICS AND STATISTICS 36 (February 1954): 1-32.

The prewar distribution of before-tax income and after-tax income is compared with that for the postwar period. The data are all compatible with those of the Office of Business and Economics. A comment by Bernard Clyman and a reply by the above authors appear in this journal, volume 38 (May 1956): 215-27.

1485a   Grampp, William D. "On Manufacturing and Development." ECONOMIC DEVELOPMENT AND CULTURAL CHANGE 18 (April 1970): 451-63.

An examination of different people's views on the place of manufacturing in economic growth, the author uses Carlyle and Ruskin, Hume and Smith, and Hamilton and Jefferson.

1486   Gwartney, James. "Changes in the Nonwhite/White Income Ratio, 1939-1967." AMERICAN ECONOMIC REVIEW 60 (December 1970): 872-83.

The author examines the values for this ratio according to sex, particular time periods, and for aggregated and regional data. The extent of educational equalization and the effects of migration are examined as well.

1487   Hagen, Everett E. "Some Facts about Income Levels and Economic Growth." REVIEW OF ECONOMICS AND STATISTICS 42 (February 1960): 62-67.

Dividing the countries into four groups, the author attempts to discuss their growth behavior relative to their per capita income.

1488   Hamberg, Daniel. "The Recession of 1948-49 in the United States." ECONOMIC JOURNAL 62 (March 1952): 1-14.

This is an examination of the factors which were underlying the recession of 1948-49. The role of consumer expenditure changes is considered most important. A comment by E.C. Bratt and J.P. Ordrechen and a rejoinder by the author appear in this journal, volume 63 (March 1953): 98-110.

1489 Hanna, Frank A. "Cyclical and Secular Changes in State Per Capita Incomes, 1929-50." REVIEW OF ECONOMICS AND STATISTICS 36 (August 1954): 320-30.

Using a sensitivity index for discussing state changes vis-a-vis national changes, the author attempts to explain variations in dispersion of state income relative to fluctuations in national income. He finds no permanent alteration in per capita incomes by state as a result of the Great Depression or World War II.

1490 _____. "State Per Capita Income Components, 1919-1951." REVIEW OF ECONOMICS AND STATISTICS 38 (November 1956): 449-64.

The composition of a state's income was found to be independent of its population size. The categories considered were wages and salaries, property income, proprietors' income, and transfer payments.

1491 Hansen, Alvin H. "Was Fiscal Policy in the Thirties a Failure?" REVIEW OF ECONOMICS AND STATISTICS 45 (August 1963): 320-23.

The author contemplates the fact although recovery occurred, it was not complete in deciding the answer to his question.

1492 Hoffman, Charles. "The Depression of the Nineties." JOURNAL OF ECONOMIC HISTORY 16 (June 1956): 137-64.

Changes in investment and consumption are examined in this paper along with interaction between the United States and the rest of the world.

1493 Hughes, Johnathan R.T., and Rosenberg, Nathan. "The United States Business Cycle before 1860: Some Problems of Interpretation." ECONOMIC HISTORY REVIEW 15 (December 1963): 476-93.

After examining the existing explanations of the cycle, the author argues that there are three forces at work: (1) over speculation; (2) reckless and excessive financial expansion; and (3) importation of cycles. He further argues that the investment in internal improvements served to create cyclical fluctuations.

1494 Johnson, D. Gale. "The Functional Distribution of Income in the United States, 1850-1952." REVIEW OF ECONOMICS AND STATISTICS 36 (May 1954): 175-82.

After adjusting all the major series of data to make them compatible with one another, the author examines the long-term shifts in income shares. He finds that the change in employee compensation has been more pronounced than the change in total labor returns.

1495   Kemmerer, Donald L. "The Changing Pattern of American Economic Development." JOURNAL OF ECONOMIC HISTORY 16 (December 1956): 575-89.

     This article is a description of the changes in the positions of relative scarcity occupied by land, labor, and capital.

1496   Kuznets, Simon. ECONOMIC GROWTH AND STRUCTURE. New York: W.W. Norton and Co., 1965. 378 p.

     This is a collection of twelve essays by the author which address all types of aspects of economic growth for the United States and the world.

1497   _____. "Measurement of Economic Growth." JOURNAL OF ECONOMIC HISTORY 7 (1947): supplement, 10-34.

     The author argues that a systematic statistical study of economic growth is both feasible and potentially fruitful, despite the obstacles. The usefulness of such a study is discussed at some length.

1498   _____. MODERN ECONOMIC GROWTH: RATE STRUCTURE AND SPREAD. New Haven, Conn.: Yale University Press, 1966. 529 p.

     This is an extensive discussion of the major variables affecting economic growth. This book considers the United States and various other developed nations.

1499   _____. NATIONAL INCOME AND PRODUCT SINCE 1869. New York: National Bureau of Economic Research, 1946. 239 p.

     Using five-year moving averages, the author estimates and presents data on the flow of goods to consumers national wealth estimates, and new commodities.

1500   _____. "National Income Estimates for the United States Prior to 1870." JOURNAL OF ECONOMIC HISTORY 12 (Spring 1952): 115-30.

     The existing national income data are rejected as inadequate and incomplete. The work by Robert Gallman (see no. 704) improves on these early data.

1501   _____. POPULATION, CAPITAL, AND GROWTH. New York: W.W. Norton and Co., 1973. 342 p.

     A collection of essays by the author, this work is devoted to the consideration of developmental problems for both the less developed and the already developed nations.

1502 _____ . "Quantitative Aspects of the Economic Growth of Nations, Distribution of Income by Size." ECONOMIC DEVELOPMENT AND CULTURAL CHANGE 11 (January 1963): 1-80.

Two major questions are considered: (1) the effect of the changes in the nature and structure of production accompanying modern economic growth on the size distribution of income; and (2) the influence of the size distribution of income on the process of economic growth. Both cross-sectional and long-term analysis are used.

1503 _____ . "Quantitative Aspects of the Economic Growth of Nations, Distribution of National Income by Factor Shares." ECONOMIC DEVELOPMENT AND CULTURAL CHANGE 7 (April 1959): 1-100.

A cross-sectional study of both interstate and international determinants of the share of income from assets, the allocation of entrepreneurial income, and employee compensation. The important question regarding the relative importance of wage shares or labor shares as the correct variable for comparison is discussed at length.

1504 _____ . "Quantitative Aspects of the Economic Growth of Nations, Levels and Variability of Rates of Growth." ECONOMIC DEVELOPMENT AND CULTURAL CHANGE 5 (October 1956): 5-94.

Using long-term series of economic data, the author considers levels of income and changes over time in the levels, all rates of population growth, national product growth, and growth per capita. Retardation and growth, in terms of long swings, are presented and discussed.

1505 _____ . SECULAR CHANGES IN PRODUCTION AND PRICES. New York: A.M. Kelley, 1967. 536 p.

Long time series of data are examined to discover the secular trends of these series and to learn which types of analysis to pursue. The chronicles of particular industries are used as sources of data. Five countries are used: Britain, Belgium, France, Germany, and the United States.

1506 Lampman, Robert J. "Changes in the Share of Wealth Held by Top Wealth-Holders, 1922-1956." REVIEW OF ECONOMICS AND STATISTICS 41 (November 1959): 379-92.

Using federal estate tax data for the number of holders and the value of wealth for selected years between 1922 and 1956, the author examines changes in the concentration of wealth and compares it to the wealth held by all persons.

1507 Leroy-Beulieu, Pierre. THE UNITED STATES IN THE TWENTIETH

CENTURY. New York: Funk and Wagnalls Co., 1906. 396 p.

From the point of view of a European the author examines the role of natural resources, population, and agriculture in the growth of the United States.

1508 Library of Congress. Congressional Research Service. THE DISTRIBUTION OF INCOME AND WEALTH: A BIBLIOGRAPHY OF RECENT MATERIALS. Washington, D.C.: Government Printing Office, 1978. 37 p.

This is a recent publication listing works which could be of use both in historical analysis as well as in modern work.

1509 Mayo-Smith, Richmond. "The Eleventh Census of the United States." ECONOMIC JOURNAL 1 (March 1891): 43-58.

Arguing that there are three classes of inquiries undertaken in the collection of census data, the author examines each and discusses the methods pursued in each.

1510 Miller, Herman P. "Factors Related to Recent Changes in Income Distribution in the United States." REVIEW OF ECONOMICS AND STATISTICS 33 (August 1951): 214-18.

Factors discussed include reduction of unemployment and increases in the number of families with more than one earner, and the relative increase in farm income.

1511 Morgan, James N. "The Anatomy of Income Distribution." REVIEW OF ECONOMICS AND STATISTICS 44 (August 1962): 270-83.

This is a thorough discussion of the pitfalls inherent in the data and measurement techniques used to understand inequality of income distribution.

1512 Morgan, T. "Distribution of Income in Ceylon, Puerto Rico, the United States, and the United Kingdom." ECONOMIC JOURNAL 63 (December 1953): 821-34.

Using Lorenz curves, the author examines the size distribution of income, sector differences, occupation differences, family size differences, and racial differences in income distribution.

1513 North, Douglas C. GROWTH AND WELFARE IN THE AMERICAN PAST. Englewood Cliffs, N.J.: Prentice-Hall, 1966. 210 p.

This is a rather general treatment of the growth process in the United States, dealing with most of the major issues of the past 175 years.

1514 _____. "Institutional Change and Economic Growth." JOURNAL OF ECONOMIC HISTORY 31 (March 1971): 118-25.

This is an assessment of the role of changing institutions in economic development, especially that of the Western world.

1515 Parker, William N. "Economic Development in Historical Perspective." ECONOMIC DEVELOPMENT AND CULTURAL CHANGE 10 (October 1961): 1-7.

The changing communication methods and the diffusion of technology, as well as some of the sequences of change are the focal points of this paper. The limiting factor has been the human capability in examining external nature.

1516 Patel, Surendra J. "Rates of Industrial Growth in the Last Century 1860-1958." ECONOMIC DEVELOPMENT AND CULTURAL CHANGE 9 (April 1961): 316-30.

Examining the performance of the industrial nations for both producer and consumer goods, the author discusses the changing shares for the world's industrial output and the prospects for the preindustrial nations.

1517 Pilgrim, John D. "The Upper Turning Point of 1920: A Reappraisal." EXPLORATIONS IN ECONOMIC HISTORY 11 (Spring 1972): 271-98.

The cycle from 1919 to 1921 is the focus of this paper, and the author argues that fiscal policy was ineffective. Monetary policy was the decisive factor.

1518 Post, John D. "The Economic Crisis of 1816-1817 and Its Social and Political Consequences." JOURNAL OF ECONOMIC HISTORY 30 (March 1970): 248-50.

This is an argument that the disturbance had its origin in an agricultural calamity which had extraordinary geographic scope. That is, the author contends that one cannot understand this crisis and that of 1819 without considering the international situation.

1519 Poulson, Barry W., and Dowling, J. Malcolm. "Background Conditions and the Spectral Analytic Test of the Long Swings Hypothesis." EXPLORATIONS IN ECONOMIC HISTORY 8 (Spring 1971): 343-52.

After discussion of the empirical framework necessary for applying spectral analytic tests of the long-swings hypothesis, the authors examine the data and conclude that their results are broadly consistent with existing literature on the topic. Suggestion are offered for further investigation, for many questions remain unanswered.

1520 _____ . "The Climacteric in U.S. Economic Growth." OXFORD
ECONOMIC GROWTH 25 (November 1973): 420-34.

Using a new approach, the authors attempt to separate the
frequency regarded as trend from those from other frequencies
in the series. Their evidence indicates retardation of U.S.
economic growth for the first third of the twentieth century.

1521 Rezneck, Samuel. "Distress, Relief, and Discontent in the United States
during the Depression of 1873-78." JOURNAL OF POLITICAL ECON-
OMY 58 (December 1950): 494-512.

This examination of the causes, the impact, and characteristics
of the depression indicate that it was second only to the one
of 1929-33 in terms of the downturn in economic activity.

1522 _____ . "The Influence of Depression upon American Opinion, 1857-
1859." JOURNAL OF ECONOMIC HISTORY 2 (May 1942): 1-23.

Speculators were the prime target of abuse along with abuses
of banking and currency procedures. The unrest of the wage
earners is discussed but the one good thing observed as a result of the depression is that it served to disabuse the mind
of illusion.

1523 Roose, Kenneth D. "The Recession of 1937-38." JOURNAL OF PO-
LITICAL ECONOMY 56 (June 1948): 239-48.

This examination of the causal factors argues that there were
many: inventory accumulation; nonexpansion of consumption
expenditure; reduction of net government contributions to income; Federal Reserve policy; and the pressure of increased
wage costs on prices and profits.

1524 Rostas, L. "Industrial Production, Productivity, and Distribution in
Britain, Germany, and the United States, 1935-37." ECONOMIC
JOURNAL 53 (April 1943): 39-54.

This article compares the scale, structure, and productivity
of manufacturing industries for these three countries. The
composition of the labor force and changes in the distribution
of income are both discussed.

1525 Rostow, Walter W., ed. THE ECONOMICS OF TAKE-OFF INTO SUS-
TAINED GROWTH. New York: St. Martin's Press, 1963. 268 p.

This is a collection of sixteen articles written by scholars
dealing with the take-off into sustained growth.

1526 _____ . THE STAGES OF ECONOMIC GROWTH. Cambridge, Engl.:
Cambridge University Press, 1971. 179 p.

This is an examination of the various supposedly observable stages in economic growth. Russia and the United States are compared with respect to the relation between growth and war.

1527 Schuller, George J. "The Secular Trend in Income Distribution by Type, 1869-1948: A Preliminary Estimate." REVIEW OF ECONOMICS AND STATISTICS 35 (November 1953): 302-24.

After applying extensive smoothing techniques to the data series, the author calculates trends for income and income shares as well. The calculations are done for both "all industries" and "private nonagricultural industries."

1528 Scott, Ira O., Jr. "A Comparison of Production during the Depression of 1873 and 1929." AMERICAN ECONOMIC REVIEW 42 (September 1952): 569-76.

By constructing ratios of the duration and amplitude of the depression in 1929 to those of 1873 for various products, the author attempts to assess the relative severity of these two disturbances.

1529 Siegel, Irving H. "The First Postwar Census of Manufactures." REVIEW OF ECONOMICS AND STATISTICS 33 (November 1951): 351-54.

This is a critical examination of the information contained in the census for 1947. The article points out that the use of the Standard Industrial Code which began in 1940 continues. A great deal of industry as well as state county and regional data are discussed.

1530 Smith, James D., and Franklin, Stephen D. "The Concentration of Personal Wealth, 1922-1962." AMERICAN ECONOMIC REVIEW 64 (May 1974): 162-67.

Using the "estate multiplier technique" to obtain wealth estimates, the author examines the changes in wealth concentration for the top 1 percent and .5 percent of the population. He concludes that the distribution became increasing more equal until about 1945, and has remained basically unchanged ever since.

1531 Soltow, James H. "American Institutional Studies: Present Knowledge and Past Trends." JOURNAL OF ECONOMIC HISTORY 31 (March 1971): 87-105.

Studying the complexities involved in decision making by business firms, the author examines the works relating to the role of government in nineteenth-century U.S. growth. The economy is judged not to have been laissez-faire.

1532   Soltow, Lee. "Economic Inequality in the United States in the Period from 1790 to 1860." JOURNAL OF ECONOMIC HISTORY 31 (December 1971): 822-39.

There was extensive inequality of wealth in the United States in 1860 and the evidence indicates that such inequality may well have prevailed since 1790. Such constant inequality requires strong assumptions about the rates of wealth accumulation and the probability of becoming a property holder.

1533   _____. "The Trend Movement in the Income Distribution in Wisconsin for a Twenty-Year Period." REVIEW OF ECONOMICS AND STATISTICS 39 (May 1957): 223-25.

This is a comparison of before-tax income between 1929 and 1949, according to particular income ranges.

1534   Sprague, O.M.W. "The American Crisis of 1907." ECONOMIC JOURNAL 18 (September 1908): 353-72.

This is an argument that it is the greater degree of speculation in a rapidly growing economy, such as the United States, that produces severe economic crises. The crisis of 1907 is compared with earlier ones in order to identify any specific differences.

1535   Supple, Barry E. "Economic History and Economic Growth." JOURNAL OF ECONOMIC HISTORY 20 (December 1960): 548-58.

This is a general discussion of how economists and historians approach the problem of examining growth.

1536   Taylor, George Rogers. "American Economic Growth before 1840: An Exploratory Essay." JOURNAL OF ECONOMIC HISTORY 24 (December 1964): 427-44.

This is primarily a nonstatistical treatment of the topic, but one which provides some insights into the time and the growth process.

1537   Temin, Peter. "The Anglo-American Business Cycle, 1820-1860." ECONOMIC HISTORY REVIEW 27 (May 1974): 207-22.

The author argues that the similarities in the Anglo-American systems were more responsible for the appearance of similarity in cycles than was the similarity of shocks experienced by the two systems. Cycles were not self-generating because each was viewed as the result of an independent shock.

1538   Weber, Bernard. "Variations in the Rate of Economic Growth in the

U.S.A., 1869-1939." OXFORD ECONOMIC PAPERS 6 (June 1954): 101-32.

The study is begun with an examination of fluctuations in the rate of secular growth of real income. Other variables examined include the transfer of resources among sectors with different productivity, variations in sector rates of growth, the long-run trend in the capital coefficient, the process of innovation, and real wage variations. Comparisons are also made with the United Kingdom for 1890-1914.

1539 Williamson, Harold F., ed. THE GROWTH OF THE AMERICAN ECONOMY. Englewood Cliffs, N.J.: Prentice-Hall, 1951. 946 p.

This collection of essays by various reknowned scholars traces the growth of the United States from colonial times to approximately the early post-World War II period.

1540 Williamson, Jeffrey G. LATE NINETEENTH-CENTURY AMERICAN DEVELOPMENT: A GENERAL EQUILIBRIUM HISTORY. New York: Cambridge University Press, 1974. 350 p.

The author uses a large-scale simulation model to examine and explain economic growth. Excellent use of the counterfactual technique.

1541 Zarnowitz, V. "Unfilled Orders, Competition, and Business Fluctuation." REVIEW OF ECONOMICS AND STATISTICS 44 (November 1962): 367-94.

This is a study of how various producers respond to changes in the demand for their output. Industry structure is felt to be a significant factor in determining the response.

1542 Zevin, Robert B. "An Interpretation of American Imperialism." JOURNAL OF ECONOMIC HISTORY 32 (March 1972): 316-60.

Outlining the history of the United States, the author compares the predictions of a Marxist approach with the realities of the U.S. experience. The conclusion is that no capitalist class exists in the U.S. economy whose purposes would be served by imperialism.

10.2 GENERAL LISTINGS

1543 Baldwin, Robert E. "Some Theoretical Aspects of Economic Development." JOURNAL OF ECONOMIC HISTORY 14 (December 1954): 333-45.

1544 Barsby, Steven L. "Economic Backwardness and the Characteristics of Development." JOURNAL OF ECONOMIC HISTORY 29 (September 1969): 449-72.

1545　Easterbrook, Thomas. "Uncertainty and Economic Change." JOURNAL OF ECONOMIC HISTORY 14 (December 1954): 346-60.

1546　Helleiner, Karl F. "Moral Conditions of Economic Growth." JOURNAL OF ECONOMIC HISTORY 11 (Spring 1951): 97-116.

1547　Hidy, Ralph W. "The Road We Are Traveling." JOURNAL OF ECONOMIC HISTORY 32 (March 1972): 3-14.

1548　Lane, Frederic C. "Meanings of Capitalism." JOURNAL OF ECONOMIC HISTORY 29 (March 1969): 5-12.

1549　Olson, Mancur, Jr. "Rapid Economic Growth as a Destablizing Force." JOURNAL OF ECONOMIC HISTORY 23 (December 1963): 529-58.

1550　Redlich, Fritz. "Arthur Spiethoff on Economic Styles." JOURNAL OF ECONOMIC HISTORY 30 (September 1970): 640-52.

1551　Schumpeter, Joseph A. "Theoretical Problems of Economic Growth." JOURNAL OF ECONOMIC HISTORY 7 (1947): supplement, 1-9.

1552　Somers, Harold M. "What Generally Happens during Business Cycles-- and Why." JOURNAL OF ECONOMIC HISTORY 12 (Summer 1952): 270-82.

1553　Tarascio, Vincent J. "Keynes on the Sources of Economic Growth." JOURNAL OF ECONOMIC HISTORY 31 (June 1971): 429-44.

1554　Usher, Abbott Payson. "The Balance Sheet of Economic Development." JOURNAL OF ECONOMIC HISTORY 11 (Fall 1951): 325-38.

1555　Wright, Quincy. "Economic and Political Conditions of World Stability." JOURNAL OF ECONOMIC HISTORY 13 (Fall 1953): 363-77.

Appendix A

ASSOCIATIONS

Although a multitude of associations are concerned directly or indirectly with the history of economic thought, only a few devote a considerable amount of time and effort to promoting this field. Consequently, I have chosen to list only the five major associations that deal with history of economic thought. The interested reader is referred to the ENCYCLOPEDIA OF ASSOCIATIONS (Gale Research Co., 1980. Annual).

Agricultural History Society, Agricultural History Group, Economics Research Service, ESA, U.S. Department of Agriculture, Washington, D.C. 20250.

American Economic Association, C. Elton Show, Secretary, 1313 Twenty First Avenue South, Nashville, Tenn. 37212.

American History Association, 400 A Street, S.E., Washington, D.C. 20003.

British Agricultural History Society, Andrew Jewell, Treasurer BAHS, Museum of English Rural Life, The University, Whiteknights, Reading, Berkshire, Engl.

Economic History Association, Richard D.William, Secretary-Treasurer, Elentherian Mills Historical Library P.O. Box 3630, Wilmington, Del. 19807.

Appendix B

JOURNALS

AGRICULTURAL HISTORY, Periodicals Department, University of California Press, Berkeley, Calif. 94720.

AGRICULTURAL HISTORY REVIEW, Andrew Jewell, Treasurer BAHS, Museum of English Rural Life, The University, Whiteknights, Reading, Berkshire, Engl.

AMERICAN ECONOMIC REVIEW, Secretary C. Elton Shaw, 1313 Twenty First Avenue South, Nashville, Tenn. 37212.

AMERICAN HISTORY REVIEW, Executive Director, American History Association, 400 A. Street, S.E., Washington, D.C. 20003.

ECONOMIC DEVELOPMENT AND CULTURAL CHANGE, University of Chicago Press, 5801 Ellis Avenue, Chicago, Ill. 60637.

ECONOMIC HISTORY REVIEW, Assistant Secretary, Economic History Society, Peterhouse, Cambridge, United Kingdom.

ECONOMIC RECORD, Brown, Prior, Anderson Pty. Ltd., 5 Evans Street, Burwood 3125, Victoria, Australia.

EXPLORATIONS IN ECONOMIC HISTORY, Academic Press, Inc., 111 Fifth Avenue, New York, N.Y. 10003.

JOURNAL OF ECONOMIC HISTORY, Richard D. Williams, Sec-Treas, Economic History Association, Elentherian Mills Historical Library, P.O. Box 3630, Wilmington, Del. 19807.

JOURNAL OF INTERDISCIPLINARY STUDIES, Journal Department, MIT Press, 28 Carleton St., Cambridge, Mass. 02142.

Journals

JOURNAL OF POLITICAL ECONOMY, University of Chicago Press, 5801 Ellis Avenue, Chicago, III. 60637.

RESEARCH IN ECONOMIC HISTORY, JAI Press, Inc., 321 Greenwich Avenue, Greenwich, Conn. 06830.

REVIEW OF ECONOMICS AND STATISTICS, North-Holland Publishing Co., P.O. Box 211, Amsterdam, The Netherlands.

AUTHOR INDEX

In addition to authors, this index includes editors, compilers, and other contributors to works cited in the text. References are to entry numbers, and alphabetization is letter by letter.

Author Index

Author Index

Author Index

Hazami, Yujiro 1160
Heald, Morrell 165
Healy, Kent T. 766–67
Heath, Milton S. 630, 768, 1445
Heaton, Herbert 20
Heilman, Ralph E. 769, 1380
Helleiner, Karl F. 1546
Hempel, Carl G. 21
Henderson, John P. 1161
Henrich, F.K. 630, 1445
Hewett, D. 857
Hexter, J.H. 22
Hibbard, B.A. 360
Hicks, John D. 1162
Hicks, Sir John R. 23
Hidy, Ralph 631–32, 928, 1163, 1547
Higgs, Robert 166–67, 361, 375, 443, 770, 1164–65, 1295
Hill, Forest G. 771
Hill, Peter J. 168
Hill, William 772, 1312
Hillard, Samuel Bowers 362
Hinderliter, Roger H. 929
Hoagland, H.E. 773
Hoffman, Charles 1492
Hoffman, I. Newton 1446
Hogan, John V. 931
Hollander, Jacob H. 932
Hollander, Samuel 564
Holyfield, James, Jr. 210
Homan, Paul T. 1059
Hoover, Edgar M., Jr. 169, 774
Hoover, Ethel D. 933
Hopkins, S.W. 476
Horowitz, Morris A. 775
Houghton, Harrison F. 633
Hourwich, Isaac A. 270
House, Albert V., Jr. 1381
Hownestine, E. Jay, Jr. 1382, 1447
Hoxie, George L. 1448
Hoxie, Robert F. 934, 1166
Hoyt, Homer 1383
Hughes, Jonathan R.T. 12, 24, 86, 634, 705, 858, 988, 1493
Hultgren, Thor 1384
Humphrey, Don D. 935
Hunt, E.H. 776
Hunt, Thomas F. 444

Hutchins, John G.B. 94, 777
Hutchinson, William K. 1167
Hyde, Francis Edwin 1168
Hynes, Allan 1200

I

Imlay, Gilbert 1169
Inman, Henry 859
Intriligator, Michael D. 511
Irwin, H.S. 363
Isard, Walter 778–79, 861

J

Jacobstein, Meyer 445
James, John A. 936, 1170
Jenks, J.W. 635, 1385
Jenks, Leland H. 780–81, 1171
Jerome, Harry 565
Jewkes, J. 512
Johnson, A. 364
Johnson, D. Gale 1494
Johnson, E.A.J. 1386
Johnson, Emory R. 862
Johnson, Hildegard Binder 271
Jones, Alice Hanson 636, 637
Jones, Ethel B. 170
Jones, Homer 940, 1060
Jorgenson, Dale W. 566, 638–39
Jorgenson, Lloyd P. 365

K

Kagel, John 309
Kalachek, E. 568
Kao, Charles H.C. 272
Karlin, S. 573
Kaun, David E. 150
Kaysen, Carl 612, 1482
Keat, Paul G. 171
Keene, Charles A. 1172
Keehn, Richard H. 320, 1102
Keller, Robert R. 682
Kelley, Allen C. 172–73
Kelley, Arthur C. 1387
Kelson, Harold 782
Kementa, Jan 783
Kemmerer, Donald L. 1495
Kemmerer, E.W. 941, 1061
Kendrick, John W. 513–14, 640

Author Index

Author Index

TITLE INDEX

This index includes all titles of books cited in the text. References are to page numbers and alphabetization is letter by letter.

Title Index

H

I

J

L

Title Index

SUBJECT INDEX

This index includes major topics covered in the text. References are to entry numbers, and alphabetization is letter by letter.

Subject Index